Letters of
Dorothy Wordsworth

Letters of
Dorothy Wordsworth

A selection edited by ALAN G. HILL

Oxford   New York

OXFORD UNIVERSITY PRESS

Oxford University Press, Walton Street, Oxford OX2 6DP

Oxford New York Toronto
Delhi Bombay Calcutta Madras Karachi
Petaling Jaya Singapore Hong Kong Tokyo
Nairobi Dar es Salaam Cape Town
Melbourne Auckland

and associated companies in
Berlin Ibadan

Selection, Introduction, and editorial material © *Oxford University Press 1981*

The text of the letters is taken from the seven published vols. of The Letters of
William and Dorothy Wordsworth, *2nd ed., general editor Alan G. Hill,*
© *Oxford University Press 1967, 1969, 1970, 1978, 1979, 1982, and 1988*

First published 1981 as an Oxford University Press paperback
Reprinted 1982, 1991

British Library Cataloguing in Publication Data
Wordsworth, Dorothy
Letters of Dorothy Wordsworth.—(Oxford paperbacks).
1. Wordsworth, Dorothy—Biography
2. Authors, English—19th century—Biography I. Title
828'709   PR5849.A8   80-41842
ISBN 0-19-281318-8

Library of Congress Cataloging in Publication Data
Wordsworth, Dorothy. 1771–1855. [Correspondence. Selections]
Letters of Dorothy Wordsworth: a selection/edited by Alan G. Hill.
p.   cm.—(Oxford letters & memoirs)
Includes bibliographical references and index.
1. Wordsworth, Dorothy, 1771–1855—Correspondence. 2. Lake
District (England)—Social life and customs. 3. Authors,
English—19th century—Correspondence. 4. Romanticism—England.
5. Wordsworth family. I. Hill, Alan G. II. Title. III. Series.
828'703—dc20   PR5849.A85 1990   [B]   90-7856
ISBN 0-19-281318-8

Printed in Great Britain by
Clays Ltd.
Bungay, Suffolk

Contents

*

List of Letters

*

vii

Acknowledgements

*

Acknowledgement is due to the following institutions holding the originals of manuscript letters: the British Library (nos. 15, 21, 23, 34–5, 37, 41–2, 46, 48, 50–1, 53, 67), Cornell University Library (no. 47), Dr Williams's Library (nos. 40, 57, 62), Edinburgh University Library (no. 61), the Henry E. Huntington Library (no. 66), the Historical Society of Pennsylvania (no. 63), the National Library of Scotland (no. 59), the New York Genealogical and Bibliographical Society (no. 12), the Pierpont Morgan Library (nos. 28–30, 38), and the Wordsworth Library, Grasmere (nos. 1–4, 7, 13–14, 16–20, 22, 24–7, 31–3, 39, 44–5, 49, 54–6, 60, 64, 69–70); and to the following individual owners of letters: Miss Maud Craig (no. 43), and Mr Jonathan Wordsworth (no. 52).

Abbreviations

D. W.	Dorothy Wordsworth
W. W.	William Wordsworth
M. W.	Mary Wordsworth (*née* Hutchinson)
C. W.	Christopher Wordsworth
S. H.	Sara Hutchinson
S. T. C.	Samuel Taylor Coleridge

Biographical Summary

*

1771 25 December, D. W. born at Cockermouth, the third of five children and sister of Richard, William, John and Christopher.

1778 After death of mother, D. W. goes to live with her cousin Elizabeth Threlkeld (later Mrs Rawson) at Halifax. (W. W. at Hawkshead G. S. from 1779.)

1783 30 December, her father John Wordsworth, attorney, dies intestate, his affairs in chaos.

1787 May, D. W. goes to live with her Cookson grandparents at Penrith, where the Hutchinsons are neighbours. (October, W. W. at St John's College, Cambridge.)

1788 December, D. W. moves to Forncett, her uncle William Cookson's rectory in Norfolk.

1794 Reunited with W. W. after his identification with, and withdrawal from, the French Revolution. April, at Windy Brow, Keswick.

1795 September, at Racedown, Dorset.

1797 July, they move to Alfoxden, nr Nether Stowey, Somerset, to be near S. T. C. D. W.'s first meetings with Charles Lamb and Southey.

1798 20 January, D. W. begins her *Alfoxden Journal*. July, August, tours of the Wye. September, they leave for Germany with S. T. C.: *Lyrical Ballads* published at Bristol. October, D. W. and W. W. arrive at Goslar. (W. W. begins *The Prelude*.)

1799 May, return to England. At Sockburn-on-Tees with the Hutchinsons. 20 December, arrival at Grasmere.

1800 January, D. W. settles with W. W. at Dove Cottage. (S. T. C. at Keswick.) 14 May, she begins *Grasmere Journal*.

1802 August, at Calais with W. W. to visit Annette Vallon and his 'French' daughter Caroline. 4 October, W. W. marries Mary Hutchinson at Brompton, Yorks. (1803–10, five children born to them at Grasmere: John, Dorothy or 'Dora', Thomas, Catharine, and William.)

1803 August–September, Scottish tour with W. W. and S. T. C. D. W. writes her *Recollections* of the tour. Lord Lowther discharges his debt to the Wordsworths. (W. W. begins to correspond with De Quincey.)

1805   5 February, death by shipwreck of D. W.'s younger brother John. (W. W. completes *The Prelude*.)

1806   October (until the following spring), at Coleorton. December, reunion with S. T. C. on his return from Malta. (W. W. prepares *Poems in Two Volumes*, 1807.)

1808   Move to Allan Bank, Grasmere. (S. T. C. lives there 1808–10, producing *The Friend*; De Quincey helps W. W. with the *Cintra* pamphlet.)

1810   July–October, D. W. at Coleorton, Cambridge and London.

1811   Rift with S. T. C. Move to the old vicarage, Grasmere.

1812   Deaths of Catharine and Thomas.

1813   May, the Wordsworths leave Grasmere for Rydal Mount. (W. W. appointed a Distributor of Stamps.)

1814   September–December, D. W. at Hindwell, Radnor. (W. W. publishes *The Excursion*.)

1816   October (until the following February), D. W. at Halifax.

1820   July–October, tour on the Continent with W. W. and M. W. November (until the following January), D. W. in London and Cambridge.

1822   September–October, second Scottish tour (with Joanna Hutchinson).

1824   February–June, at Coleorton, Oxford, London and Cambridge.

1826   February–September, at Brinsop, Herefordshire.

1828   June–July, D. W. visits Isle of Man. November (until the following spring), keeping house for her nephew John Wordsworth at Whitwick Rectory, Leics.

1829   April, first serious illness. July–September, at Halifax.

1830–5 Progressive decline in health (onset of arteriosclerosis).

1850   23 April, W. W. dies at Rydal Mount.

1855   25 January, death of D. W. at Rydal Mount.

Introduction

*

Wordsworth's 'exquisite sister', as Coleridge called her, made no claim to superior talents of any kind, in spite of the golden opinions which others had of her. 'I should detest', she wrote, 'the idea of setting myself up as an author.' If Dorothy Wordsworth was at all conscious of her literary gifts, she could never bring herself to court public favour by exposing her feelings to strangers; and her letters, like her journals, were addressed to those few individuals whose sympathy and understanding she could take for granted. 'I have not those powers which Coleridge thinks I have—I know it,' she protested to Lady Beaumont. 'My only merits are my devotedness to those I love and I hope a charity towards all mankind.' What can a reader today expect to get from letters that were so professedly occasional and unassuming in character?

Wordsworth himself thought that the importance of 'Letters' in modern times had been vastly exaggerated: 'If they are good and natural as letters, they will seldom be found interesting to other minds beyond the persons, or the circle, to which they are immediately addressed.' And no doubt Dorothy agreed with him. Yet how wrong they both would have been in her own case. Though her name is now part of history, and the world she knew has passed away for ever, countless admirers still fall under the spell of her personality and find in her letters, taken together, the most authentic biography of her that we have and a unique picture of the circles she moved in. No other observer was so close to Wordsworth and Coleridge, or shared so completely their feelings and aims; and no one else had such an eye for the landscapes which inspired them, or could furnish the living materials for poetry out of her own observations. Her letters seem so spontaneous and uncontrived that she might be talking out aloud to absent friends. But as De Quincey remarked, they are models of good sense and just feeling, and full of the kind of shrewd comment and lively detail that will appeal to a reader at any time.

Early in life Dorothy Wordsworth spoke of domestic happiness as her highest ideal, and her letters mirror her outgoing personality and the talents which she put to the service of others. A more introspective writer would have distorted the picture by bringing herself forward, but Dorothy had learnt to keep her eye on the scene in front of her and not parade her own feelings for inspection. The earliest extant letters are, admittedly, somewhat mannered. The separation from her brothers in her grandparents' house at Penrith was a test of stamina from which indeed she emerged unbruised; but given her impulsive nature, it is hardly surprising that she tended to dramatise her predicament in novelistic terms. The phase did not last, however. In the more sympathetic atmosphere of her uncle's household at Forncett and Windsor her writing became natural and outward-looking, and once she had accepted Wordsworth at Windy Brow as sole guardian of her future and they had set up house together at Racedown, all wishes of her own seem to have been merged in the wider purpose of ministering to him and reviving his poetic powers after his withdrawal from the French Revolution. Thereafter, she rarely speaks of herself, her own hopes or expectations. If she had any deeper longings, she kept them entirely to herself.

She built her life on foundations which she knew instinctively were right *for her*. That is why she makes it appear so rounded and complete. And she built durably: the bond with her brothers (William and John particularly), home, friendships, the natural scene—all were supremely satisfying to her and grew more meaningful over the years. The substance of all her hopes was realized with her brother 'home at Grasmere', in the workaday world of Dove Cottage, where they found together

> A portion of the blessedness which love
> And knowledge will, we trust, hereafter give
> To all the vales of earth and all mankind.

Wordsworth's marriage to Mary Hutchinson, their childhood friend, only seemed to extend further the spirit of comradeship which he had celebrated in *Tintern Abbey* at the climax of the *annus mirabilis* of 1798. Amid a widening circle of relations and friends, which included the Coleridges and Southeys at Keswick and the Clarksons at Eusemere, Dorothy found a new role caring for his growing family. She was always happy in the company of children. Though 'the set was broken' with the death of John, the sailor brother, and there were further domestic tragedies and estrangements to follow, the survivors only seemed to grow closer together in undisturbed harmony. There was something almost heroic about their commitment to a simple country life, which lasted on almost unchanged in the superior comforts of Rydal Mount. As the seasons passed, each with its own pleasures and consolations, the pattern of their days seemed to embody the 'natural piety' which the poet had aspired to when they first made their home at Dove Cottage.

Dorothy Wordsworth was not much acquainted with the wider world. A winter in Germany, an excursion to France during the Peace of Amiens, and a Continental tour after the Napoleonic War comprised all her travels abroad with her brother. She also visited Scotland twice, on the first occasion in his and Coleridge's company. But she was happiest among the landscapes of her own country. A special place in her affections was always reserved for Coleorton, Sir George and Lady Beaumont's estate in Leicestershire, where memories of poetry, scenery and friendship mingled happily together. She always looked back with gratitude to the Wordsworths' residence at the Home Farm during the winter of 1806–7, when her brother laid out the winter garden while preparing his poems for the press, and Coleridge joined them on his return from Malta. She also loved Brinsop Court, the moated farmhouse of the Hutchinsons in the Welsh border country, and Trinity Lodge in Cambridge, home of her youngest brother Christopher and her gifted nephews, where she met some of the leading minds in the University. Her letters show her delight in fresh surroundings, but also how much she enjoyed returning to familiar landmarks, like the moss-seat in the Dove Cottage garden, with its view of Helm Crag, or the terrace at Rydal Mount which eventually, in her decline, marked out the limits of her outdoor life. In fact she found (like Thoreau at Concord) that she did not have to travel far in search of what she needed. A walk over the fells or a coach-ride by moonlight would people her imagination with unforgettable impressions, and amid the lakes and mountains of her native region she achieved a profound sympathy with the great men who were her daily companions. Such natural rapport would have been impossible in more sophisticated society.

She expressed no wish to change her circumstances. 'Happily', she once noted in her journal, 'we cannot shape the huge hills, or carve out the valleys according to our fancy.' The power that formed the scene around her had also determined her place within it. That was the message she read in the lives of simple country folk, who accepted the discipline of circumstances as a law of Nature. It made her think deeply about the education of children, though not after the fashion of the received wisdom of her day. For the 'march of mind' in the nineteenth century passed her completely by. While she felt a profound sympathy with the poor and oppressed, and sought them out almost compulsively as if their hardships held the key to understanding the human situation, she had no 'views' on the problems of the age. The distant rumblings of the European war hardly impinged on her settled existence, except when threats of a French invasion led to the formation of the Grasmere Volunteers, largely (one gathers) on her brother's initiative. In politics, as in so much else, she was quite content to follow his lead, enjoying a county election as much perhaps for the colour and animation of the scene as for the niceties of political principle involved. Her letters are too intimate and domestic to give a panorama of the period. They do, however, convey her faith in a traditional rural life-style which was increasingly to be threatened by urban values and tourism as the nineteenth century progressed. What concerned her most of all were 'the common things that round us lie', in her brother's words, the simple familiar things that are so often overlooked by the townsman or the tourist, who is in too much of a hurry to notice them. As De Quincey put it, 'She was content to be ignorant of many things; but what she knew and had really mastered lay where it could not be disturbed—in the temple of her own most fervid heart.'

In her own lifetime Dorothy Wordsworth's letters remained unknown outside her immediate circle, and their importance was not fully recognized until the beginning of the present century, when William Knight published his *Letters of the Wordsworth Family* (3 vols., 1907). This was replaced in due course by Ernest de

Selincourt's larger and more accurate collection, *The Letters of William and Dorothy Wordsworth* (6 vols., 1935–9), which is now in turn being re-edited and enlarged as new letters come to light, and it is on this new edition that the present selection is based. From the hundreds of Dorothy's letters which are now available, seventy have been chosen to provide a portrait of the writer and her milieu which can be read as a continuous narrative with the minimum of editorial commentary. By no means all her letters are suitable for this purpose. Some which are indispensable to the student of Wordsworth's poetry are in other respects uneven in quality.and interest. Others are too full of the minutiae of daily life to appeal to a modern reader, though they have their value for the specialist. She wrote hurriedly, and owing to the cost of postage shrank from leaving blank space at the bottom of her sheet. Every free corner was likely to be crammed with last-minute postscripts, many of them almost indecipherable. In these circumstances an editor might be tempted to abridge the text by selecting striking passages from letters which are otherwise unsuitable; but to do so would be to destroy their authentic flavour and shape, and this procedure has been unhesitatingly rejected in the present volume. Apart from a few fragments of letters that have not survived in their entirety, this selection consists entirely of complete letters, reproduced as nearly as possible as they were written, and chosen not only for the interest of their subject-matter but also to indicate the range of her correspondents.

What is the most memorable impression that a reader will take away from these letters, having followed the course of Dorothy's life from youth until the onset of her last tragic illness? They obviously cannot tell us all we would like to know about the manifold influences that helped to shape Wordsworth's mind and art,—his political and poetic development, his experiences in France, and his love affair with Annette Vallon, for example. Some letters which could have illuminated these issues simply have not survived. Nor do the extant letters entirely explain Dorothy's crucial influence on his poetic development from the Racedown period onwards. The reader will get a vivid sense of their daily life together, especially if he turns to the *Journals* as well; but her inspiration worked its way into his poems in ways we do not always see and cannot analyse, and their relationship will always pose something of an enigma. Perhaps it is best left as Wordsworth himself described it in *The Prelude*. Certainly, the efforts of some modern commentators to explain it away in post-Freudian terms have been peculiarly insensitive and maladroit.

What the letters abundantly and openly proclaim is her abiding sense of her brother's genius. But she depicts him in a very human and down-to-earth way, in relation to everyday circumstances. The poets may be at their work, but the cow has to be milked, the carpets shaken, and the children fed. Unlike so many Victorian critics, she does not build Wordsworth up into a prophet of Nature as Benjamin Robert Haydon succeeded in doing in his famous painting *Wordsworth on Helvellyn*. Nor does she present him as a genius struggling to preserve his disintegrating vision, in the way of some modern critics. She leaves us instead with a renewed sense of Wordsworth's humanity, and of the familiar things in which his art was rooted. He is essentially 'a man speaking to men.' The picture is refreshingly uncomplicated and carries its own air of truth.

Her portrait of Coleridge is similarly life-like and shrewdly drawn. The letters recapture both the exhilaration of her first contact with him, and the tragic disillusionment that crept in later. He was not an easy addition to any family circle. She was only too aware of the weaknesses that threatened to destroy him,—his pathetic love for Sara Hutchinson, the break-up of his marriage, his dilatory habits, the mysterious illnesses, the drug addiction. But she never ceased to believe in his genius, partly wasted though it may have been. She paints an unforgettable picture of daily life at Allan Bank as Wordsworth (assisted by De Quincey) put together his pamphlet *On the Convention of Cintra* and Coleridge struggled to keep up the instalments of his periodical *The Friend*, while the chimneys smoked incessantly and the whole household was thrown into confusion. It is because she had utter confidence in the permanent value of what they were all doing that she made no attempt to over-dramatize the situation. A modern biographer might be tempted to depict them as picturesque bohemians, or cut them down to size. Dorothy quite unaffectedly shows the human face of true genius. She always tried to bring out the best in people.

Perhaps her greatest quality of all is the magnanimity which shines out from all her letters. No one is exempted from her generosity of feeling. It was indeed by keeping her friendships in constant repair (following Dr Johnson's advice) that she helped to create a congenial atmosphere around her brother in which he could do his work. 'Do not make loving us your business,' she wrote to Mary Hutchinson just before her marriage to Wordsworth, 'but let love of us make up the spirit of all the business you have.' This same spirit transfigured all her dealings with others. It comes out in her tributes to Southey's industry and to the remarkable endowments of Coleridge's children, Hartley and Sara. It underlies her instinctive appreciation of the tie that bound Charles and Mary Lamb together in their tragic predicament. But it also appears when the reader may least expect it, as in her compliment to Thomas Monkhouse, the London merchant, who won an easy way into her regard: 'He is in no danger of being so wedded to gain as to shut out good affections'. This unvaried aura of magnanimity may be hard to come to terms with today, when emotion is more rigorously suppressed and may even be mistaken for insincerity, but it has somehow to be reckoned with if one is to understand the inner dynamics of the Wordsworth circle.

Dorothy Wordsworth really needs no further introduction. She can now be left to speak for herself. Cardinal Newman once remarked that a person's true life is in his or her letters: 'not only for the interest of a biography, but for arriving at the inside of things, ... contemporary letters are facts.' Dorothy's letters enable the reader to dispense with much modern theorising and conjecture, and to meet a remarkable group of geniuses face to face, so that he may come to appreciate their priorities and rethink his own. To have brought such a circle so vividly before our eyes is surely one of her greatest achievements.

Alan G. Hill

List of Correspondents

*

Beaumont, Lady (1756–1829), of Coleorton Hall, Leics.: wife of Sir George Beaumont, 7th Bt. (1753–1827), amateur painter, patron of the arts, and W. W.'s benefactor.

Clarkson, Catherine (1772–1856), wife of Thomas Clarkson (1760–1846), the abolitionist: lived successively at Eusemere, nr Pooley Bridge, Bury St Edmunds, and Playford Hall, Ipswich.

Coleridge, Samuel Taylor (1772–1834), poet and philosopher.

Crackanthorpe, Mrs Christopher (1756–1843), of Newbiggin Hall, D. W.'s aunt: wife of 'Uncle Kit', joint guardian of the Wordsworth children.

De Quincey, Thomas (1785–1859), essayist, author of *Confessions of an English Opium Eater*.

Hutchinson, Elizabeth (1820–1905), of Brinsop, D. W.'s niece.

Hutchinson, Mary (1770–1859) of Penrith: later, wife of William Wordsworth.

Hutchinson, Sara (1775–1835), D. W.'s sister-in-law.

Jewsbury, Maria Jane (1800–33), authoress and contributor to the annuals.

Johnson, the Revd William (1784–1864), schoolmaster in Grasmere and London, 'the Patriarch of National Education'.

Jones, the Revd Robert (1769–1835), Welsh clergyman and College friend of W. W.'s.

Kenyon, John (1784–1856), patron of poets.

Laing, Mary (d. 1871), sister of David Laing (1793–1878), the Edinburgh antiquary and bibliographer.

Lamb, Mary (1764–1847), sister of Charles Lamb (1775–1834), the essayist, and joint author of the *Tales from Shakespeare*.

Monkhouse, Thomas (1783–1825), M. W.'s cousin, a London businessman.

Pearson, William (1780–1856), of Crosthwaite, nr Kendal, farmer and naturalist.

Pollard, Jane (1771–1847) of Halifax: later, wife of John Marshall (1765–1845), linen manufacturer of Leeds and M.P.

Poole, Thomas (1765–1837), tanner, of Nether Stowey, Somerset.

Quillinan, Edward (1791–1851), half-pay officer and occasional writer: married W. W.'s daughter Dora as his second wife in 1841.

Rawson, Mrs William, *née* Threlkeld (1745–1837), of Halifax, D. W.'s 'aunt', actually her mother's cousin.

Robinson, Henry Crabb (1775–1867), barrister and diarist.

Scott, Sir Walter (1771–1832), novelist.

Wade, Josiah (d. 1830), linen-draper of Bristol, S. T. C.'s early friend.

Wordsworth, Christopher (1774–1846), D. W.'s youngest brother, Master of Trinity College, Cambridge, from 1820.

Wordsworth, Christopher, jnr. (1807–85), D. W.'s nephew, later Bishop of Lincoln.

Wordsworth, Dora (1804–47), D. W.'s niece.

Wordsworth, Capt. John (1772–1805), the 'sailor brother', drowned in the wreck of the East Indiaman, the *Earl of Abergavenny*, in Weymouth Bay.

Wordsworth, Priscilla, *née* Lloyd (1781–1815), wife of Christopher.

Wordsworth, Richard (1768–1816), D. W.'s eldest brother, solicitor in Staple Inn.

Wordsworth, William (1770–1850), D. W.'s elder brother, the poet: Poet Laureate, 1843, in succession to Southey.

Letters of
Dorothy Wordsworth

*

1. *To* Jane Pollard

[Penrith, 6 and 7 Aug. 1787]
Monday Evening ten o'clock.

Have you not my Dearest Girl, have you not thought me unpardonable for not having wrote to you on the appointed day? Yes, I fear you have, I fear you have said, "before I could forgive her for neglecting to write to me on the day fixed; but a repeated offence I cannot pardon". Ah! Jane, if this has been your resolution let me entreat you to read with patience my excuses and beg you in your next Letter to tell me you forgive me. Yesterday morning I parted with the kindest and most affectionate of Brothers, I cannot paint to you my Distress at their departure, I can only tell you that for a few hours I was absolutely miserable, a thousand tormenting fears rushed upon me, the approaching Winter, the ill-nature of my Grandfather[1] and Uncle Chrisr.,[2] the little probability there is of my soon again seeing my younger Brother,[3] and the still less likelihood of my revisiting my Halifax Friends, in quick succession filled my mind. Could I write to you while I was in this situation? My dear Jane's feeling heart will I am sure at once tell her, "No," After dinner I begun a letter of which I wrote one side before Church time. As I was returning home in the afternoon two young Ladies engaged me to walk with them, I was in low spirits I thought a walk would perhaps put off for a while my melancholy reflections, therefore I consented; I rose early this morning, and I should cer-

[1] William Cookson (1711–87), mercer.
[2] Christopher Crackanthorpe, (1745–99), 'Uncle Kit', joint guardian of the Wordsworth children.
[3] John was about to leave Hawkshead G.S., and enlist as a merchant seaman.

tainly have employed my time in addressing you my Dear Jane if I had not had some work to finish before my Grandmother's coming down stairs, it was what I had neglected doing while my Brothers were here, as when they were with me I could always employ my time much more agreeably than in mending an old shirt. She did not know that I had not finished it and if I had not done it this morning she would have found me out, today I went out a visiting and when I came home it was too late for the post. My Grandmother is now gone to bed and I am quite alone. Imagine me sitting in my bed-gown, my hair out of curl and hanging about my face, with a small candle beside me, and my whole person the picture of poverty (as it always is in a bed-gown) and you will then see your friend Dorothy. It is after eleven oclock. I begin to find myself very sleepy and I have my Hair to curl, so I must bid my very Dear Friend a good night.

Tuesday evening. I have stolen a moment again to take up my pen to write to my Dear Jane and I hope to be able to finish my Epistle before the post goes off, though I am sure I could not write in a dozen sheets all I have to say to her, and perhaps if I was to be able to tell her all I wish she would think I only troubled her with trifles. You know not how forlorn and dull I find myself now that my Brs are gone neither can you imagine how I enjoyed their company when I could contrive to be alone with them which I did as often as possible. Ah! Jane if the partial affection of a Sister does not greatly magnify all their merits, they are charming boys, particularly the three youngest (William, John, and Kit). No doubt I discern in them merits which will by every body else pass unheeded. I often say to myself "I have the most affectionate Brothers in the world, while I possess them, while I have you my Dear Dear Jane to whom I will ever lay open all the secrets of my heart can I ever be entirely miserable?" but "no", no one can deprive me of the sweet consolation of pouring out my sorrows into the bosom of a brother or a friend; I, (young as I am) flatter myself that Halifax contains several real friends to me, but it is indeed mortifying to my Brothers and me to find that amongst all those who visited at my father's house he had not one real friend; would you think it Jane? a Gentleman of my father's intimate acquaintance, who is not worth less than two or three thousand a year, and who always

professed himself to be the real friend of my father refused to pay a
bill of seven hundred pound to his Children without considerable
deductions; when my Father died his affairs were in a very unsettled
way and Lord Lonsdale[1] does not owe us less than 4 thousand 7
hundred pounds of which I daresay we shall never receive a farthing, we shall however have about 600 pounds a piece, and I am sure
as long as my Brothers have a farthing in their pockets I shall never
want. My Br Wm goes to Cambridge in October but he will be at
Penrith before his departure, he wishes very much to be a Lawyer
if his health will permit, but he is troubled with violent head-aches
and a pain in his side, but I hope they will leave him in a little time.
You must not be surprized if you see him at Halifax in a short time,
I think he will not be able to call there in his way to Cambridge as
my Uncle Wm[2] and a young Gentleman who is going to the same
Colledge will accompany him. When I wrote to you last I had some
faint hopes that he might have been permitted to stay with me till
October. You may guess how much I was mortified and vexed at
his being obliged to go away. I absolutely dislike my Uncle Kit who
never speaks a pleasant word to one, and behaves to my Br Wm in
a particularly ungenerous manner.

I thank you my Dear Jane for your inquiries after my health, I
have been perfectly well since I came to Penrith excepting for a pain
in my head now and then, but I think crying was the cause of it I
hope in your next letter you will acquaint me with your perfect
recovery.

I am also mu[ch] obliged to you for your literary intelligence. I
do not [remember] having heard of the conversations of Emily.[3] I
ha[ve] a very pretty little collection of Books from my Brothers [   ]
which they have given me. I will give you a Catalog[ue]. I have the
Iliad, the Odyssey, [?] works, Fielding's works, Hayley's[4] poems,
Gil Blas (in French), Gregory's Legacy to his Daughters,[5] and my
Brother Ric[hard] intends sending me Shakespeare's Plays and the
Spec[tator.] I have also Milton's Works, Dr. Goldsmith's poems,

[1] James Lowther, 1st Earl of Lonsdale (1736–1802).
[2] The Revd William Cookson (1754–1820).
[3] Louise La Live D'Épinay, *The Conversations of Emily. Translated from the French*,
1787.
[4] William Hayley (1745–1820), friend of Cowper.
[5] John Gregory, M.D., *A Father's Legacy to his Daughters*, 1774.

[and] other trifling things, I think I hear you say "how will [you] have time to read all these?" I am determined to re[ad a] great deal now both in French and English. My Grandmr sits in the shop in the afternoons and by working par[ticularly] hard for one hour I think I may read the next, withou[t be]ing discovered, and I rise pretty early in a morning so I [hope] in time to have perused them all. I am at present [reading] the Iliad and like it very much, My Br Wm read [a part] of it.

So, you have got high-heeled shoes [? I do not] think of having them yet a while I am so little, and wish to appear as Girlish as possible I wear my hair curled about my face in light curls friz'd at the bottom and turned at the ends. How have you yours? I have tied my black hat under the chin, as it looked shabby in its former state.

I really think it is better not to have any stated time for writing one may so easily be disappointed, but always take the first opportunity we have, so I entreat you to write to me very, very soon. I will not fix the day for fear I should be disappointed but do not defer it longer than till next Monday or Tuesday. Now mind this is to be the latest, write sooner if possible.

I am obliged to conclude this ill-written scrawl immediately or I shall be too late for the post. Adieu my Dearest, Dearest Girl.

My very best Love to all your Family.

Write soon, Can you read this?

[*Unsigned*]

2. *To* Jane Pollard

[Forncett] Monday Evening Jany 25th [and 26, 1790]

Your goodness quite overpowers me, my very dear Friend. Oh Jane! how kind you are; to remember one with such tender affection; who could scarcely have reproached you had you cast her off as utterly unworthy of your regard—believe me, no decrease of friendship has occasioned my apparently unfriendly behaviour. I have no excuse to offer but that poor one, (indolence) which being the best I could possibly have, your love for me suggested to you. I will not pain you or myself by a review of my conduct. I trust from the kindness you have shown me, that I shall be entirely forgiven by you.

4

I rejoice with you on the prospect of your dear Father's perfect recovery. I did indeed sympathize with you in your distress for I too well know how irreparable is the loss of an indulgent parent. I hope your next Letter will confirm what you told me in your last and that I shall hear of his continued amendment. I think I have a great deal to tell you it is so long since I wrote to you. I say to myself where shall I set forward? but first I will answer your letter and begin with what most nearly concerns me; my Aunt's[1] displeasure. You are indeed very kind to impute my silence to the true cause. I fear she is very angry with me as indeed she has great reason; but I will not enter into particulars as I should only swell my letter to no purpose. You know my heart too well to doubt my gratitude to her and affection for her and I hope I know her too well to allow me to be mistaken when I say I trust that *"she does not think that all my professions"* of regard *"were insincere"*; indeed Jane, I am much hurt with what you tell me my Cousins[2] say of me; to assert that my assurances of affection were all insincere, I confess I think unfriendly and more unkind than my behaviour upon a candid consideration has merited. If they had said that I now seemed to have lost that affection for them which I formerly possess'd; for that I would have found many excuses, but for what they have now said I can only discover one; which is this, that the assertion was made without due consideration; I, however, heartily forgive them when I consider how much more attention and kindness they had a right to expect from me than I have lately shewn them. I have written to my Aunt but have taken no notice of that part of your letter.

I have every reason my dear Jane to be satisfied with my present situation; I have two kind Friends[3] with whom I live in that retirement, which before I enjoyed I knew I should relish. I have leisure to read; work; walk and do what I please in short I have every cause to be contented and happy. We look forward to the coming of our little relation with anxious expectation; I hope to be a good nurse, though by the bye I must make considerable improvement before I arrive at any degree of excellence; I verily believe that I never took an infant in my arms that did not the moment it was there by its

[1] Elizabeth Threlkeld, later Mrs William Rawson, (see List of Correspondents).
[2] The Fergusons.
[3] The Revd and Mrs William Cookson.

cries beg to be removed. My Brother John, I imagine sailed for India on Saturday or Sunday in the Earl of Abergavenny: he wrote to me the other day while on board her in excellent spirits. William is at Cambridge, Richard in London,[1] and Kitt at Hawkshead, how we are squandered abroad.

Perhaps you know that we are engaged in a Law suit with Lord Lonsdale, which is not likely to end in less than three years, it may be much longer. I cannot say I feel myself very anxious as to the issue of it; I have entirely reconciled myself to whatever may be my lot, for if we have sufficient to provide for my Brothers on them I know I may depend; and I have good Friends who will do every thing for me in the intermediate space.

Did I ever tell you that I had got a little school; indeed when I recollect, it is not possible that I should have told you, as I have only kept it six months. I will give you my plan. I have nine scholars, I had at first ten but I dismissed one and during the winter I did not think it prudent to supply her place. Our hours in winter are, on Sunday mornings from nine till church time: at noon from half past one till three: and at night from four till half past 5: those who live near us come to me every Wednesday and Saturday evening.

I only instruct them in reading and spelling and they get off prayers hymns and catechisms. I have one very bright scholar, some very tolerable, and one or two very bad. We distribute rewards such as books, caps, aprons etc. We intend in a little time to have a school upon a more extensive plan—so that this of mine is only a temporary thing. We are to have a mistress who is to teach them spinning, knitting etc in the week days, and I am to assist her on Sundays, when they are to be taught to read. Mr Wilberforce[2] has been with us rather better than a month, tell your Father I hope he will give him his vote at the next general election. I believe him to be one of the best of men.

He allows me ten guineas a year to distribute in what manner I think best to the poor, it is a very nice sum by which I [am] enabled to do more good than perhaps might ever have been in my

---

[1] Articled to a firm of solicitors.

[2] William Wilberforce (1759–1833), politician and abolitionist, a College friend of Cookson.

power—remember all this is between ourselves, therefore don't mention it.

I am very sorry to hear that E. T.—d[1] is so poorly. Give my kind love to her.

I shall look forward to the time of my receiv[ing] another letter from you, with anxious expectation that I trust you will be as good as your word. You do not [mention] your own health, therefore I hope it is perfectly reesta[blished.] pray tell me what has been your complaint and if [you are] now perfectly well. Let me have a long letter from you and assure me you entirely forgive me; Oh Jane you are very dear to me. I love you if possible better than ever since your last arrived I would not leave a scrap of paper unfill'd if I had time to say. more, but I every moment expect to have my letter call'd for—adieu my dear Girl.

D. Wordsworth

My kind remembrance to each of your Family. Do write soon—can you read this scrawl?

Tuesday Morning.

I find I have a little more time therefore I will not omit telling you that I have seized the first opportunity I have had of getting a letter conveyed to the office. Be very particular in telling me how you go on. What are you reading? Do you walk much? are your Sisters all well. Do you often see our Family? what does my Aunt say of me? in short tell me every thing—and continue to love me—my dearest Jane.

3. *To* Jane Pollard

Forncett Sunday Morng June 26th. [1791]

I am so much indebted to you, my dear Jane, for the steadiness of your friendship that I am at a loss for words to thank you. Believe me, however, my dearest girl, I am fully resolved in future never to

---

[1] Elizabeth Threlkeld, a cousin (see Letter 4 below), to be distinguished from 'Aunt' Threlkeld.

put your affection for me to so severe a trial. I will not say that I have suffered as much as I deserve, but I have suffered so much as I hope will make me very unwilling to throw myself again into a similar situation. I am very happy to hear that your father's health continues to improve, and that your mother (of whom I heard by my aunt) continues to preserve her health and evenness of spirits. Long may you enjoy that domestic comfort uninterrupted for which your family is so remarkable, and which is in fact the only thing which deserves the name of happiness.

I hope you will perform your promise of letting me have another letter from you very soon. I am anxious for a further account of my old friends. Poor Betsy Ferguson[1] is probably dead ere this. It is very long since I have received so severe a shock as from the account you give me of her. Oh Jane how short a time has elapsed since she was as strong as healthy and perhaps more gay than we are. How are her sisters affected by her melancholy fate? I used to think that there was not that disinterested affection for each other amongst them which one always wishes and expects to see in children of the same family. Do not forget to answer all the questions I put to you in my last which you had not room to reply to. I hope you will have a pleasant jaunt to Leeds. Do let me hear often from you, I never indeed my dearest Jane, will be so negligent in future. Be so good as tell my Aunt that I have expected a letter from her some time. I would have written to her if I had not been prevented by the expectation of a letter every post. I often hear from my brother William who is now in Wales where I think he seems so happy that it is probable he will remain there all the summer, or a great part of it: Who would not be happy enjoying the company of three young ladies in the Vale of Clewyd and without a rival? His friend Jones[2] is a charming young man; and has *five sisters*, three of whom are at home at present, then there are mountains, rivers, woods and rocks, whose charms without any other inducement would be sufficient to tempt William to continue amongst them as long as possible. So that most likely he will have the pleasure of seeing you when he visits Halifax, which I hope he will do in his road to the

---

[1] A cousin.
[2] Robert Jones (see List of Correspondents), W. W.'s companion on the 'pedestrian tour' to France and Switzerland the previous summer.

North; he thinks with great pleasure of paying that place a visit where I have so many friends. I confess you are right in supposing me partial to William. I hope when you see him you will think my regard not misplaced; probably when I next see Kitt I shall love him as well, the difference between our ages at the time I was with him was much more perceptible than it will be at our next meeting; his disposition is of the same cast as William's and his inclinations have taken the same turn, but he is much more likely to make his fortune; he is not so warm as William but has a most affectionate heart, his abilities though not so great perhaps as his brothers may be of more use to him as he has not fixed his mind upon any particular species of reading, or conceived an aversion to any. He is not fond of Mathematics but has resolution sufficient to study them because it will be impossible for him to obtain a fellowship without a knowledge of them. William you may have heard lost the chance, indeed the certainty of a fellowship by not combating his inclinations, he gave way to his natural dislike of studies so dry as many parts of the mathematics, consequently could not succeed at Cambridge. He reads Italian, Spanish, French, Greek and Latin, and English, but never opens a mathematical book. We promise ourselves much pleasure from reading Italian together at some time, he wishes that I was acquainted with the Italian poets, but how much have I to learn which plain English will teach me. William has a great attachment to poetry; indeed so has Kitt, but William particularly, which is not the most likely thing to produce his advancement in the world; his pleasures are chiefly of the imagination, he is never so happy as when in a beautiful country. Do not think from what I have said that he reads not [at] all, for he does read a great deal and not only poetry and those languages he is acquainted with but history etc etc. Kitt has made a very good proficiency in his learning and is certainly a very clever young man, he is just seventeen, so that October 92 we shall have him at Cambridge.

When I last wrote to you I told you that our affairs wore a promising aspect; they are now in a very critical state; our trial is to come on at the next Carlisle assizes, where we hope the justice of our cause will carry us through. Lord Lonsdale has retained all the best counsel, who except one, are engaged to serve him upon all occasions, and that one he had just engaged the moment before my brother went to him. We have got a very clever man on our side but as he is young he will not have much authority, his name is Christian,[1] he is a friend of my Uncle, knows my brother William very well and I am very well acquainted with him and a charming man he is; I hope, however, that what he wants in experience will be made up in zeal for our interest. You may perhaps have seen his name in the reviews; a pamphlet which he published lately upon the question whether Hastings'[2] trial was to go on was highly spoken of. He is professor of common law in the university of Cambridge. We have been some time expecting tidings of my brother John; but have not any cause for uneasiness though we hear nothing of him as the East India vessels have been detained in consequence of the expected war with Spain. My Aunt and I are at present pleasing ourselves with the thoughts of riding a good deal this summer; she is to ride double, and I upon a little horse of my Uncle's. The country about us though not romantic or picturesque is very pleasing, the surface is tolerably varied, and we have great plenty of wood but a sad want of water.

I think I once mentioned the Miss Burroughes's to you, I am more intimate with them than any other young people; indeed we have only two other young women in our neighbourhood; and one of them I dislike very much and the other is at too great a distance to allow us to have much communication with each other. I find [the Miss] Burroughes's improve much upon a further knowledge of the[m. They] are indeed very agreeable girls; I had a very pleasant walk with them on Friday evening and I hope for another this evening as I am going to call upon them. I cannot help often regretting that I have not a more intimate friend near me; but I am convinced that I shall never form a friendship that will not appear trifling indeed compared with that I feel for you. You are the friend of my childhood, and Oh! how endearing a thought is that. You shared all my little distresses and were the partner of all my pleasures. It gives me great concern when I think that I ever gave you pain by my attachment to Peggy Taylor; surely I never appeared to give her the preference. I am well convinced that she never held so large a share of my affection as you by many degrees.

[1] Edward Christian (1758–1823).
[2] Warren Hastings.

You are disappointed that I do not think of visiting Halifax sooner than the spring of the year 93. I do assure you that nothing but the most powerful reasons could tempt me to defer the execution of my plan so long. By that time I shall be my own mistress and though I would do nothing inconsistent with the duty I owe my Uncle and Aunt, yet I shall then be able to do it of myself without all the difficulty which I should have before my coming of age. I shall also by that time know what is the amount of my possessions and can square my proceedings accordingly, for in the present uncertain state of our fortunes I should be certain of meeting with a refusal on account of the expence attending so long a journey. We shall either be very well off in regard to money matters or be left without a farthing except Richard's estate,[1] for what money we have if the trial goes against us will be swallowed by the gentlemen of the law. Whatever is the result of this tedious suit I am prepared to meet it; I fear not poverty in my youth and why should I expect it in age, when I have 4 Brothers all of whom have received good educations and suitable to their situations in life, and who are all sincerely attached to me; while I am young I thank God I am not destitute of the means of supporting myself, independent of the assistance which I may expect from my Gmr. and the rest of my friends therefore I can bear the worst with fortitude and put myself into a situation by which I may procure a livelihood till my Brothers are able to assist me; you shall hear more of this if we are unfortunate, but which I hope is not likely, in the mean time do not say anything of the hint I have given you. I was indeed greatly mortified on hearing of Mr W's bad success,[2] every friend to humanity must applaud his zeal and lament that it failed in its effect. I beg my dear Friend, that you will write as soon as possible and a long letter.

　　　　　　　　　　　　　　Yours unalterably　　D W

　　　　　　　　　　　　　　Monday Eveng.

I am very sorry to hear you have ever so troublesome a complaint as a pain in your side, pray tell me particularly what is the general state of your health in your next. I am indeed very healthy.

[1] At Sockbridge, nr Penrith.
[2] Wilberforce's motion to abolish the slave trade had been defeated.

I am going to Stratton this eveng and shall put my lr. into that office. I go alone, am not I daring? Love to all yr Family and you.

4. *To* Jane Pollard

Forncett, February 16th [1793]

Your affectionate Letter, my dear Friend, afforded me more Satisfaction than I usually receive even from your Letters, for though there is a certain Pleasure attending the Conviction that one is not forgotten by the person one loves after having long sought and wished for it, yet we have both experienced that the Price at which this Pleasure is purchased is much too painful; I trust, then, that in future we shall prevent each others wishes by writing sooner than our Letters may fairly be expected, and never again put the Attachment of our Hearts to so severe a Trial as it has often gone through. Your Letter found me happy in the Society of one of my dear Brothers and one of the dearest of my Brothers.[1] I think I have told you that Christopher and I had been separated nearly five years last Christmas; judge then of my transports at meeting him again, and judge too of my Happiness during the Time we spent together when I inform you that he is a most amiable young Man, sensible, affectionate, and engaging. By the Bye I know not whether I have not exaggerated a little in this last Article of Praise, for his Modesty is so extreme as almost to amount to absolute Bashfulness; and though my Partiality for him teaches me to account this as rather a Merit than otherwise (and as in a youth of eighteen no body perhaps would *profess* to contradict me), yet it certainly makes the word *engaging* not quite proper, for it would be some Time before a stranger would discover half his merits or perhaps find him out to be agreeable. He is like William: he has the same traits in his Character but less highly touched, he is not so ardent in any of his pursuits but is yet more particularly attached to the same Pursuits which have so irresistible an Influence over William, which deprive him of the Power of chaining his attention to others discordant to his feelings. Christopher is no despicable Poet, but he can become a

[1] C. W., now at Trinity College, Cambridge.

Mathematician also, he is not insensible of the Beauties of the Greek and Latin Classics, or of any of the charms of elegant Literature but he can draw his mind from these fascinating studies to others less alluring; he is steady and sincere in his attachments, William has both these Virtues in an eminent degree; and a sort of violence of Affection if I may so Term it which demonstrates itself every moment of the Day when the Objects of his affection are present with him, in a thousand almost imperceptible attentions to their wishes, in a sort of restless watchfulness which I know not how to describe, a Tenderness that never sleeps, and at the same Time such a Delicacy of Manners as I have observed in few Men. I hope you will one day be much better acquainted with him than you are at present, much as I have talked to you about him. I look forward with full confidence to the Happiness of receiving you in my little Parsonage,[1] I hope you will spend at least a year with me. I have laid the particular scheme of happiness for each Season. When I think of Winter I hasten to furnish our little Parlour, I close the Shutters, set out the Tea-table, brighten the Fire. When our Refreshment is ended I produce our Work, and William brings his book to our Table and contributes at once to our Instruction and amusement, and at Intervals we lay aside the Book and each hazard our observations upon what has been read without the fear of Ridicule or Censure. We talk over past days, we do not sigh for any Pleasures beyond our humble Habitation "The central point of all our joys".[2] Oh Jane! with such romantic dreams as these I amuse my fancy during many an hour which would otherwise pass heavily along, for kind as are my Uncle and Aunt, much as I love my sweet little Cousins, I cannot help heaving many a Sigh at the Reflection that I have passed one and twenty years of my Life, and that the first six years only of this Time was spent in the Enjoyment of the same Pleasures that were enjoyed by my Brothers, and that I was then too young to be sensible of the Blessing. We have been endeared to each other by early misfortune. We in the same moment lost a father, a mother, a home, we have been equally deprived of our patrimony

---

[1] D. W. was dreaming of keeping house for W. W. in the event of his taking holy orders. He had recently returned from revolutionary France to superintend publication of *An Evening Walk* and *Descriptive Sketches*.

[2] *Descriptive Sketches* (1793), l. 571.

by the cruel Hand of lordly Tyranny. These afflictions have all contributed to unite us closer by the Bonds of affection notwithstanding we have been compelled to spend our youth far asunder. "We drag at each remove a lengthening Chain"[1] this Idea often strikes me very forcibly. Neither absence nor Distance nor Time can ever break the Chain that links me to my Brothers. But why do I talk to you thus? Because these are the thoughts that are uppermost in my Breast at the moment, and when I write to the companion of my childish Days I must write the Dictates of my Heart. In our conversations so full of tenderness I have never constrained my Sentiments; I have laid open to her the inmost Recesses of my Heart then why should I impose a Restraint upon myself when I am writing to her? But is it not possible that these details of my Feelings and my little Griefs may be insipid to her? she cannot relieve them, she perhaps may think them unreasonable.

By this Time, you have doubtless seen my Brother Williams Poems, and they have already suffered the Lash of your Criticisms. I should be very glad if you would give me your opinion of them with the same Frankness with which I am going to give you mine. The Scenes which he describes have been viewed with a Poet's eye and are pourtrayed with a Poet's pencil; and the Poems contain many Passages exquisitely beautiful, but they also contain many Faults, the chief of which are Obscurity, and a too frequent use of some particular expressions and uncommon words for instance *moveless*,[2] which he applies in a sense if not new, at least different from its ordinary one; by moveless when applied to the Swan he means that sort of motion which is smooth without agitation; it is a very beautiful epithet but ought to have been cautiously used, he ought at any rate only to have hazarded it once, instead of which it occurs three or four times. The word *viewless*,[3] also, is introduced far too often, this, though not so uncommon a word as the former ought not to have been made use of more than once or twice. I regret exceedingly that he did not submit the works to the Inspection of some Friend before their Publication, and he also joins with

---

[1] Goldsmith, *Traveller*, l. 10.

[2] *Evening Walk*, ll. 104, 206; *Descriptive Sketches*, l. 266.

[3] *Evening Walk*, l. 148; *Descriptive Sketches*, ll. 36, 92, 227, 548, 648. All were later taken out.

me in this Regret. Their Faults are such as a young Poet was most likely to fall into and least likely to discover, and what the Suggestions of a Friend would easily have made him see and at once correct. It is however an Error he will never fall into again, as he is well aware that he would have gained considerably more credit if the Blemishes of which I speak had been corrected. My Brother Kitt and I, while he was at Forncett, amused ourselves by analysing every Line and prepared a very bulky Criticism, which he was to transmit to William as soon as he should have added to it the Remarks of his Cambridge Friends. At the Conclusion of the Evening Walk, I think you would be pleased with those lines, "Thus hope first pouring from her blessed Horn" etc. etc. You would espy the little gilded Cottage in the Horizon, but perhaps your less gloomy Imagination and your anxiety to see your Friend placed in that happy Habitation might make you overlook the dark and broad Gulph between. If you have not yet seen the Poems pray do not make known my opinion of them—let them pass the fiery ordeal. Mr. Griffith[1] desired my Br to send him half a Dozen copies as soon as they should be published which I have no doubt he has done, and by his means you most probably have seen them. I am sure I ought to ask your forgiveness for dwelling thus lon[g] on what relates merely to myself or my Brothers.

I look [?forward] to the latter end of next summer with a full confidence of [? meeting the] beloved Friend of my happiest Days, our conversa[tion will indeed] be interesting, we shall live over again those hours [? of which the remem]brance will ever be dear to me. "Then hope itself was all I knew of Pain"[2]—I look forward with much Pleasure to an [   ] [? with] Harriot,[3] I am sure she was always a very great [   ] [and pro]mised to be Just the Woman you describe. I am very [? sorry to hear] such an account of poor Elizabeth Threlkeld,[4] I say [   ] is really much to be pitied, as I am sure the Fa[mily] [? indispo]sition may in great measure be laid to the charge [   ] mistaken Indulgence. You never described her per[son: is] she as tall as Miss Bolland? She

---

[1] A cousin.
[2] See *Evening Walk*, l. 32.
[3] Jane's younger sister.
[4] D. W.'s cousin, Mrs Rawson's niece.

must by this Time [? have put] on the Woman's dress which I think will not sit [   ] her. Does she wear Powder? or in what sort of P[   ] appear? I was much affected with the History of [   ] I often think of her, and with tears I have mourned her Fate. *She* herself perhaps does not suffer so much now as before her loss of Reason, but dreadful indeed must have been her previous sufferings when they were driving her to such a State.

You are very good in inquiring after our little People. I wish I could introduce them to you. They are the sweetest children I ever saw—healthy and strong to a remarkable degree, and of course very lively. They have never known an Hour's illness since their Birth except when they had the small-pox.

Give my kind love to my Cousins when you see them and to Mrs. Rawson. Pray tell Mrs R. that I wish to hear from her and to have her opinion of my Brothers Poems. If she *has* already read them, I wish you would tell her what I have said of them— if not wait till she has formed her own judgment. I am sure you must think that there are some very glaring Faults but I hope too, that you will discover many Beauties, Beauties which could only have been created by the Imagination of a *Poet*.

Remember me very affectionately to your Father and Mother, and Sisters. Tell them that I look forward with much Pleasure to seeing them again—adieu my dear Girl,

Believe me unalterably yours

D Wordsworth.

Pray write immediately.

5. *To* unknown correspondent

[Windy Brow, Apr. 1794]

After having enjoyed the company of my brother William at Halifax, we set forward by coach towards Whitehaven, and thence to Kendal. I walked with my brother at my side, from Kendal to Grasmere, eighteen miles, and afterwards from Grasmere to Keswick, fifteen miles, through the most delightful country that was ever seen. We are now at a farm-house,[1] about half a mile from Keswick. When I came, I intended to stay only a few days; but the country is so delightful, and, above all, I have so full an enjoyment of my brother's company, that I have determined to stay a few weeks longer. After I leave Windy Brow (this is the name of the farm-house), I shall proceed to Whitehaven.

6. *To* Mrs Christopher Crackanthorpe

Windy Brow April 21st [1794]

My dear Aunt,

I should have answered your letter immediately after the receipt of it, if I had not been upon the point of setting forward to Mrs Spedding's[2] of Armathwaite where I have been spending three days. I am much obliged to you for the frankness with which you have expressed your sentiments upon my conduct and am at the same time extremely sorry that you should think it so severely to be condemned. As you have not sufficiently developed the reasons of your censure I have endeavoured to discover them, and I confess no other possible objections against my continuing here a few weeks longer suggest themselves, except the *expence* and that you may suppose me to be in an unprotected situation. As to the former of these objections I reply that I drink no tea, that my supper and breakfast are of bread and milk and my dinner chiefly of potatoes from choice. In answer to the second of these suggestions, namely that I may be supposed to be in an exposed situation, I affirm that I consider the character and virtues of my brother as a sufficient protection, and besides I am convinced that there is no place in the world in which a good and virtuous young woman would be more likely to continue good and virtuous than under the roof of these honest, worthy, uncorrupted people so that any guardianship beyond theirs, I should think altogether unnecessary.

[1] Windy Brow belonged to W. W.'s schoolfriend William Calvert, brother of Raisley Calvert (1773–95), whose timely legacy to W. W. enabled him to be a poet instead of entering the Church.

[2] Mother of W. W.'s schoolfriend, John Spedding.

I cannot pass unnoticed that part of your letter in which you speak of my "rambling about the country on foot". So far from considering this as a matter of condemnation, I rather thought it would have given my friends pleasure to hear that I had courage to make use of the strength with which nature has endowed me, when it not only procured me infinitely more pleasure than I should have received from sitting in a post-chaise—but was also the means of saving me at least thirty shillings.

In mentioning the inducements which I have to stay at Windy Brow a few weeks longer it will be unnecessary to speak of the beauty of the country or the pleasantness of the season. To these are added the society of several of my brothers friends from whom I have received the most friendly attentions and above all the society of my brother. I am now twenty two years of age and such have been the circumstances of my life that I may be said to have enjoyed his company only for a *very few* months. An opportunity now presents itself of obtaining this satisfaction, an opportunity which I could not see pass from me without unspeakable pain. Besides I not only derive much pleasure but much improvement from my brother's society. I have regained all the knowledge I had of the French language some years ago, and have added considerably to it, and I have now begun reading Italian, of which I expect to have soon gained a sufficient knowledge to receive much entertainment and advantage from it. I am much obliged to you and my Uncle for your kind invitation which I shall accept with great pleasure at my return from Whitehaven. I have received the kindest civilities from Mrs Spedding of Armathwaite. She has made me promise that if it is in my power I will spend a little while with [   ] I know of nothing that would make me more happy than to cultivate the acquaintance of the Miss Speddings who are most amiable women. I beg my love to my Uncle and the children, and my compliments to Miss Cust.[1] Believe me, my dear Aunt

Affectionately yours

D Wordsworth

---

[1] Mrs Crackanthorpe's sister.

7. *To* Mrs John Marshall

My dearest Jane,

If the *intention* of writing may excuse my long silence I am to be excused, for I really never more fully intended any thing in my life than to write to you very soon after my arrival at Racedown. I certainly had no right to expect to hear from you till I myself had informed you of my address. Before I begin to tell you anything of my own affairs let me congratulate you upon your happy escape. I cannot conceive any thing much more distressing than your situation during the fire, accompanied with the alarm of your mother's indisposition. Perhaps this accident may in fact be a piece of good fortune as it will increase the caution of the people engaged in your *large concern*, and may prevent future and more important mischief. We are now surrounded by winter prospects without doors, and within have only winter occupations, books, solitude and the fireside, yet I may safely say we are never dull. Basil[1] is a charming boy, he affords us perpetual entertainment. Do not suppose from this that we make him our perpetual play-thing, far otherwise, I think that is one of the modes of treatment most likely to ruin a child's temper and character. But I do not think there is any Pleasure more delightful than that of marking the development of a child's faculties, and observing his little occupations. We found every thing at Racedown much more complete with respect to household conveniences than I could have expected. You may judge of this when I tell you we have not had to lay out ten shillings for the use of the house. We were a whole month without servant, but now we have got one of the nicest girls I ever saw; she suits us exactly, and I have all my domestic concerns so arranged that everything goes on with the utmost regularity. We wash once a month. I hire a woman, to whom I give ninepence for one day, to wash, on the next we have got the clothes dried and on the third have finished ironing. It is the only time in which I have any thing to do in the house, but then I am very active and very busy as you will suppose. I have been making Basil coloured frocks, shirts, slips, etc, and have a good

---

[1] Son of Basil Montagu (1770–1851), lawyer and author. W. W. was tutoring the boy.

deal of employment in repairing his clothes and putting my brothers into order. We walk about two hours every morning—we have many very pleasant walks about us and what is a great advantage, the roads are of a sandy kind and are almost always dry. We can see the sea 150 or 200 yards from the door, and at a little distance have a very extensive view terminated by the sea seen through different openings of the unequal hills. We have not the warmth and luxuriance of Devonshire though there is no want either of wood or cultivation, but the trees appear to suffer from the sea blasts. We have hills which seen from a distance almost take the character of mountains, some cultivated nearly to their summits, others in their wild state covered with furze and broom. These delight me the most as they remind me of our native wilds. Our common parlour is the prettiest little room that can be; with very neat furniture, a large book[case?] on each side the fire, a marble chimney piece, bath stove, and an oil cloth for the floor. The other parlour is rather larger, has a good carpet, side boards in the recesses on each side the fire, and has upon the whole a smart appearance, but we do not like it half so well as our little breakfast room. I have only had one great disappointment since I came and that was about the little girl. I lament it the more as I am sure if her father knew all the circumstances he would wish her to be placed under our care. Mr. Montague had intended being with us a month ago but we have not seen him yet; we hope however that he will be with us before Christmas. I have the satisfaction of thinking that he will see great improvements in Basil. Our nearest neighbours have called upon us; I do not think we shall be much benefitted by their society, as they do not seem much inclined either to go out or see their friends; nor indeed if they were would they be any great advantage to us, as though they are very good kind of people, and seem desirous of doing us any thing in their power, they have not much conversation. William has had a letter from France since we came here. Annette[1] mentions having despatched half a dozen none of which he has received. My aunt Cookson was brought to bed of a girl nearly three weeks ago. She has now five children. She was doing

---

[1] Annette Vallon, mother of W. W.'s 'French' daughter Caroline (b.1792).

very well when my uncle wrote to me.

The greatest inconvenience we suffer here is in being so far from the post office; with respect to household conveniences we do very well, as the butcher coming from Cruikhern[1] brings us every thing we want. With respect to letters we are however, more independent than most people as William is so good a walker, and *I* too have walked over twice to Crewkhern (the distance is 7 miles) to make purchases, and what is more we turned out of our way three miles, in one of our walks thither to see a house of Lord Powlett's and a very fine view. We were amply repaid for our trouble. If you want to find our situation out, look in your maps for Crewkhern, Chard, Axminster, Bridport and Lime; we are nearly equidistant from all those places. A little brook which runs at the distance of one field from us divides us from Devonshire. This country abounds in apples; in some of our walks we go through orchards without any other enclosure or security than as a common field. When I spoke of the sea I forgot to tell you that my brother saw the West India fleet sailing in all its glory before the storm had made such dreadful ravages. The peasants are miserably poor; their cottages are shapeless structures (I may almost say) of wood and clay—indeed they are not at all beyond what might be expected in savage life. You must not find fault with this small paper, for I have written so close that my letter contains more than your large sheet, but if I had had any other I should not have made use of this, for I feel as if I had yet a great deal more to say. How does your mother's health continue in general? When do you expect to see Harriot? Give my kind love to all at Ovenden. Perhaps you may be there when this letter reaches you. Remember me affectionately to Mrs Marshall, Mr M and Ellen.[2] I of[ten] think of the happy days I spent [with] you and of the hospitality and kind[ness]. Excuse miserable writing. William desires his best compliments to you and Mr M.—adieu—my dear Jane believe me ever your faithful friend

D. Wordsworth

---

[1] i.e. Crewkerne.
[2] Jane's elder sister.

8. *To* Mary Hutchinson [?]

Racedown, [June, 1797]

... You had a great loss in not seeing Coleridge. He is a wonderful man. His conversation teems with soul, mind, and spirit. Then he is so benevolent, so good tempered and cheerful, and, like William, interests himself so much about every little trifle. At first I thought him very plain, that is, for about three minutes: he is pale and thin, has a wide mouth, thick lips, and not very good teeth, longish loose-growing half-curling rough black hair. But if you hear him speak for five minutes you think no more of them. His eye is large and full, not dark but grey; such an eye as would receive from a heavy soul the dullest expression; but it speaks every emotion of his animated mind; it has more of the 'poet's eye in a fine frenzy rolling' than I ever witnessed. He has fine dark eyebrows, and an overhanging forehead.

The first thing that was read after he came was William's new poem *The Ruined Cottage*[1] with which he was much delighted; and after tea he repeated to us two acts and a half of his tragedy *Osorio*. The next morning William read his tragedy *The Borderers*.[2] ...

9. *To* Mary Hutchinson [?]

[Nether Stowey, July 4th, 1797]

... There is everything here; sea, woods wild as fancy ever painted, brooks clear and pebbly as in Cumberland, villages so romantic; and William and I, in a wander by ourselves, found out a sequestered waterfall in a dell formed by steep hills covered with full-grown timber trees. The woods are as fine as those at Lowther,[1] and the country more romantic; it has the character of the less grand parts of the neighbourhood of the Lakes. ...

[1] Later embodied in Bk. i of *The Excursion*.
[2] Publ. 1842.
[3] Seat of Lord Lonsdale, nr Penrith.

10. *To* Mary Hutchinson [?]

Alfoxden, near Nether-Stowey, Somersetshire,
August 14, 1797.

Here we are in a large mansion, in a large park, with seventy head of deer around us. But I must begin with the day of leaving Racedown to pay Coleridge a visit. You know how much we were delighted with the neighbourhood of Stowey. ... The evening that I wrote to you, William and I had rambled as far as this house, and pryed into the recesses of our little brook, but without any more fixed thoughts upon it than some dreams of happiness in a little cottage, and passing wishes that such a place might be found out. We spent a fortnight at Coleridge's; in the course of that time we heard that this house was to let, applied for it, and took it. Our principal inducement was Coleridge's society. It was a month yesterday since we came to Alfoxden.

The house is a large mansion, with furniture enough for a dozen families like ours. There is a very excellent garden, well stocked with vegetables and fruit. The garden is at the end of the house, and our favourite parlour, as at Racedown, looks that way. In front is a little court, with grass plot, gravel walk, and shrubs; the moss roses were in full beauty a month ago. The front of the house is to the south, but it is screened from the sun by a high hill which rises immediately from it. This hill is beautiful, scattered irregularly and abundantly with trees, and topped with fern, which spreads a considerable way down it. The deer dwell here, and sheep, so that we have a living prospect. From the end of the house we have a view of the sea, over a woody meadow-country; and exactly opposite the window where I now sit is an immense wood, whose round top from this point has exactly the appearance of a mighty dome. In some parts of this wood there is an under grove of hollies which are now very beautiful. In a glen at the bottom of the wood is the waterfall of which I spoke, a quarter of a mile from the house. We are three miles from Stowey, and not two miles from the sea. Wherever we turn we have woods, smooth downs, and valleys with small brooks running down them through green meadows, hardly ever intersected with hedgerows, but scattered over with trees. The hills that cradle these valleys are either covered with fern and bilberries, or oak woods, which are cut for charcoal. .... Walks extend for miles over the hill-tops; the great beauty of which is their wild simplicity: they are perfectly smooth, without rocks.

The Tor of Glastonbury is before our eyes during more than half of our walk to Stowey; and in the park wherever we go, keeping about fifteen yards above the house, it makes a part of our prospect.

11. *To* Mary Hutchinson [?]

Alfoxden. Nov 20 1797

We have been on another tour: we set out last Monday evening at half past four. The evening was dark and cloudy: we went eight miles, William and Coleridge employing themselves in laying the plan of a ballad,[1] to be published with some pieces of William's. ....
William's play is finished, and sent to the managers of the Covent Garden Theatre. We have not the faintest expectation that it will be accepted.

12. *To* Mrs William Rawson

Allfoxden 13th June [and Bristol 3 July] 1798.

My dear Aunt,

It is useless to tell you what were my resolutions upon the receipt of your last letter. I resolved to answer it immediately but, this resolve slipping from me, I have been induced by various circumstances to delay from time to time till three months are gone by. Of late I have wanted to give you precise information respecting our future destination. You know that we are obliged to quit Allfoxden at Midsummer. It is not, however, on account of the taxes, for we could get rid of them by appealing, but because the house has been taken by another person. At first we regretted this circumstance very much as every thing has contributed to attach us to this place,

---

[1] *The Rime of the Ancient Mariner.*

the society of Coleridge and the friendly attentions of a Mr. Poole[1] who is a man of uncommon virtue and good sense, the exceptional beauty of the country, and the excellent opportunities we have of getting books; but as we are now determined upon going into Germany along with Mr and Mrs Coleridge and their family we are glad that we are not shackled with the house.

We have long wished to go into that country for the purpose of learning the language, and for the common advantages to be acquired by seeing different people and different manners. Coleridge has had the same wish; and we have so arranged our plans that I hope we shall sail in two or three months. Our first intention was to have gone *immediately* to the neighbourhood of one of the universities; but as we find that the price of lodgings etc. is much greater in the towns where there are universities we have resolved to go into some small town or village, till we have acquired the language, which we imagine we shall have a good knowledge of in about twelve months, and afterward, to draw near a university, when William and Coleridge will then be better able to profit by the instructions they may have an opportunity of receiving.

We are advised to go into Saxony. Some parts of that country are extremely beautiful and boarding is very cheap. It is our intention (William's and mine) to board in some respectable family for the benefit, or rather the obligation of talking German constantly. The Coleridges, if they can, will take a ready-furnished house as they have two children and must of course keep a servant.[2]

Such are our plans for one year, at least; what we shall do afterwards it is impossible at present to say. If the state of Europe will permit we shall endeavour to get into Switzerland; at any rate we shall travel as far as the tether of a slender income will permit. We hope to make some addition to our resources by translating from the German, the most profitable species of literary labour, and of which I can do almost as much as my Brother.

Poor Basil! We are obliged to leave him behind as his father, on account of having altered the course of his pursuits in the law, will not be able to pay the additional expences which we should incur on his account. This, however, might be got over as he has friends

---

[1] Thomas Poole (see List of Correspondents).
[2] In the event S. T. C. left his wife and children at Nether Stowey.

who would do it for him, but as the experiment of taking a child of his age into a foreign country is at any rate hazardous, and might be prejudicial if we were not so placed that he might see much of other children, we think upon the whole that it is better that he should not go, taking into the calculation the certain expense.

I am convinced it is not good for a child to be educated alone after a certain age. Basil has in some respects, I think suffered from it, though no doubt in others he has gained; he has a most excellent temper, is quite free from selfishness, is extremely active, and never fretful or discontented. Much of his good temper must be owing to our regularity of temper, and the consequent equable treatment which he receives from us. If he had been more with children whose minds were upon *the same level with his own* I think he could scarcely have been without selfishness. As to his activity I believe that the solitude of Racedown tended considerably to increase it. Till a child is four years old he needs no other companions, than the flowers, the grass, the cattle, the sheep that scamper away from him when he makes a vain unexpecting chase after them, the pebbles upon the road, etc. etc. After the age of about four years he begins to want some other stimulus than the mere life that is in him; his efforts would be greater but he must have an object, he would run but he must run *races*, he would climb a wall but he has no motive to do it when he is alone; he must have some standard by which to compare his powers or he will have no pleasure in exercising them, and he becomes lifeless and inactive.

Basil as to bodily exertion has had this advantage since we came to Allfoxden; he has played a great deal with a little boy who lives near us. He is a very naughty spoiled child but I think Basil has not suffered so much from him morally, as we expected, and he has certainly gone on improving in physical strength. The situations of the two children at home are so totally different as to prevent all comparison, one source of selfishness and Basil is so well convinced that to be [good? ...]

The two pages which you have just been reading were written about three weeks ago at Allfoxden. We have left that Dear and beautiful place and are now at Bristol where we arrived last night, after having spent a week at Mr Coleridge's after our departure from Allfoxden. We are going into lodgings at Shirehampton, a very beautiful place in this neighbourhood.

I wonder whether we are likely to see Mr. Rawson during our two months residence in this neighbourhood. I fear there is not much chance of it as he generally makes his journey later. I need not say what pleasure it would give me to see him. I wish he had ever contrived to visit us at Allfoxden, if he had had no other motive than that of seeing an interesting country he would not have been disappointed. I have not often felt more regret than when we quitted Allfoxden; I should however have felt much more if we were not likely in so short a time to have again the pleasure of Coleridge's society, an advantage which I prize the more, the more I know him.

You ask me if I am acquainted with Southey.[1] I know a little of him personally, that is I dined three times at his house when I was in town and called there once or twice; and I know a good deal of his character from our common friends. He is a young man of the most rigidly virtuous habits and is, I believe, exemplary in the discharge of all Domestic Duties, but though his talents are certainly very remarkable for his years (as far as I can judge) I think them much inferior to the talents of Coleridge.

I am writing in a front room, in one of the most busy streets of Bristol. You can scarely conceive how the jarring contrast between the sounds which are now for ever ringing in my ears and the sweet sounds of Allfoxden makes me long for the country again. After three years residence in retirement a city in feeling, sound, and prospect is hateful.

We shall certainly not stay at Shirehampton more than three months; we talk of being on board the vessel in two months but I do not think this is very probable, as I have no doubt that many things will delay the Coleridges which they have no idea of at present.

I think Mr Rawson has correspondents in Germany; perhaps by their means I should be able to hear from and write to you post free. Otherwise I fear letter-writing will be so expensive that I must very much abridge the quantity of letters which I write. In writing letters in foreign countries the expense is much more than doubled for one is obliged to pay both for the letters sent and received. Perhaps I

---

[1] Robert Southey (1774–1843), the poet, S. T. C.'s brother-in-law.

shall be able to get letters sent by means of the Wedgwoods[1] who are to give us letters of introduction to some Hamburgh merchants. At any rate I must so manage that when one of my friends hears from me the rest must hear either of or from me.

Give my kind love to Elizabeth Threlkeld.[2] Tell her she shall hear from me very soon. I ought to have written to Mrs Marshall some time ago. I can scarcely say why I have neglected it but I will certainly write to her from Shirehampton.

I was very happy to hear of poor Mr Pollard's release. Will his family continue at Ovenden? I have thought that they would perhaps go to Leeds.

When I am just upon the point of concluding my letter I recollect that you may perhaps think that we are going upon an expensive scheme into Germany and that our income will not suffice to maintain us. I must put you to the expense of a double letter to explain this to you. Notwithstanding Mr Montagu, (from having changed the course of his application to the law) has not been able to fulfil his engagement respecting Basil, we have lived upon our income and are not a farthing poorer than when we began house-keeping. We can live for less money in Germany while we are stationary than we can in England, so that you see our regular income (independent of what we may gain by translation) will be sufficient to support us when we are there, and we shall receive, before our departure much more than sufficient to defray the expenses of our journey, from a bookseller[3] to whom William has sold some poems that are now printing, for which he is to have a certain present price and is to be paid afterwards in proportion to their sale. Our expenses last year 23£ for rent, our journey to London, clothes, servant's wages etc included, only amounted to 110£. We have parted from our servant. Poor Girl! it was a hard trial for her. She would have gone to the world's end with us. I believe she was much more attached to us than to any other beings in the world. She was married a year ago and is now with child so she would have left us, if we had even been in England.

---

[1] Thomas and Josiah Wedgwood, of the Staffs. pottery family, S. T. C.'s benefactors.

[2] Mrs Rawson's niece.

[3] Joseph Cottle, publisher of *Lyrical Ballads*, 1798.

Remember me very affectionate[ly] to the Fergusons. Perhaps we may see Edward. I heard that he was at Bristol last year. [Why did not he] come to Allfoxden? The distance by the ferry below Bridgwater is only 36 miles.

I am very glad to hear that Mr. Griffith [   ] in his wife and child. Remember me to them when you write.

God bless you my dear Aunt, [and]
Believe me

Your very affectionate
D. Wordsworth.

Bristol, July 3rd
    Direct to me at Mr Cottle's,
    Wine Street Bristol.

13. *To* Christopher Wordsworth

Goslar, Feb 3rd 1799

My dear Brother

As we have prolonged our stay at Goslar so much beyond our expectations, we regret extremely that we limited you to writing within the two months. We wish extremely to hear from you, as we are yet uncertain respecting your success in the struggle for a fellowship. My Aunt Cookson, in a letter which I had from her about two months ago, says that you have got two pupils, one the son of the Bishop of Norwich, but she says not a word about the fellowship.[1] Now we do not know whether to argue from her silence that you have gained or lost the point, as either event would certainly have been worthy of a particular communication.

For more than two months past we have intended quitting Goslar in the course of each week, but we have been so frightened by the cold season, the dreadful roads, and the uncovered carts; that we needed no other motives (adding these considerations to our natural aversion to moving from a place where we live in comfort and quietness) to induce us to linger here. We have had a succession of excessively severe weather, once or twice interrupted with a cold

[1] C. W. was elected Fellow of Trinity in 1798.

thaw; and the cold of Christmas day has not been equalled even in this climate during the last century. It was so excessive that when we left the room where we sit we were obliged to wrap ourselves up in great coats etc in order not to suffer much pain from the transition, though we only went into the next room or down stairs for a few minutes. No wonder then that we were afraid of travelling all night in an open cart! I do not believe that we should yet venture to move if we had not hit upon another plan, namely that of walking the first 30 or 35 miles of our journey, by which means we shall save the distance of 20 miles, a circuit which the diligence makes, and shall also travel through a much pleasanter country. Nordhausen a city in Upper Saxony is the place to which our foottravels tend. We shall there meet with covered Diligences to all the considerable towns of Saxony. We are not yet exactly decided whither we shall go. We have letters to Weimar, but there are other places which seem to promise equal advantages, and where living is much cheaper as Erfurt, Eisnach etc. We do not, however much expect to find any thing that will induce us to prolong our stay more than a couple of months, before we return to Hamburgh; but having advanced so far into the country we are unwilling to remain here without seeing something more. We have gone on advancing in the language, the main object of our journey, in tolerably regular progress, but if we had had the advantage of good society we should have done much more, this, however is a benefit which we have now given up all expectation of attaining, as we find that when a *man and woman* are received into society, they are expected, being considered as a sort of family, to give entertainments in return for what they receive. Now this, in conjunction with the expence of travelling, is absolutely out of our power, though I believe that we could do it, being stationary, for as little expense as we could live for, entirely without company, in England. We have then bounded our desires to seeing a little more of the country and getting into a family pretty much resembling this, in which we now are with whom, as now, we may talk upon common subjects. Perhaps if the weather is fine and we do not find travelling very expensive, we may not fix more than a fortnight in one place; but make a little circuit from town to town. At present however the weather is not very favourable for such a plan, as though it is very good for walking the set distance which we have to go, yet it is not sufficiently inviting to induce us to ramble much about. It is hard frost and the snow is still lying upon the ground. We have sent off our luggage; and shall take a guide with us. We shall set off on Saturday morning.

The climate of this part of Germany appears to me to be much colder than that of England but I daresay the difference *seems* to be greater than it is, on account of the stoved rooms, whose summer warmth makes a contrast with the external air, that sets the flesh a creeping, even when you go through the passages and staircases. Our room has never been heated so much by many degrees as the rooms of Goslar in general are, but I got a severe cough in the seasoning. I am now however quite well and can bear any transitions. We walk at least an hour every day, often much more. William has a green gown, lined throughout with Fox's skin, and I wrap myself up in furs that defy the cold.

Goslar is not a place where it is possible to see any thing of the manners of the more cultivated Germans, or of the higher classes. Its inhabitants are all petty tradespeople; in general a low and selfish race; intent upon gain, and perpetually of course disappointed. They cannot find in their hearts to ask of a stranger a fair price for their goods. The woman of this house who is a civil and good kind of a respectable woman *in her way* could not refrain from cheating us of halfpence and farthings when we first came. She is a widow with 5 children, and keeps a linen draper's shop, which I daresay barely serves to support them decently. Yet she dresses herself out very fine in artificial flowers on a Sunday, and spent half a Louis on a jaunt in a traineau[1] a luxury which I suppose it would be almost a disgrace not to enjoy once in a winter. When the snow first fell the whole town was in commotion, traineaus every where! but the people are not rich enough to keep to it long, all is now quiet. Coleridge is in a very different world from what we stir in, he is all in high life, among Barons counts and countesses. He could not be better placed than he is at Ratzeberg for attaining the object of his journey; but his expences are much more than ours conjointly. I think however he has done perfectly right in consenting to pay so much, as he will not stay longer in Germany than till March or

[1] A sledge.

April. It would have been impossible for us to have lived as he does; we should have been ruined. *We* shall certainly return to England before the end of summer, but very probably in the spring. As soon as we are perfectly satisfied with our knowledge of the language we shall think about returning, unless we should meet with so pleasant a residence in Saxony as should induce us to stay there longer than seems at present likely. If we do not, we shall go to Hamburgh at the end of two months; and take lodgings somewhere in that neighbourhood till we can sail for England, which will probably be immediately if we improve sufficiently in the language; if not, as soon as we have attained that end. William is very desirous to know that his tragedy is safe in your hands. It was entrusted to Richard when we left London, to be sent to Mr Josiah Wedgwood at Stoke near Cobham and Mr W. was requested to forward it to you by the coach. If by any unfortunate accident you should not have received it Wm. desires you will make use of every possible exertion to get it. Write to Richard immediately to know what he has done with it; and if he has forwarded it to Mr Wedgwood, write to Mr W.—in short neglect no step to procure it. You know that Wm has no copy with him, and if it were lost, the work would be irrecoverably gone. Pray write to us immediately. You had best address to us at Hamburgh, as if we should prolong our stay in Saxony your letter can be forwarded to us; if not, we shall find it there when we go. Direct to me to the care of Mr Remnant at the English library in Hamburgh.

Have you heard anything of Peggy our Servant? Be very particular in your accounts of what you are, and have been, doing. Every thing is interesting at this distance.

William has been mixing with his German employments a good deal of english poetical composition. We have lived very happily and comfortably, but not sufficiently differently from our English way of life. A young man an apprentice in the house comes up to sit with us every evening, but we have no other society except that of a French Emigrant Priest, and what we find in our daily intercourse with this family. Do not fail to tell us whether the tragedy is safe— and write immediately for even if we do not stay longer than two months in Saxony, we may receive your letter before our departure thence.

William begs his best love. God bless you, my dear Brother. Believe me

most affectionately yours
D. Wordsworth.

Be so good as to forward this letter to Richard. I write to my Aunt Cookson by the same post so it is unnecessary that you should trouble yourself to inform her of your having heard from me.

14. *To* S. T. Coleridge

Nordhausen Wednesday evening
27th February [1799]

My dear Coleridge,

We have at last received your long desired letters. Our patience was rewarded, or our cowardice flattered, by a most delightful morning which made its appearance last Saturday. Our baggage had been long ready, packed and repacked. We had gone to bed, the friday night being very stormy, without any hope. I called William in the morning; he saw the sun shining upon the garden, up he got, we put together our last parcel, conveyed it to the posthouse, and set off on foot in the afternoon at one o'clock. Goslar lies on the edge of some high hills; mountains they cannot be called, at the skirts of the Hartz Forest. After walking about a mile we began to ascend through a pine forest which with the accompaniments of tiny waterfalls alias "kittenracts"[1] might as Wm says, remind a traveller of the Alps in the same way as a little kitten may suggest recollections of a full-grown tiger. Some of the pine-trees are extremely beautiful. We observed that when they seemed to be past maturity, and perhaps sooner in a close situation their boughs which had before ascended, making an acute angle with the trunk, descend till they shoot out horizontally or make an obtuse angle with the upper part of the tree. This is effected by the twigs, which from the weight of their foliage drag down the boughs, and hang like long threads of ivy in festoons of different lengths, the upper part of the branch being always bare. Some of these threads appear

[1] S. T. C.'s word for a small cataract.

to be two or three yards long. In the very old trees the festoons are interwoven with grey or green moss, giving to the whole tree a very venerable and impressive appearance. We observed that the brilliant green of the earth-moss under the trees made our eyes ache after being so long accustomed to the snow. The peasants in the *plains* adjoining to Goslar are extremely well clothed and decent in their appearance. We had often seen in Goslar women inhabitants of the hills, but we did not imagine them to be so rude and barbarous a race as we found them. They carry enormous burthens in square baskets hung over their shoulders, their petticoats reach very little below their knees, and their stockings are dangling about their ankles without garters. Swellings in the throat are very common amongst them which may perhaps be attributed to the straining of the neck in dragging those monstrous loads. They rarely travel without a bottle of German brandy, Schnapps as they call it; many of them go weekly from Clausthall to Brunswick, they perform this journey, a distance of thirty five miles in two days, carrying ass loads, parcels, etc, and letters clandestinely. These people are chiefly inhabitants of Clausthal, a large Hanoverian town cursed with the plague of a vicious population. We arrived there in the dusk of the evening, found an excellent inn, with beautiful bedlinen, good coffee, and a decent supper. The charge was about the same rate as in England, perhaps a little cheaper. This town lies in the centre of the Hartz forest. We left it on sunday, a mild morning, saw little that was remarkable till we came to the decaying posts of an old gibbet. We had scarcely passed it when we were saluted with the song of the lark, a pair of larks a sweet, liquid and heavenly melody heard for the first time, after so long and severe a winter. I ought to have said that before this we had a view of the Brocken, the Mont Blanc of the Hartz forest, and the glory of all this part of Germany. I cannot speak of its height compared with any of our British mountains, but from the point from which we saw it, it had nothing impressive in its appearance. The day continued chearing and delightful, and we walked through a country presenting forest views of hill and valley, one of which a deep valley with a village built of wood scattered in the bottom was very interesting. We lingered under the shades of the trees and did not arrive at Osterode till four o'clock in the afternoon. It is also a Hanoverian possession, a small *city* lying at the edge of the Hartz forest, in a kind of low wide valley. The appearance of the people as we passed through the streets was very little favorable, they looked dirty, impudent, and vulgar, and absolutely the whole town being at the windows or in the streets as we unluckily met them coming from church, we were stared completely out of countenance, at least I was; William stoutly denies that he was at all uncomfortable; however this was we had not courage to stop at an inn till we had walked through the whole town, and just on the other side of the city gates, we called at one where they told us they could give us nothing to eat. While we stood pondering what we should do, inquiring for another Wirtshaus, and half resolved to go a league further where we were told we could be accommodated, one of the under-officers of the town, who was drinking with a sort of rabble, in the Wirts-haus where we had been refused admittance, accosted us, and civilly assured us that we should be admitted into the house, but he brought out one of his comrades a little step above him in place and about equal in self-importance and insolence, who questioned us respecting our business etc etc, and would not let us pass without a pass-port. He conducted William to the Burgomaster who promised to grant him the said pass-port in the morning after he had seen our letters which were to come by the post-waggon, with our trunk in the evening. In the mean time I was left in one of those towers which you always see at the entrance of cities, amongst a set of soldiers who were furbishing their dress, a woman who was engaged in some kind of Taylor's business, and a man who had an iron ring and chain hanging to his hand, I suppose as a punishment for some felony. You may be sure I was not a little impatient for William's return, he brought back his friend the officer in great good humour both with himself and him, for he took care to flatter his vanity, and we were admitted into the Wirts-haus; where we had some cold veal to supper, *decentish* beds, and a large quantity of excellent coffee in the morning for the value of one shilling and elevenpence English money. Though we rose at seven o'clock, owing to the delays of office, we did not leave our inn till after ten. It was a mild morning, the sun shone occasionally through the patches of broken clouds, and the larks regaled us with a never-ceasing song. We had still the Hartz forest on our left, and crossed a very delightful valley through which our road ought to have taken us but the floods had swept away the bridge. The country through which we passed was in general pleasant and tolerably peopled, but the ways dreadful, we were often obliged to walk as in the mines at Stowey, above the ankles in water, and sometimes as high in clay. We left the town of Hartzberg[1] on our left; it has a huge decaying castle, built upon the edge of a steep hill richly wooded and commanding a very fine prospect of hills clothed with Beech wood, and a wide meadow valley through which runs a respectable river,[2] after we left this place the roads grew worse and worse, the darkness came on, and we were near being stopped by a water when a waggon overtook us which conducted us safely to an Inn at Schazefeld,[3] where we got a good supper, that is cold beef, indifferent soup, and cabbage, straw beds and coffee and bread and butter for 1 shilling and tenpence. In the night we had a hard frost and the first part of our yesterdays journey was very delightful; the country charming, something like the widest of the Welsh valleys, the widest and tamest, but afterwards the roads grew worse, still however we had a pleasant walk, and reached our inn at 4 in the afternoon. We had sausages and boiled milk to supper, coffee etc for 1 shilling and ninepence, we slept in company with our host and hostess and four children, a facetious shoe-maker, a Prussian tax-gather[er] and a journeyman hat-maker, who had travelled all over Germany working a month here, and a few days there, to see the world. William advised him to go to England as he was so fond of travelling. "England? was ist das für ein land gehört es an dem Konig von Danemark? wo liegt es? nein, nein, man ist nicht ruhig darin." If my report does not exactly accord with the strict rules of German Grammar I hope you will be so good as to attribute it to the hatmaker. Our landlord had been in the Prussian service, a fine look-ing man, extremely fond of his children, and seeming to be very happy with a very good-tempered wife. We were struck with the extreme folly of people who draw conclusions respecting national character from the narrow limits of common observation. We have been much with German hosts and hostesses and notwithstanding the supposed identifying tendency first of national manners, and

---

[1] Herzberg.
[2] The Sieber.
[3] Scharzfeld.

of particular occupations, these persons appeared in every respect as if made in contrast to each other, but this will be a more proper subject for conversation. This morning was very rainy, so we got into the post-waggon, in which conveyance we travelled ten miles, and arrived at the post-haus in the afternoon. We are now at a tolerable inn but we don't know what we have to pay; I have thus brought down the little history of our lives since Saturday morning. I now come to something of more importance, the subject of your letters—but let me first speak of the joy we felt at seeing your handwriting again; I burst open the seals and could almost have kissed them in the presence of the post-master, but we did not read a word till we got to the inn when we devoured them separately, for at least two hours. With the experience we have had of the possibility of travelling for a very trifling expence, we cannot but think you have done wisely in quitting Ratzeberg, both on your own account and that of Chester.[1] Gottingen seems to be the best possible place for your purpose.

    William now takes the pen. God bless you Dear Dear Coleridge.

[Unsigned]

15. *To* Thomas Poole

Sockburn July 4th [1799]

My dear Mr Poole,

    Ever since our arrival in England it has been William's intention to write to you yet his delaying disposition has so got the better of him that though we have been two months on English ground you have heard nothing of us from ourselves. Knowing how much you are interested in our welfare I can no longer refrain from taking up the pen to inform you *where* we are and that we are in good health. We found living in Germany, with the enjoyment of any tolerable advantages, much more expensive than we expected which determined us to come home with the first tolerable weather of the Spring. We left Coleridge and Mr Chester at Göttingen ten weeks ago, as you probably have heard, and proceeded with as little delay

---

[1] John Chester, S. T. C.'s travelling companion.

as possible, travelling in a German Diligence, to Hamburgh, whence we went down the Elbe in a boat to Cuxhaven, where we were not detained longer than we wished for our necessary refreshment, and we had an excellent passage to England of two days and nights. We proceeded immediately from Yarmouth into the North where we are now staying with some of our early friends[1] at a pleasant farm on the Banks of the Tees. We are very anxious to hear from Coleridge,—he promised to write to us from Göttingen, and though we have written twice we have heard nothing of him. We hope that having delayed writing to us longer than he intended, he now delays because he is on the point of returning to England. When we were at Göttingen he received a letter from Mrs Coleridge by which we had the pleasure of hearing that she and dear little Hartley[2] were well. Poor Berkeley! I was much grieved to hear of his death. It gave us sincere joy to learn (from Coleridge) that your good mother was in better health three months ago than she had ever been for some time. I hope that we shall again have the same good accounts of her.—We are yet quite undetermined where we shall reside—we have no house in view at present. It is William's wish to be near a good library, and if possible in a pleasant country. If you hear of any place in your neighbourhood that will be likely to suit us we shall be much obliged to you if you will take the trouble of writing to us.

We are very glad to hear that Mr Wedgwood is going to settle not far from Stowey.

William joins with me in kind remembrances to your Mother, and Mrs Coleridge, and yourself.

I will not make any apology for this short and unentertaining letter. I know you will not receive it without pleasure. Believe me, my dear Sir,

> Yours affectionately
> Dorothy Wordsworth.

Pray remember us to Mr Ward[3]—and request Coleridge to write when he arrives at Stowey.

[1] The Hutchinsons.
[2] Hartley Coleridge (1796–1849), poet. His baby brother Berkeley had died the previous Feb.
[3] Poole's apprentice.

Our address—at Mr Hutchinsons, Sockburn near Northallerton, Yorkshire. To be left at Smeaton.

16. *To* Mrs John Marshall

[Grasmere] Wednesday morng. September 10th [and 12, 1800]

My dear Jane, I will say nothing of my sorrow and remorse for having neglected you so long; you know that I have always been an irregular correspondent, perpetually warring against habits of procrastination, and still submitting to them, and you know much of me and of my character and disposition; so I trust you will not find it difficult to withdraw that harsh insinuation that I might have become indifferent to you. Professions are idle and useless; you are disposed to love and to forgive me and I feel that I must trust to those kindly dispositions for your *entire* pardon.

I shall dismiss this subject. In my firm confidence in your affection for me, I trust that all such subjects as are most interesting and most pleasing to me will be so to you and that you will be glad to turn your thoughts from what must be painful to us both.

At a qu[arte]r past eight yesterday morning Molly put your letter into my hands. I read the first sentence of it with extreme joy for it informed me that your husband was the bearer of it. Without reading one word more, I dispatched a little girl with a note requesting that he would come and breakfast with us, and as soon as William was dressed he followed her to the Inn. Mr Marshall had, however, breakfasted. It grieved me very much that I had not seen him pass the door. I was just going to make breakfast, and, busy about something or other, I had not heard the horse's feet.

Before his arrival I had read and reread your letter, and believe me, most glad should I have been if you had told me ten times as much about your children, those dear little dear creatures. I wish I could see them, and I do hope that before next autumn is over I may have that pleasure. We meditate a journey to the neighbourhood of Scarborough to see our Friends, the Hutchinsons[1] who are settled there; we shall then extend our journey further and stop with

[1] Mary H. and her brother Thomas were now living at Gallow Hill, a farm nr Brompton, Yorks.

you at Leeds. Our plan is to purchase a taxed cart, which we can have for 7 guineas and hire a horse, if we cannot afford to buy one, but this being altogether a very grand scheme a large sum will be necessary to execute it, and it will depend entirely upon William's success with the booksellers.

How fat your husband looks! if I had met him in the lane I should not have known him. We enjoyed his company very much yesterday, and wish exceedingly that he could have stayed another day with us. We could have taken him today to a very fine valley and waterfall which he has never seen, and still we should have left enough unseen to induce him to come again.

Yesterday morning after we had sat together half an hour my Brothers accompanied Mr M. round the two lakes, Rydale and Grasmere, by which means he saw them in many new points of view and in much greater beauty than he had seen them before. I was left at home to make pies and dumplings, and was to follow them when I had finished my business, but as they could not tell exactly which way they should go I sought them in vain, and after we had all walked far enough to get very good appetites we met together at two o'clock at our own house to dinner. After dinner, Wm and Mr Marshall and I rowed over the water to the island, the lake was very rough but upon the whole the day was fine. We returned to tea, and after tea John and Mr M and I walked up to the head of our vale, which makes one small green, retired, woody valley where the lake is not to be seen. I never had more pleasure in accompanying any one to see these places than Mr M he seemed to enjoy them so much, and from the excessively accurate ideas which he had of the relative situations of places we knew that they had in former times been deeply impressed upon his mind. William was not quite well which was the reason that he [did] not walk with us in the evening. He is better this morning and he and John are gone with Mr M to Keswick, they will leave their horses at Wytheburn and go on the other side of Thurlemere water. They will dine with Coleridge at Keswick, and my Brothers will both accompany Mr M to Buttermere, Ennerdale, and Wassdale if Wms. horse can manage it, but it is lame and we do not know how it will perform the journey— if Wm. cannot go on he will return tomorrow morning and John is to proceed with Mr M. I wished exceedingly to go along with them but we could not manage it.

Mr Marshall will give you a fuller description than I can by letter of our dwelling[1] and our manner of life—but I will not keep back what I have to tell you from the fear that you may hear it twice over as that will not I know be tiresome to you. We are daily more delighted with Grasmere, and its neighbourhood; our walks are perpetually varied, and we are more fond of the mountains as our acquaintance with them encreases. We have a boat upon the lake and a small orchard and a smaller *garden* which as it is the work of our own hands we regard with pride and partiality. This garden we enclosed from the road and pulled down a fence which formerly divided it from the orchard. The orchard is very small, but then it is a delightful one from its retirement, and the excessive beauty of the prospect from it. Our cottage is quite large enough for us though very small, and we have made it neat and comfortable within doors and it looks very nice on the outside, for though the roses and honeysuckles which we have planted against it are only of this year's growth yet it is covered all over with green leaves and scarlet flowers, for we have trained scarlet beans upon threads, which are not only exceedingly beautiful, but very useful, as their produce is immense. The only objection we have to our house is that it is rather too near the road, and from its smallness and the manner in which it is built noises pass from one part of the house to the other, so that if we had any visitors a sick person could not be in quietness. We have made a lodging-room of the parlour below stairs, which has a stone floor therefore we have covered it all over with matting. The bed, though only a camp bed, is large enough for two people to sleep in. We sit in a room above stairs and we have one lodging room with two single beds, a sort of lumber room and a small low unceiled room, which I have papered with newspapers and in which we have put a small bed without curtains. Our servant is an old woman 60 years of age whom we took partly out of charity and partly for convenience. She was very ignorant, very foolish, and very difficult to teach so that I once almost despaired of her, but the goodness of her dispositions and the great convenience we knew we should find if my perseverance was at last successful induced me to go on. She has now learnt to do everything for us mechanically, except those

[1] Dove Cottage.

...ing in which the hands are much employed, for in-
...prepares and boils the vegetables and can watch the meat
...it is made ready for roasting, looks to the oven etc. My Brother
...in has been with us 8 months during which time we have had a
good deal of company, for instance Mary Hutchinson for 5 weeks,
Coleridge a month, and Mr [and] Mrs C and their little boy nearly
a month. During all this time we have never hired any helpers either
for washing or ironing and she has washed all the linen of all our
visitors except the Family of the Coleridges during that month. I
help to iron at the great washes about once in 5 weeks, and she
washes towels stockings, waistcoats petticoats etc once a week such
as do not require much ironing. This she does so quietly in a place
apart from the house and we know so little about it as makes it very
comfortable. She sleeps at home which is a great convenience in our
small house and in winter it is a considerable saving of fire that her
home is so near, for after the dishes are washed up, we let the kitchen
fire go out and we never light it till it is time to dress the dinner, and
she employs herself at home. She is much attached to us and honest
and good as ever was a human being.

My Brother Christopher is now in Norfolk. It is true that he is
desperately in love and engaged to marry Miss Lloyd, the Sister of
the author Charles Lloyd,[1] and Daughter of one of the Lloyds of
Birmingham, but it is not likely that the marriage will take place for
two or three years, as he must wait for a living. I have never seen
this Miss Lloyd (Priscilla she is called) but from what I have heard
of her I believe her to be an interesting and amiable young woman.
Her Brother is coming to live at Ambleside; he has a wife and child,
his wife is very highly spoken of by everybody but we are by no
means glad that they are to be our neighbours (this between ourselves) because Charles Lloyd is a man who is perpetually forming
new friendships, quarrelling with his old ones, and upon the whole
a dangerous acquaintance. Priscilla is to come with them and after
paying a visit to Mrs Clarkson[2] at Ulswater she is to spend the
winter with her Brother and Sister at Ambleside. Christopher is so
deeply engaged in college business that he could not contrive to

[1] Charles Lloyd (1775–1839), author of *Edmund Oliver*, who had lodged with
S. T. C. at Bristol in 1796.
[2] Catherine Clarkson (see List of Correspondents).

come and see us this summer, but I hope he will spend some time with us next year. My Friends at Forncett are going on as usual. They have a fine family of children. I have not seen my Uncle but I am told he looks much more like a Doctor of Divinity than he used to do. He was at Penrith at the death of my Uncle Crackanthorp. When John leaves us he intends spending some time at Forncett. But he will stay with us as long as he can which will be no longer than till the arrival of the Abergavenny, which is expected this month or next. You may have heard that my Uncle Crackanthorp left me 100£—it was a small sum compared with all that we have lost, but I daresay he would have done much more if he had been a free agent in the making of his will. He did not so much as name the name of his Brother or one of his nephews! Poor man! I shed many a tear for him during his sickness and when I heard of his death. My Aunt Crackanthorp is despised by every body about Penrith from her excessive pride. William the eldest child is the darling of all who know him, he is lively, sensible, excessively affectionate, and it is not in the power of his mother or his aunt to give him the least atom of pride.

My Brother William is going to publish a second Edition of the Lyrical Ballads with a second volume. He intends to give them the title of "Poems by W. Wordsworth" as Mrs Robinson[1] has claimed the title and is about publishing a volume of *Lyrical Tales*. This is a great objection to the former title, particularly as they are both printed at the same press and Longman is the publisher of both the works. The first volume sold much better than we expected, and was liked by a much greater number of people, not that we had ever much doubt of its finally making its way, but we knew that poems so different from what have in general become popular immediately after their publication were not likely to be admired all at once. The first volume I have no doubt has prepared a number of purchasers for the second, and independent of that, I think the second is much more likely to please the generality of readers. Williams health is by no means strong, he has written a great deal since we first went to Allfoxden, namely during the year preceding our going

---

[1] Mary Robinson (1758–1800) actress and royal mistress. W. W. did not change his title after all.

into Germany, while we were there,[1] and since our arrival in England, and he writes with so much feeling and agitation that it brings on a sense of pain and internal weakness about his left side and stomach, which now often makes it impossible fo[r] him to [write] when he is in mind and feelings in such a state that he could do it without difficulty.

We have spent a week at Mr Coleridge's since his arrival at Keswick. His house[2] is most delightfully situated, and combines all possible advantages both for his wife and himself, *she* likes to be near a Town, *he* in the country—it is only $\frac{1}{2}$ a qr of a mile from Keswick and commands a view of the whole vale. Mrs Coleridge is going to lye in, her little boy, Hartley, who is an original sprite is to come and stay with us during that time, he is a sweet companion, always alive and of a delightful temper, I shall find it very difficult to part with him when we have once got him here.

William and John were in Yorkshire last summer, at Gor Dale Yordas, etc, thence they went to see our Friends the Hutchinsons and were absent a whole month. They talked about paying you a visit, but they found they had stayed so long at Scarborough that they did not like to leave me alone any longer. During their absence, I felt myself very lonely while I was within doors, I wanted my little companion Basil, and poor old Molly did but ill supply to me the place of our good and dear Peggy who was quite as a friend to us. Basil is with an Uncle in Huntingdonshire—we wish his father to send him to some school, if possible in the North of England that he may be near us.

We are very comfortably situated with respect to neighbours of the lower classes, they are excellent people, friendly in performing all offices of kindness and humanity and attentive to us without servility—if we were sick they would wait upon us night and day. We are also upon very intimate terms with one family in the middle rank of life, a Clergyman[3] with a very small income, his wife, son and daughter. The old man is upwards of eighty yet he goes a fishing to the Tarns on the hill-tops with my Brothers, and he is as active as many men of 50. His wife is a delightful old woman, mild and

---

[1] W. W. wrote the Lucy Poems at Goslar, and began *The Prelude*.
[2] Greta Hall, where the Southeys joined them in 1803.
[3] The Revd Joseph Sympson, vicar of Wythburn.

gentle, yet chearful in her manners and much of the gentlewoman, so made by long exercise of the duties of a wife and a mother and the charities of a neighbour, for she has lived 40 years in this vale and seldom left her home. The daughter, though much inferior to her mother is a pleasant kind of woman, and the son is an interesting man, he is about 40, manages his Father's glebe land, reads a little and spends much time in fishing. When we were at Keswick Mrs Spedding[1] had not left her room after her lying-in so we did not see her. Margaret Spedding was not at home, but we saw Miss Spedding when we called, she also called upon me but I was not at home, and we took a walk with her one morning. I hope the Coleridges will find them pleasant neighbours but we are too far from them to receive much benefit from their society. My Brother William has seen Mrs Spedding several times and I think he was a good deal pleased with her. Old Mrs Gibson was there when I called. I was excessively struck with a certain forbidding stateliness in her manner, very unlike your good mother in law Mrs Marshall, whose mild good sense and humble gentle manners I can never cease to remember with pleasure. The thought of what you have lost brings me once again to you. I think I have talked long enough about myself and my own concerns. You must indeed feel most sensibly the want of so pleasing a companion and so kind a friend as Mrs Marshall, but you have great cause of comfort and thankfulness in having made her latter days easy. It might look a little like flattery when I praise your own husband to you if you were not my old friend Jane Pollard—he is indeed an interesting man, so gentle, so mild, and with so much genuine feeling, simplicity, and good sense. My Brothers quite take to him. I wish heartily that he could have stayed longer with us, he seemed to enjoy what he saw so deeply. I tried to persuade him to bring you along with him next summer but I could not make him promise. When you see any body who is likely to write to Mr Threlkeld[2] (I understand that Mrs T and her daughters are not at home) pray desire them to tell him that we hope he will come by Grasmere in his road from Scotland, or perhaps Harriot may be writing to Elizabeth and she will take the trouble of mentioning it.

---

[1] Sarah Spedding, *née* Gibson, wife of W. W.'s schoolfriend, of Mirehouse, Bassenthwaite.

[2] Mrs Rawson's brother, father of Elizabeth.

I am extremely glad to hear that your mother enjoys so good a state of health. Pray make my kind remembrances to her and all your sisters, particularly my best love to Ellen and Harriot. I found that one sheet of paper would not contain half of what I [had to say] to you; I am sorry to charge you with double postage, [but I think] you will pay it willingly after our long silence. Give y[our little] William a kiss for me. God bless you my dear F[riend.] believe me with sincere affection, your Friend,

D. Wordsworth.

I take up the pen again as I have not, I find, answered all your questions. With respect to passing our time I can [not ?] tell you how we pass it because though our employ[ments] are not very various yet they are irregular. We walk [every] day and at all times of the day, we row upon the water, and in the summer sit a great part of our time under the apple trees of the orchard or in a wood close by the lake-side. William writes verses, John goes a fishing, and we read the books we have and such as we can procure. I read German, partly as preparatory to translating, but I am unfit for the task alone, and William is better employed so I do not know when it will turn to much account. If Wms name rises amongst the Booksellers we shall have no occasion for it. We often have our friends calling in upon us. Anthony Harrison[1] of Penrith (E Threlkeld knows him) came last Saturday but one and stayed till Sunday—on the Friday after Mr and Mrs James Losh[2] of West Jesmond near Newcastle called, and we breakfasted with them the next morning at Ambleside, and on that same day Mr and Mrs Clarkson came to dinner, and stayed with us till after dinner on Monday. Mr Clarkson is the man who took so much pains about the slave trade, he has a farm at Ulswater and has built a house. Mrs C. is a pleasant woman. We are going there next Wednesday and shall probably stay till the Sunday after. We intend walking over the mountains and Mr and Mrs Clarkson will meet us with a boat at Patterdale.

When you see Mrs Rawson give my kind love to her, tell her I have received her letter which crossed mine on the road, and that

---

[1] A solicitor: author of *Poetical Recreations*, 1806.
[2] James Losh (1763–1833), W. W.'s early radical friend.

I will write to her shortly. Once more adieu my dear Jane. .
written till my fingers ache, and I fear unless you have wonq.
patience I have written far more than you can read. God bless yₑ
for ever.

D. W.

My Brothers and Mr Marshall have a delightful day. I hope they
are now with Coleridge at Keswick.

I have told you that I was surprized to see your husband grown
so fat. I should have added that I thought he looked very well. He
will tell you that I am much thinner than when I last saw you. I
first lost my flesh in Dorsetshire having [caught] a violent cold
attended with a swelled face, violent toothach and many symptoms
of fever. I was never fat afterwards though less thin than I am at
present, and I am afraid I shall never regain the stone and a
quarter of flesh which I have lost. My pens and Ink are the worst
that ever were written with and William has run away with the pen
knife.

Give my kind love to the Fergusons.

Friday afternoon. I went yesterday afternoon to drink tea with
Mrs Simpson, and at my return found William. He had parted from
Mr Marshall and John in Borrowdale and crossed the mountains
home. He regretted very much that he was obliged to leave them,
but he was too ill to go on—he looked dreadfully when he reached
home and his side and stomach were very bad but today he is better.
John accompanied Mr M to Buttermere—we expect him at Grasmere tomorrow evening. Both my Brothers and Mr M had a
delightful walk on Wednesday morning half round Thurlemere
water, they dined at the Royal Oak at Keswick, and drank tea and
supped at Coleridge's. I suppose that John and Mr M will part at
Keswick tomorrow I am much grieved that Wm was not able [to]
stay with them, both on his account and Mr Ms. I shall send off this
letter today. You will have heard from your [hus]band by this time;
he closed a letter to you [at Gra]smere. Wms kind remem[brances.]
God love you! We expect Sarah Hutchinson[1] in the Spring. I hope
she will stay 3 or 4 months.

[1] Mary H.'s younger sister.

47

17. *To* Mary Hutchinson

My dearest Mary,

We left poor Coleridge on Monday evening; we had been with him a week and a day. You know that I wrote to Sara on the Friday Evening before we went to Keswick giving her the joyful tidings that C was better, but alas! on Saturday we had a sad account of him. I was determined not to give you unnecessary uneasiness therefore I did not write. We left home at one o'clock on Sunday—and reached Keswick at about six. We both trembled, and till we entered the door I hardly durst speak. He was sitting in the parlour, and looked dreadfully pale and weak. He was very, very unwell in the way that Sara can describe to you—ill all over, back, and stomach and limbs and so weak as that he changed colour whenever he exerted himself at all. Our company did him good and the next day he was much better. Since that time he has been upon the whole greatly improved in his looks and strength but he was never quite well for more than an hour together during the whole time we were there, tho' he began to form plans and schemes for working but he was unable to do any thing. The weather was very fine when we were there such as one would have thought might have set him up at once but these frequent attacks make him more weak in recovering from them. I do think he will never be quite well till he has tried a warm climate. If he were to live for six months at Lisbon in the South of France at one of the Western Isles he would probably be restored to perfect health and might keep himself well with tolerable care. He and Hartley are to come over in the first returned Chaise after tomorrow. Hartley is to stay some time with us and to go to Grasmere school. Dear little fellow! he will be as happy as a young lamb playing upon the green turf in the church-yard with our bonny little lasses. We hope that C. will grow well in a short time after he comes to us, but there is no security for his continuing so. We should have stayed longer at Keswick but our company not being so new did not do him so much good as at first, and then we are never comfortable there after the first 2 or 3 days. This of course we do not mind while we are of any essential service to him, but the same cause which makes us uncomfortable at Keswick prevents him from having good from us that he otherwise would have. Mrs C. is in excellent health. She is indeed a bad nurse for C., but she has several great merits. She is much very much to be pitied, for when one party is ill matched the other necessarily must be so too. She would have made a very good wife to many another man, but for Coleridge!![1] Her radical fault is want of sensibility and what can such a woman be to Coleridge? She is an excellent nurse to her sucking children (I mean to the best of her skill, for she employs her time often foolishly enough about them). Derwent[2] is a sweet lovely Fatty—she suckles him entirely—he has no other food. She is to be sure a sad fiddle faddler. From about $\frac{1}{2}$ past 10 on Sunday morning till two she did nothing but wash and dress her 2 children and herself, and was just ready for dinner. No doubt she suckled Derwent pretty often during that time. When I say I would not give you any unnecessary uneasiness about Coleridge, do not fear that I shall not inform you at all times when he is very ill, but as his relapse was only a common one I did not like to give you pain. I will write to you immediately after he arrives; and I hope and trust I shall be able to tell you he is better. We found a letter from John on our arrival at home at 12 o'clock on Monday night. We had *such* a walk! so delightful! We left Keswick at $\frac{1}{2}$ past 5 in order that we might avoid the heat of the day, and we rested again and again by the road-side. We had the full round moon before us just above Helvellyn. The night was very clear, and it was so light that I read John's letter without a candle at William's room window, and his hand is not a very legible one. We rouzed Molly and Sally Ashburner out of bed and gladly they rose, as it was to receive us. We found the garden much improved in our absence. Our cabbages look well and we have two crops of peas up. The flowers are in thriving condition. I have sowed plenty of scarlet beans. I would give a good deal that they might be as nice as last year and that you might see them. The garden looks well indeed but the Vale is miserable. It is scorched and burnt as brown as an autumn stubble-field.

[1] S. T. C. had already met and fallen in love with Sara Hutchinson.
[2] Derwent Coleridge (1800–83), schoolmaster and divine.

We had left the Vale of Keswick fresh green and beautiful, and we expected to find this Vale so, but oh! the heavy disappointment. The days are intensely hot and the nights are frosty every body prays for rain which God send soon! it would be a woful season if we should have another time of scarcity. You will be glad to hear that our good friend, Mr Griffith has sent us a barrel of the best flour from America—it is now at Liverpool.

My dearest dear Mary I look forward with joy to seeing you again, you *must* come in Autumn or before—how I wish Joanna[1] could be spared you might then come on here from Middleham it is but a half way journey, but all the way from Gallow Hill is terrible! How glad I shall be to hear that you are with Sara—she is a dear good creature. I wish from my heart that William and I could be with you—pray tell us every thing about Middleham and do not fear dear Mary that you ever write too often; or can write too often. William is better than he was a while ago—he is taking a stomachic medicine which I hope will do him good but his digestion is still very bad— he is always very ill when he tries to alter an old poem— but new composition does not hurt him so much. I hope he will soon be able to work without hurting himself. I am quite well and indeed I am inclined to write you a long letter but I am so thrown back with being at Keswick, where I can do nothing, that I have not time. I am going to write to Sara—I must write Mr Griffith, Miss Griffith and Mrs Rawson and I have just finished a long sheet to John filled as full as possible with poems and letter.

The thrushes are singing divinely in the orchard. It is 7 o'clock. Wm is lying upon the outside of the bed that has its back to the window I have the little round green table beside him. We are going to tea and then for a walk. Wm will take the pen while I prepare the tea. When we return from walking I shall write to Sara. My kindest love to Tom.

God bless you. I wish that you were here that you were both here to walk with us, you and dearest Sara.

[*Unsigned*]

---

[1] Mary H.'s youngest sister.

18. *To* Richard Wordsworth

Grasmere 10th June [1802]

My dear Brother,

William received your letter on Monday morning. I am considerably better than I was when I wrote to you last, though far from well. I have had the most severe cold I have ever had in all my life, and it has taken hold both of my strength and my looks.

I will make no comments upon the intelligence which William communicated to you in his last, except, that I do not doubt that, if his health is so good that he can go on with those employments in which he has lately been engaged, his marriage will add to his comfort and happiness. Mary Hutchinson is a most excellent woman—I have known her long, and I know her thoroughly; she has been a dear friend of mine, is deeply attached to William, and is disposed to feel kindly to all his family.

As you express a desire to know what are my wishes or expectations respecting a settlement upon me I will explain to you frankly how I feel, though, relying as I do and have ever had reason to rely, upon the affection of my Brothers and their regard for my happiness, I do not doubt that, according to their power, they would meet the full extent of my wishes, without my making them known myself. I shall continue to live with my Brother William—but he, having nothing to spare nor being likely to have, at least for many years, I am obliged (I need not say how much he regrets this necessity) to set him aside, and I will consider myself as boarding through my whole life with an indifferent person. Sixty pounds a year is the sum which would entirely gratify all my desires. With sixty pounds a year I should not fear any accidents or changes which might befal me. I cannot look forward to the time when, with my habits of frugality, I could not live comfortably on that sum (Observe I am speaking now, of a provision or settlement for life, and it would be absurd at my age (30 years) to talk of any thing else). At present with 60 pounds per ann. I should have something to spare to exercise my better feelings in relieving the necessities of others I might buy a few books, take a journey now and then—all which things though they do not come under the article of absolute necessaries, you will easily perceive that it is highly desireable that a person of my age and with my education should occasionally have in her power. As to the *mode* of doing this for me, I will say no more than that it seems to be absolutely necessary, to give it any effect, that it should, as much as possible, be independent of accidents of death or any other sort that may befal you or any of my Brothers, its principal object being to make me tranquil in my mind with respect to my future life. Having dealt thus openly with you, my dear Brother, I must add that I should be very loth to be oppressive to you, or any of my Brothers, or to draw upon you for more than you could spare without straitening yourselves—I am sure that John will meet your utmost wishes in the business, and Christopher will do all that he can afford. But when he marries he will be in a different situation from what he is in now, and though he may, and probably will, be as rich, or richer, even as a married man, yet this is uncertain; therefore, he may not be able at this present time to make a *permanent* and unconditional engagement. I received 10£ from him the year before last and 20£ last year, and he promised me the same sum annually as long as he should continue a Fellow of Trinity.

You never talk about coming to see us—I wish you would. Grasmere is a sweet place, and you would have plenty of sport in fishing, if [you] have not lost the art. We have been advised to send a statement of our Case to Lord Lonsdale's Executors and Heirs. Mr Clarkson talked to my Uncle Myers[1] about it, who approves of its being done, but William will write to you about it. In a fortnight's time we are going into Yorkshire to Mr Hutchinson's to spend a couple of months before William is married—he will be married just before our return home. Pray write before we go. I shall stand in need of the money which John intended for me, having calculated upon it—The sum he gave me reason to expect to receive by this time was twenty pounds—God bless you!

    I am my dear Brother,

your affecte Sister D Wordsworth.[2]

---

[1] The Revd Thomas Myers, vicar of Lazonby.
[2] This is part of a joint letter: W. W.'s contribution followed.

19. *To* Mrs John Marshall

My dear Friend,

I cannot express how grievously I am mortified at not having had the happiness of seeing you when you were at Scarborough. We reached Gallow Hill on Friday evening, and truly distressed I was indeed to learn that you had been here the Sunday before and were gone. What a pleasure would it have been to me to see my old Friend and her dear little children!

My Brother desires me to send his kind remembrances to you and Mr Marshall and to assure you that he was exceedingly sorry that he had not the pleasure of seeing you both.

I should have written to you from London, but that I always indulged the hope of meeting you here and at Scarborough, and was always also unable to speak with any certainty of the time of our return. We were detained in London by a succession of unexpected events, first the arrival of my Brother Christopher, then of my Brother John, and last of all (which was, indeed, the only unfortunate one) by my being exceedingly unwell, in a violent cold caught by riding from Windsor[1] in a long-bodied coach with 12 passengers. This cold detained us in town till last Wednesday. I am now perfectly well, except that I do not feel myself strong, and am very thin, but my kind Friends help me to take such good care of myself that I hope soon to become as strong as any body.

We leave Gallow Hill on Monday morning, immediately after my Brother William's marriage,[2] we expect to reach Grasmere on Wednesday Evening. William, Mary and I go together in a post chaise, and after Mr Hutchinson's harvest is over (when we shall have got completely settled in our own home) he and his Sister Sara will follow us and spend some time at Grasmere and Keswick. My dear Jane, if this letter reaches you before next Monday you will think of me, travelling towards our own dear Grasmere with my most beloved Brother and his Wife. I have long loved Mary Hutchinson as a Sister, and she is equally attached to me this being so, you will guess that I look forward with perfect happiness to this Connection

---

[1] Their uncle Cookson was now a Canon of Windsor.
[2] At Brompton Church on 4 Oct.

between us, but, happy as I am, I half dread that concentration of all tender feelings, past, present, and future which will come upon me on the wedding morning. There never lived on earth a better woman than Mary H. and I have not a doubt but that she is in every respect formed to make an excellent wife to my Brother, and I seem to myself to have scarcely any thing left to wish for but that the wedding was over, and we had reached our home once again. We have, indeed, been a long time absent. It was, however, a delightful thing to us to see all our Brothers, particularly John, after his return from India. He was in perfect health and excellent spirits. We spent two days with my Uncle and Aunt Cookson at Windsor, and saw Mary, and their three youngest children, as good and as sweet a set of children as ever I was with. Mary is a delightful, lovely, affectionate, and sensible Girl. My Uncle and Aunt were both well, my Uncle looks scarcely worse than when I left Forncett. We did not see the Nicholsons.[1] I knew that Caroline (whom I should have liked dearly to see and whom I love and respect very much) was at Guildford, and I guessed that the rest of the family were there, it being the time of year in which they always are, therefore I did not attempt to seek out their house.

No doubt you have heard that we have every prospect of settling our affairs with Lord Lowther[2] entirely to our satisfaction. Our claim *in Law* is as good as ever, and, what is of more consequence, Lord L. is a just man and disposed to repair as much as lies in his power, the Damage done by his predecessor. I am going to write to Mrs Rawson this afternoon. Remember me kindly to your Sister Catherine, and all your Sisters—again my Love to your husband, and kisses to all your children. God bless you my dear Jane! Your affectionate and faithful friend,

D. Wordsworth

---

[1] Samuel Nicholson, a London haberdasher, and his family, friends of W. W.
[2] Lord Lonsdale's cousin and heir, Sir William Lowther, Bt. (1757–1844), created Viscount Lowther.

20. *To* John Wordsworth[1]

Grasmere—May 1st. 1803.

My dear John,

Richard has informed me that you are [gone] down to Gravesend, to return no more from your ship. God send a blessing on you and your whole voyage and bring you back to us again in health and prosperity! We have thought about you continually of late, and have been anxious to hear from you, but, though you have never written to us, we have not supposed that you have thought much less about us than if you had. My Letters to Richard will have explained to you fully my sentiments respecting my money being adventured without Richard's security to me for it, therefore I need say nothing to you about it. I am sure, my dear Brother, that I need not speak of my affection for you, of the deep love I bear you, and you know well that there are few sacrifices that I should be unwilling to make on that score. But this is not an affair to be weighed in the balance of my affection for you, nor have I been called upon to advance the money on that score. It is an affair of prudence. As such, I have no doubt, and merely as such you have considered it, though we have come to different conclusions.

Sara Hutchinson left us on Thursday. Coleridge is ill in a rheumatic fever, and all his family have got the Influenza. We are all tolerable, but it is a sad unhealthy season and nobody is quite well. My general health is, however, much better than it was a few months ago. Mary's health is very good upon the whole. She and William send their kindest love to you. The Sympsons and old Molly never forget to inquire after you. Molly says "if I could but see Maister John I would send all the money that ever I have for a venture with him!"—you must know she has more than seven pounds. Mr Wedgewood has written to Coleridge requesting that you would have the goodness to bring him home a dozen China Pens. They were to be of different sizes, and one of them was to be large enough for some purpose or other but I have forgotten what—I suppose, however, that it was to be a large one. Farewell!

---

[1] Added to a letter to Richard Wordsworth.

again and again God bless you. Believe me ever your affectionate Sister Dorothy Wordsworth.

21. *To* Mrs Thomas Clarkson

Grasmere. 17th July [1803]

My dear Friend

Mary and I have never ceased to regret that you did not see our own darling child[1] before your departure from this country. It would have been very sweet to us to think that you had carried away an image of what we so dearly love. When you see him he will be a different creature and we should have liked that you had known perfectly what he is now; or rather what he was then, for he is much grown since that time, though indeed he does not appear to us to be much altered. He has blue eyes, a fair complexion, (which is already very much sunburnt,) a body as fat as a little pig, arms that are thickening and dimpling and bracelets at his wrists, a very prominent nose, which *will be* like his Father's, and a head shaped upon the very same model. I send you a lock of his hair sewed to this letter. To-day we have all been at Church. Mary was *churched* and the Babe christened—Coleridge my Brother Richard, and I were God-fathers and Godmother, old Mr Sympson answered for my Brother Richard, and had a hearty enjoyment of the christening cake, tea and coffee, this afternoon. The Child sleeps all night, and is a very good sleeper in the day. I wish you could see him in his Basket which is neither more nor less than a meat Basket which costs half a crown. In this basket he has (Not like Moses in his cradle of rushes, but in a boat, mind that. W. W.)[2] floated over Grasmere water asleep and made one of a dinner party at the Island, and we often carry it to the orchard-seat where he drops asleep beside us. My dear Friend, we are very anxious to hear how you have borne the journey. This letter will most likely reach Bury before your arrival there but I hope if it does that you will have written to us before you receive it. We are also very anxious to know the opinion of Physicians respecting your disease, and the remedies to be used. Poor Mr Clarkson. I often think

[1] W. W.'s son John.
[2] Added in the margin.

of him and his Solitude. I hope he goes on with his Book[1] which will be [the] only thing that can keep him in comfort. Luff[2] was here for a couple of hours on Thursday, and we expect him again to-morrow to meet Coleridge. C is much better in health and spirits than he has been for some time past. We expect to set off on our Scotch Tour in about ten days—William and C talk of it with thorough enjoyment, and I have no doubt I shall be as happy as they when I am fairly off, but I do not love to think of leaving home, and parting with the dear Babe who will be no more the same Babe when we return—besides, Sara does not come. This is a sad mortification to us particularly as she had given us the strongest reason to expect her, however we still hope for Joanna who can be very easily spared from Gallow Hill. Our dear Mary does not look forward to being left alone with one gloomy thought—indeed how should she with so sweet a Babe at her Breast? But both for her sake and Sara's we earnestly wished that they might have been together. You will rejoice to hear that the affair with Lord Lowther is entirely settled, except for signing releases and a few Law forms. We are to receive eight thousand five hundred pounds. The whole of the money is to be paid in a year. I cannot tell you yet what our Shares will be as there will be some deductions. I will write to you when we are on our Tour—you will like to know what we see and do. God bless you my ever dear Friend. May God restore you to health and may you come back to us with a Body as fit for enjoyment among these noble and quiet Mountains and Vales as your heart is. Best respects to your Father and Mother. Love to your Brother Robert who is a huge favorite of mine, little though he be! and to your dear Son.

Yours ever and ever Dorothy Wordsworth.

22. *To* Lady Beaumont

Grasmere May 25th [and 29th] 1804

My dear Madam

    I thank you from my heart for the pleasure we have all received from your most kind letter. I left home two or three days after its

---

[1] *A Portraiture of Quakerism*, 1806.
[2] A Patterdale friend.

arrival, and during a delightful journey over the mountains, under
the crown of Helvellyn, to Patterdale, and along the shore of Ulswater, it was one of my most pleasing thoughts that when I was
safely lodged at the house of my Friend I would recount to Lady
Beaumont the history of my journey and tell her about the dear
Friends whom I had left at home—not all at home either for I
parted with my Brother at Airey Force; we had walked over the
Hills together lodged at Patterdale, and the next morning we rode
on horseback as far as Liulph's Tower,[1] walked up to the Force, he
struck over the hills to Keswick and I went onwards down the Lake
and two miles further. My Brother spent three days at Keswick with
Mrs Coleridge; she is well and in good spirits, and the children,
Hartley especially, seem to be in good health; he goes to school, and,
I believe, takes to the performance of his duty even as other children
of his years. My Brother says he should scarcely have known Sara[2]
(the last time he saw her was the very day of your departure from
Keswick) she is no longer, as I daresay you remember her, all peace
and meekness, the gentle "Lady Abbess", but a little quick creature
here, and there, and everywhere, as lively as Hartley himself. She
is thin and very small. Our Baby who is six months younger is
almost twice her size. When I began to write, but I have wandered
from my purpose, I was going to tell you why I had not answered
your letter much sooner but indeed except for the satisfaction of my
own heart that knows full well the claims your kindness has upon
me, I should have said nothing about it for you will be half inclined
to smile at me for talking of business and want of leisure in this
solitude. I must first tell you however that I only mean want of
leisure to perform a duty which I could not resolve to perform
without making a pleasure of it, for I have had time to write a
hundred letters if I could have been contented to sit down without
the quiet possession of myself and my own thoughts. I was a fortnight from home with my Sister's Sister, who is just come with her
Brother to a farm three miles from Penrith.[3] She was fitting up his
house and I went to welcome her into the country, and help her
with her work, such as fitting up beds, curtains, etc etc etc.—we

[1] Lyulph's Tower, above Ullswater, built by the Duke of Norfolk in 1780.
[2] Sara Coleridge (1802–52), author of *Phantasmion*.
[3] Park House.

worked diligently all day and in the evenings were glad to walk out together. I am pleased to think that when I tell you of this Friend of ours you are prepared with a ready interest for she is one of whom you must have heard Coleridge speak Miss Sara Hutchinson, one of his most dear and intimate friends, even before she was so nearly connected with us by my Brother's marriage. You will be glad to hear that she is come to be an inhabitant of this country both for his sake and ours, she is fixed at a very sweet place, and seems to be perfectly contented; and pleased with every thing around her. Since my return home I have had no leisure, I had almost said no comfort till today. I have really been overwrought with positive labour. Our old Servant, whom you may have chanced to hear Coleridge speak of as a drollery belonging to the Cottage, has left us, and we have been engaged in a Whitsuntide cleaning, colouring and painting etc etc before the coming of our new Servant whom we expect today. It is an affair of great consequence to us that we should be well served and that all things in our little establishment should be regularly arranged, which has not been the case for the last six weeks while we have had no servant but a little Girl, therefore, my Sister not being very strong, I was glad to take upon myself the charge of putting things in order. A long story you will say, and indeed, though as I have said I explained my long silence for my own satisfaction, I should not have said so much about it if at the same time I had not been giving you some idea of the manner in which we live and had an opportunity of speaking of Miss Hutchinson who is so much esteemed by our common Friend; for I think one of the dullest things in the world is a letter filled with apologies for not writing sooner.

My dear Madam, I was most happy to find by your last letter that you had not, as we had feared from what Mrs C had told us, given up the thought of coming into Cumberland this Summer. My Sister and I long ardently for the pleasure of seeing you, and knowing *more* of you, for already we seem to be well acquainted with you. I cannot express how much pleasure it has given us that my Brother's Poems have afforded so much delight to you and Sir George. I trust in God that he may live yet to perform greater and better things for the benefit of those who shall come after us, and for the pure and good of these times. You will rejoice to hear, that he has gone on regularly, I may say rapidly, with the poem[1] of which Coleridge shewed you a part, and that his health, though at present he is troubled with a weakness in one of his eyes, is upon the whole good. He tells me that he intends writing to Sir George immediately; but as he is so apt to procrastinate I dare not say that it will certainly be within this fortnight, but he may speak for himself before I close my letter; at present he is walking, and has been out of doors these two hours though it has rained heavily all the morning. In wet weather he takes out an umbrella, chuses the most sheltered spot, and there walks backwards and forwards, and though the length of his walk be sometimes a quarter or a half a mile, he is as fast bound within the chosen limits as if by prison walls. He generally composes his verses out of doors, and while he is so engaged he seldom knows how the time slips away, or hardly whether it is rain or fair. I wrote so far several days ago. We have since had the satisfaction of hearing that our Friend was arrived at Gibralter.[2] No doubt he has written to you. It is a great comfort to us to know that he has got so far on his voyage, but indeed the accounts he gives of the state of his health are not very chearing. Only the very day before he wrote he had been bowed down as before by a rainy afternoon, and as soon as the rain abated he was well again. I fear indeed; too much I fear that the change of climate will work no permanent cure, but that when he returns to England again he will be as subject to the weather as heretofore. I agree with you, woful as the change will be to him, that, unless a thorough change be wrought in his habit of Body, it will be wise and proper that he should fix his residence in the dryest part of our Island. We have had nothing but rainy weather for this fortnight past—to make us some amends the mountains are more than usually beautiful, almost as green as the valley itself, but we shall be tired out if we have not a little more sunshine before another fortnight is over. My Brother and sister and the little Boy are only waiting for fair weather to make the same journey from which I am returned. My Sister and the child will be absent three weeks, a long time for me! I do not know how the house will sound without his voice. I shall find a loss even of the very worst he can do—his passionate cries and screams—he is a turbulent Fellow, and often when he is in my arms

[1] *The Prelude.*
[2] S. T. C. was bound for Malta in search of health.

I wish for a little quietness, but when he is away the heartsomeness of the house will be gone too, at least so it will seem for a little while, especially when I am quite alone, but my Brother will not stay more than a week or ten days. I wish I could tell you that we had had the pleasure of drinking of the brown Stout. It is not yet tapped, but we are now drinking the last Cask of our own ale. We shall, as you were so good as to direct, put a tea cup full of sweet Oil into the Cask. I hope my dear Madam that before the summer is over we shall have the great delight which we talk much about of conducting you into the recesses of our Vale,—beautiful as it shews itself to the Traveller passing through you will say that its richest treasures are only found when sought after. I ought to beg your pardon for sending a sheet so full of blunders—written with so bad a pen—I do indeed presume upon your goodness, or I should keep this back and write another letter. My Brother and sister unite with me in most respectful remembrances and every good wish to you and Sir George. Believe me my dear Madam, Very sincerely yours

Dorothy Wordsworth. May 29th

23. *To* Mrs Thomas Clarkson

Park house January 6th 1805.

My dear Friend,

It is near seven o'clock, Sunday night, we have just put our two Children to bed and William, Mary, Sara, Joanna, Tom, and George Hutchinson[1] with Hartley Coleridge are making a Christmas party round the fire. My thoughts are with you and have often been with you since we came here; how would it have enlivened our fireside if you had been one of us, and so near your own home! We came to Parkhouse in the Irish Car on Wednesday. The day before New Year's day was one of the most delightful days that ever was felt we were all taking our pleasure upon the ice. William and George Hutchinson pushed us along in their skates on the ice (Grasmere Water is entirely frozen over) and we carried the children on our knees, John and even little Dorothy.[2] In our good spirits we

---

[1] M. W.'s youngest brother.
[2] Dora, b. the previous Aug.

resolved with true courage, and perhaps a little rashness it might
seem, to come to see Sara the next day if the weather was not
changed. It proved a fine morning, and we had a delightful journey,
the children were no worse—but owing to our being over heated in
climbing Kirkstone both Mary and I suffered for it. She has been
ill in the tooth ache unable to stir out ever since we came, and I
caught a very bad cold. All this would have been spared if William
would have allowed us a little more time, but he was so much afraid
of our being too late at night and hurried us up the hill. I carried
Dorothy in my arms, Mary had enough to do to carry herself and
her clothes, William bore Johnny and G Hutchinson took care of
the horse. We shall return by the other Road and shall not have any
hills to climb, so I hope we shall be no worse for our journey home.
Sara is very well—and looks well. We are all exceedingly anxious
about Coleridge—no letters have arrived, we believe him to be at
Malta and William assures us that if they do not manage like Idiots
the fever may be kept out of that small Island. Your letter affected
us very much and I was very proud of Tom.[1] Give my kind love to
him and tell him we are all very glad that he remembers his old
Friends with so much affection, he writes very nicely and I hope he
will go on improving. The next time I write to you I shall write him
a letter also, at present I have not time to do more than just tell you
how we are going on for the person is waiting who is to carry this
letter to the post-office. When I write to Tom I shall take a large
sheet of paper and write plain that he may have the pleasure of
reading the letter as well as calling it his own. William and I walked
this morning up the Vale of Dacre to Hutton John. We had a
delightful walk, the more delightful for those mingled recollections
painful yet sweet of the walk we had through that vale when we
came from Keswick to see you at Eusemere. Oh my dear Friend!
when we saw the white spot at the foot of Ulswater, your house, as
we came along in the twilight[2]—I remembered most vividly the first
time we visited you and many other times—when we came from
Watermillock for instance and saw the lights before us in the
windows—yet we have reason to be thankful that you have had the
resolution to part with it for I am sure it would never more have

[1] Mrs Clarkson's son.
[2] On 12 July 1802, according to D. W.'s *Grasmere Journal*.

done you good. We now have little thought of leaving our cottage till Coleridge's Return which surely will not be long, we shall go wherever he goes—and why may not you be near us too? This moment they have come in to hasten me, the man must be off. God Bless you my dear Friend, I will write again very soon—and do let us hear from you as often as you can with comfort write a few lines.

My dear Friend farewell

Yours ever more
Dorothy Wordsworth.

24. *To* Mrs John Marshall

[Grasmere] Friday [15th and Sunday 17th] March [1805]

I summoned up my heart a few days ago and began with courage to write to Mrs Rawson intending also to write to you—but I could not, therefore I desired her to forward the letter to you after she had read it. I cannot rest till I have written, so I choose a time in which my thoughts are calm and settled, and I will endeavour to *keep in* the grief which gushes out of me so many times in the day. I will tell you wherein my consolation is, and all that I can to comfort your tender heart. My good and dear Friend, your letter was a soothing gift, it drew a flood of tears from us, while we sate round our melancholy fire, and after they had passed away, we were in some sort cheered by your sympathy—it does me good to weep for him:[1] it does me good to find that others weep, and I bless them for it. Enough of this, it is not now the time, if I go on I shall do no better than before.

Yet I know not what to write—it is with me when I write as when I am walking out in this Vale once so full of joy. I can turn to no object that does not remind me of our loss. I see nothing that he would not have loved with me and enjoyed had he been by my side; and indeed, indeed my consolations rather come to me in gusts of feeling, than are the quiet growth of my Mind. I know it will not always be so—the time will come when the light of the setting sun

---

[1] John Wordsworth, drowned in the shipwreck of the *Abergavenny* in Weymouth Bay on 5 Feb.

upon these mountain tops will be as heretofore a pure joy—not the same *gladness*, that can never be—but yet a joy even more tender. It will soothe me to know how happy *he* would have been could he have seen the same beautiful spectacle. I shall have him with me, and yet shall know that he is out of the reach of all sorrow and pain, can never mourn for us—his tender soul was awake to all our feelings—his wishes were intimately connected with our happiness. We know not then what anguish might have been his lot if he had lived longer—he was taken away in the freshness of his manhood, pure he was;—and innocent as a child, I may even say, for among the impure he lived uncontaminated. Never human being was more thoroughly modest, and his courage I need not speak of, it served him in the hour of trial, he was seen "speaking with apparent chearfulness to the first Mate a few minutes before the ship went down", and when nothing more could be done he said "the will of God be done" and I have no doubt when he felt that it was out of his power to save his life, he was as calm as before if some thought of what we should endure did not awaken a pang. Our loss is not to be measured but by those who are acquainted with the nature of our pleasures and have seen how happily we lived together those eight months that he was under our Roof—he loved solitude and he rejoiced in society—he would wander alone among these hills with his fishing-rod, or led on merely by the pleasure of walking, for many hours—or he would walk with William or me, or both of us, and was continually pointing out with a gladness which is seldom seen but in very young people something which perhaps would have escaped our observation, for he had so fine an eye that no distinction was unnoticed by him, and so tender a feeling that he never noticed any thing in vain. Many a time has he called me out in an evening to look at the moon or stars, or a cloudy sky, or this vale in the quiet moonlight—but the stars and moon were his chief delight,—he made of them his companions when he was at Sea, and was never tired of those thoughts which the silence of the night fed in him—then he was so happy by the fire-side, any little business of the house interested him, he loved our cottage, he helped us to furnish it, and to make the gardens—trees are growing now which he planted. Oh! my dear Jane! I must not go on. I do not in this way perform the task I assigned myself. He was with us when Mr Marshall was here, and as I daresay he has repeated to you since his death, accompanied Mr M to Buttermere—he stayed with us till the 29th of September, having come to us about the end of January.[1] During that time Mary Hutchinson now Mary Wordsworth stayed with us six weeks. John used to walk with her every where, and they were exceedingly attached to each other—so my poor Sister mourns with us, not merely as we have lost one of the family who was so dear to William and me, but from tender love of John and an intimate knowledge of his virtues. Her hopes as well as ours were fixed on John—we never thought of him but with hope and comfort, and this is now our sorrow—but at the same [time] it is our best consolation and will in the end be a never-failing source of pleasing contemplations. It is good for us to think upon the virtuous. I trust our hearts will be mended by what we know of his. The News-papers have given contradictory and unintelligible accounts of the dismal event—this was very harassing to us. We knew that our Brother would do his duty, of this we were confident—that he would not lose his presence of mind, or blunder, or forget, but we wanted to have all cleared up, to know *how* it was. This as far as concerned ourselves— and then for the sake of the relatives of those poor three hundred who went down with him we were greatly distressed. It cut us to the heart to think that their sorrow should be aggravated by a thought that his errors or weakness, or any other misconduct should have occasioned or encreased the calamity. God be praised we are now satisfied in our own knowledge—we know how it was, and I hope that many of those who have mourned for their friends may have received such information as may have settled their minds also. It is "a memorandum respecting the Loss of the Earl of Abergavenny" by Gilpin one of the Mates which has been transcribed from a pamphlet and sent to us, which has explained to us the manner of the ship's going down. There have been two Narratives published, one of no value at all, the other, though I believe drawn up without much feeling, may in many respects be depended on

---

[1] See Letter 16 above.

as it is done by a person high in the India House. I do not know the title but the motto is taken from Clarence's Dream,[1] by which you will know if you have the right one, for I wish you to send for it.

I am afraid I have written a letter that will give you pain in the reading for I have been so much affected with the thoughts of my poor Brother as I went along, that I am sure I must have written what will affect you with fresh sorrow—do forgive me—I shall be better—I *am* better—I have walked out today and had less of anguish than I have ever had in any walk since we have been in our trouble. I nurse the Baby and do what I can, I am even now comforted while I write to you, though I have been often scarcely able to see my paper.

And now again my dearest Jane let me bless you for your letter. *Your* letter and Mrs Rawsons have given me inexpressible consolation—the consolation which sympathy always affords. I should like very much to see you among your Children. May they live to be blessings to you and each other! I was much affected by your having called your daughter by my name, especially as she has yours also. I cannot talk about coming to see you at present, for I cannot think of any separation from my Brother and sister. We do not think we shall stay long at Grasmere. Our house is too small for us and there is no other in the Vale, so we must move at some time, and the sooner it is done the better for us as we now are. We shall most likely go southward, and we will endeavour to take that opportunity of visiting our friends at Halifax and you and Mr Marshall—but we do not talk of change and we shall find it hard to resolve.

Remember me affectionately to your Mother and Sisters. William joins with me in kindest regards to Mr Marshall. May God bless you, my dear Friend believe me ever your affectionate and faithful friend.

D. Wordsworth

Write to me again I pray you.

My Brother Richard says that there is no reason to think that we shall any of us suffer in our property. This is a great comfort to us for our poor John's sake, who I am sure would have one pleasing

---

[1] See *Richard III*, I. iv. 21–24.

thought on that account when he knew that all he carried ‹
him would be lost. As for ourselves, we ventured nothing t‚
could not well have done without, nor would John for the ‹
have taken a single hundred pounds of William's or mine at ‚ ‚
hazard of depriving us of our independence. My Brother Richard
lent him a considerable Sum, but *he* could well have born the loss.
Christopher also, as I have since learnt had lent him all his
property, but he would not have suffered from the loss, having a
very sufficient income—but all is insured.

I send off this letter on Sunday. I can think of nothing but our
Dear Departed Brother, yet I am very tranquil today—I honour
him, and love him, and glory in his memory.

Far[ew]ell my dear dear Friend. I shall be very glad to hear from
you—tell me about your children. Kiss them all for me, and clasp
little Jane Dorothy to your heart. Do you continue to suckle her?
Mary has not yet weaned our Dorothy. I know not that there is any
thing in this letter that was not in that I wrote to Mrs Rawson. If
there be you will not think it any trouble to transcribe it—again
God bless you!

25. *To* Lady Beaumont

Grasmere June 11th, 1805.

My dear Friend,

It will give you pleasure to hear that I have delayed writing to
you in consequence of full employment. I do not mean employment
that made it impossible or inconvenient; but I had determined
within myself not to write till our work was ended. In the first place
we turned to the melancholy garden, and put it into order; the
orchard hut, which had remained unfinished since last autumn, we
have completed, and our own dwelling-house which had fallen into
disorder like other things, we have had set to rights. While these
labours were going on I took a small share in them, but nursing was
my chief business. Since that time I have been engaged in finishing
a copy of a journal of our Tour in Scotland—this was at the first
beginning a very painful office,—I had written it for the sake of
Friends who could not [be] with us at the time, and my Brother

John had been always in my thoughts, for we wished him to know every thing that befel us. The task of re-copying this journal, which at first when it was proposed to me after his death, I thought I could never do, I performed at last and found it a tranquillizing employment. I write to you from the Hut, where we pass all our time except when we are walking—it has been a rainy morning, but we are here sheltered and warm, and in truth I think it is the sweetest place on Earth—the little wrens often alight upon the thatch and sing their low song, but this morning *all* the Birds are rejoicing after the rain. Before my eyes is the Church and a few houses among trees, and still beyond the hollow of Easedale which I imagine but cannot see, and the quiet mountains shutting all up. Where I sit I have no view of the Lake, but if I chuse to move half a yard further along the seat, I can see it, and so on, going all round, we have a different view. My Brother is at Patterdale, he took his fishing-rod over the mountains, there being a pass from Grasmere thither. My Sister and I accompanied him to the top of it, and parted from him near a Tarn[1] under a part of Helvellyn—he had gone up on Saturday with a neighbour of ours to fish there, but he quitted his companion, and poured out his heart in some beautiful verses to the memory of our lost Brother,[2] who used to go sometimes alone to that same Tarn; for the pleasure of angling in part, but still more, for his love of solitude and of the mountains. Near that very Tarn William and I bade him farewell the last time he was at Grasmere, when he went from us to take the command of the ship. We were in view of the head of Ulswater, and stood till we could see him no longer, watching him as he *hurried* down the stony mountain. Oh! my dear Friend, you will not wonder that we love that place. I have been twice to it since his death. The first time was agony, but it is now a different feeling—poor William was overcome on Saturday—and with floods of tears wrote those verses—he parted from us yesterday (Monday) very chearfully, and indeed his spirits are far better than I could have thought possible at this time. He will return to us we hope in three days. He went for the sake of relaxation, having finished his long poem,[3] and intending to pause a short time before

[1] Grisedale Tarn.
[2] *Elegiac Verses in Memory of my Brother, John Wordsworth*, publ. 1842.
[3] *The Prelude.*

he begins the other.[1] You will judge that a happy change has been wrought in his mind when he chuses John's[2] employments, and one of John's haunts (for he delighted in the neighbourhood of Patterdale) for such a purpose. We have had no news of Coleridge's Return, further than a confirmation of his intention, but no time was spoken of, and the letter from Miss Stoddart,[3] who sees him probably almost daily, was dated the 5th of March. We conclude now, that he will be at Malta when the tidings of my Brother's death and the loss of the Abergavenny reach that place; and we have no doubt that he will come by the first Ship afterwards. We expect Mrs C at the end of this week—she is to bring the little Darling Sara with her, who has by the mercy of God escaped from an accident that you will shudder to hear of. She slipped from the Servant who was playing with her near the Forge at the bottom of the field, ran upon a wooden Bridge which I believe has been built since you were at Keswick and fell into the Greta—the Bridge is very high above the Stream, and the water was low—it is almost miraculous that she was not dashed to pieces. A man from the forge went a considerable way down the river and took her out. She was put to bed immediately and soon recovered, but she has never been *perfectly* well since, Mrs C. hopes however that change of air will entirely restore her. What a shock, for her poor Father, if after his sorrowful voyage, he had heard the tidings of *her* death too!

Perhaps this letter may not find you in London. I should wish it to be so except for Coleridge's sake, to whom it would be such a comfort to see you when he returns; but it is all uncertain when that will be, and we must try to be easy and patient. We are often, in spite of all we can do, very painfully anxious about him. I said I should wish this letter might not find you in London—you would guess my reason, it seems as if the springtime were almost wasted for those who are obliged to be in a large city. We have had delicious weather and I may truly say that we never more deeply enjoyed the blessing. As soon as breakfast is over we come up hither, stay all day, and after our walk in the evening return, and often linger here till

---

[1] *The Recluse.*

[2] i.e. his brother, who had been keen on fishing.

[3] Sister of Sir John Stoddart (1773–1856), King's Advocate for Malta, later married to Hazlitt.

the stars appear. I do not expect that we shall see you this summer, and indeed I cannot even *wish* that you should come for so short a time merely *to see us*, but it will be different when Coleridge is at home also. William has returned our thanks to you and Sir George for the print of Coleridge[1] and I believe, told you what we think of it. It seems to me to be in parts far better than any other likeness except that painted by Hazlitt[2] which is so dismal that I shrink from the sight of it. I thought of Coleridge dying, and not merely dying, but dying of sorrow and raised up upon his bed to take a last farewell of his Friends. My Sister's pleasure at the first sight of the print was equal to what the painter himself, I think could have desired; but the whole face, when seen all at once, seems to *me* scarcely to resemble Coleridge, though the forehead and outline of the *shape* of the face are very much like him. We have read Madoc[3] with great delight, but I will tell you more of my own particular sentiments of it when I have read it again to myself. I had one painful feeling throughout, that I did not care as much about *Madoc* as the Author wished me to do, and that the characters in general are not sufficiently distinct to make them have a separate after-existence in my affections. We were all exceedingly interested for young Lewellyn, but the women, except Erillyab, do not seem to me to differ much from women as represented in our better modern novels, and I could not discover that the characters of Emma and Goervyl were discriminated from each other. Yet the manner of telling the story is exceedingly spirited, and the attention is always kept awake. As you observe the descriptions are often exceedingly beautiful,—they are like resting-places both for repose and delight. The language occasionally, nay *frequently* gave me pain, and mostly in cases where it seemed that a very little trouble might have removed the faults. I have not the Book here or I would take down a few of those expressions which I complain of. They are a sort of barbarisms which appear to belong to Southey himself. But indeed I seem to be talking very conceitedly and almost as if I thought I were a great Critic—so I must end with saying again that we have read the Poem with the greatest delight,

[1] From James Northcote's portrait (1804).
[2] William Hazlitt (1778–1830), the essayist. It was painted for Sir George Beaumont at Keswick in 1803.
[3] Southey's poem.

and I expect much more from reading it alone, for there is a weakness in my mind which makes it exceedingly difficult for me to remember or even *understand* a story when it is read aloud. I do not think I lost much of the spirit of it in this first reading, I mean of the *manner* etc. but many of the incidents escaped from me. I have written a long letter all about ourselves. I should have taken a larger sheet, if I had not thought I should have given over much sooner, for I am sorry to make a double letter of it. I have not mentioned your dear Sister's name, but she has been often in my thoughts. May God restore her to you for years of happiness! I wish very much to know the degree of confinement in which she is detained, and whether she suffers much personal inconvenience from it. I hope I shall hear from you soon, but if I knew you were still in London I should not be uneasy at your silence, therefore do not let the thought of my expecting a letter from you press on you in the throng of your many engagements. If Sir George should be ill or any evil should happen, I am sure that by some means you will take care [that] we shall know it.

Farewell, believe [me] ever with sincere love and esteem, your faithful Friend

Dorothy Wordsworth.

My sister sends her kind remembrances. My Brother has written some small poems which I think you will like, since he finished that long one on his own early life and education.

26. *To* Lady Beaumont

Grasmere—Christmas day—[and 26 Dec.] 1805.

Your kind and interesting letter gave me true pleasure; indeed, my dear Lady Beaumont, the proofs which I so frequently receive from you of your sympathy in my daily feelings and common concerns are very affecting to me. You yourself are far removed from many of the cares, anxieties, and even pleasures that occupy my mind, which makes your sympathy doubly touching; and for that cause I am the more grateful for it. I began this letter yesterday, on Christmas-day, but was interrupted. It is a day of dear and interesting remembrances, and to me peculiarly, therefore I was unwilling to take another sheet of paper for the Date's sake. I yesterday completed my thirty fourth year—a birthday is to every body a time of serious thought, but more so, I should think, when it happens to be upon a day of general festivity, and especially on Christmas-day, when all persons, however widely scattered, are in their thoughts gathered together at home. I can almost tell where every Birth-day of my life was spent, many of them even *how* from a very early time. The Day was always kept by my Brothers with rejoicing in my Father's house, but for six years (the interval between my Mother's Death and his) I was never once at home, never was for a single moment under my Father's Roof after her Death, which I cannot think of without regret for many causes, and particularly, that I have been thereby put out of the way of many recollections in common with my Brothers of that period of life, which, whatever it may be actually as it goes along, generally appears more delightful than any other when it is over. Poor Coleridge was with us two years ago at this time. He came over with Derwent on his way to London, and was detained week after week by sickness. We hear no further tidings of him, and I cannot help being very uneasy and anxious; though without any evil, many causes might delay him; yet it is a long time since he left Malta. The weather is dreadful for a sea voyage. Oh my dear Friend, what a fearful thing a windy night is now at our house! I am too often haunted with dreadful images of Shipwrecks and the Sea when I am in bed and hear a stormy wind, and now that we are thinking so much about Coleridge it is worse than ever. My Sister is not yet returned, we expect her at home tomorrow if the day be tolerable, but wind rain and snow are driving down the vale, and the chimney every now and then roars as if it were going to come down upon us. I am very anxious that this boisterous day should be followed by a gentle one (as often happens). I should be exceedingly disappointed if My Sister should not come home,—she has stayed much longer than she intended,[1] and is anxious to be with us again, and to see the Children. John is grown very much during her absence, and Dorothy, till within these three days, has been advancing rapidly, but she is now very poorly, having caught cold, and will be quite thrown back again, when her

[1] At Park House.

Mother sees her, which is mortifying to me. You are very good in taking so much thought about us. It is true that Miss Hutchinson will be of great use in assisting us in the care of the Children; not that when we are both well we are over-fatigued with them but, even at a[ll] times it would be better if we had more time for the cultivation of our minds by reading. I do not read much—very little, indeed; but in this house it would be exceedingly unpleasant to have two Servants, not to speak of an *insurmountable* objection, the want of room for another person; but as soon as we can meet with a suitable house in a situation that we like, we are resolved to remove, and by keeping a couple of cows (even if my Sister should have no more children) we shall have sufficient employment for two Servants, and she and I might have much more leisure. I have been summoned into the kitchen to dance with Johnny and have danced till I am out of Breath. According to annual custom, our Grasmere Fidler is going his rounds, and all the children of the neighbouring houses are assembled in the kitchen to dance. Johnny has long talked of the time when the Fiddler was to come; but he was too shy to dance with any Body but me, and though he exhibited very boldly when I was down stairs, I find they cannot persuade him to stir again. It is a pleasant sound they make with their little pattering feet upon the stone floor, half a dozen of them, Boys and Girls; Dorothy is in ecstasy, and John looks as grave as an old Man. I am very glad that you hear so frequently from your Sister. If the Lyrical Ballads do but give her half the pleasure which you have received from them it will be very gratifying to me. I have no thoughts more soothing than those connected with the hope that my dear Brother and Coleridge may be the means of ministering consolation to the unhappy, or elevating and worthy thoughts to many who live in solitude or retirement; or have too much of the bustle of the world without unhappiness. I have transcribed two thirds of the Poem addressed to Coleridge,[1] and am far more than pleased with it as I go along. I often think of the time when William shall have the pleasure of reading it to you and Sir George. He is very anxious to get forward with The Recluse,[2] and is reading for the nourishment

---

[1] *The Prelude.*

[2] The long poem on Man, Nature and Society, of which only the second part, *The Excursion*, was completed.

of his mind, preparatory to beginning; but I do not think he will be able to do much more till we have heard of Coleridge. My Brother returns his best thanks to Sir George for his letter—he intends answering it very soon; he talked of writing immediately after the receipt of it, to explain what he had said before, as he feared that he had so expressed himself that Sir George had misunderstood his sentiments respecting large houses.

I was exceedingly interested with your Extract from the News-paper concerning Lord Nelson's last moments[1]—how very affecting the noble Creature's thoughts of his early pleasures, and the happy Fair-day at [his] home! My Brother was at Park House when I received it—he had [seen] the same account at Penrith; but it was not in the Courier, the Paper we have at Grasmere, therefore your kind attention was a great gain to me.

The day grows worse and worse—I fear we shall have sad tidings from the Sea-coast. Heaven grant that Coleridge may be somewhere or other safe on Land! Adieu my dear Friend. May you enjoy many years of life with health and tranquillity! Coleridge, I believe, was at Dunmow[2] about five weeks after this time two years ago. Oh! that he were with you there now!

Yours ever
Dorothy Wordsworth.

December 26th

P.S. I had almost forgotten one of the main objects for which I wrote, or rather the only matter of business. My Brother sent the Houbraken[3] by a Gentleman, a Friend of ours, who is to leave it at my Brother's Chambers No. 11 Staple Inn London. We did not part with it without anxiety as we had not time to pack it up, for the Gentleman came unexpectedly and did not get out of his Carriage, it being late at night; but we gave him the strictest charge to get it properly packed at Kendal, and to take all possible care of it. We have lately had a lesson how little Carriers are to be trusted, having lost a parcel which contained five Books of my Brother's Poem, and the third part of my Journal of our Scotch Tour. Of course we

---

[1] At the battle of Trafalgar on 21 Oct.
[2] In Essex, where the Dowager Lady Beaumont lived.
[3] A biographical dictionary, named after the engraver of the portraits.

should not have ventured the Poems if we had had no other Copy, and a Friend[1] of mine has thought it worth while to take a copy of my Journal, so it is rather a vexatious business than a serious loss, though attended with some inconvenience, for my Friend who has the Journal is in Norfolk and we are obliged to employ her to get it recopied and send it to us by the Coach. We think it safest that the Book should remain in my Brother's chambers till it be convenient to you to send for it, otherwise we should have desired him to see that it was delivered.

27. *To* Lady Beaumont

Grasmere. Saturday afternoon
4 o'clock. April 20th [1806]

Many thanks, my dear Friend, for your kind letter! You cannot doubt but that it delighted us to hear of the pleasure you had received from seeing my Brother;[2] and it was very kind of you to find a moment to write to me among your many engagements. I am seated in a *shady* corner of the moss hut (for it fronts the west and towards evening the sun shines full into it) and but that Mr Crump's ruinous mansion[3] (has my Brother told you that one third of it is fallen down?) stares me in the face whenever I look up there is not any object that is not chearful and in harmony with the sheltering mountains and quiet vale. The lake is perfectly calm, two or three ploughs are at work, the fields scattered over with sheep and lambs. Within three days the flowers have sprung up by thousands. William's favourite, the little celandine,[4] glitters upon every bank, the fields are becoming green, the buds bursting; and but three days ago scarcely a trace of spring was to be seen. We have had two days and nights of gentle rain with a South wind; and now that the sun shines again the change seems almost miraculous. We are so proud of it that we have scarcely been in the house ten minutes together the whole day, and I, you see, have lost no time in taking possession

[1] Mrs Clarkson.
[2] W. W. had been staying with the Beaumonts in Grosvenor Square.
[3] Allan Bank, just completed by J. G. Crump, a Liverpool merchant.
[4] See *To the Small Celandine* and *To the Same Flower*, composed 1802.

of our summer abode. Ever since my Brother left us the weather has been unusually severe, much colder than it was at christmas; and it has been a very sickly time, and we in our family have not escaped bad colds. John and Dorothy were exceedingly poorly for several days. John is recovered entirely and has been roaming about as happy as the young lambs all this fine day, and we hope that Dorothy is in the way of mending. I wish I could say the same of their Mother who has a bad cough, which is particularly troublesome to her in her present state; we trust however that, if the wind does not shift to its old quarters in the North, she may soon get rid of it.

My Brother has received so much pleasure in your house, had so many proofs of your affectionate regard that my heart is overcome with gratitude! he has sent us the history of every day that he has passed with you, and we are very happy in the thought of his being now so near to you, so very near that it is almost the same thing as if he were under your roof. I am truly glad that my Brother's manuscript poems give you so much pleasure—I was sure that you would be deeply impressed by the Ode.[1] The last time I read it over, I said: 'Lady Beaumont will like this'. I long to know your opinion and Sir George's of Benjamin, the Waggoner;[2] I *think* you will be pleased with it, but cannot be so sure of this—And you would persuade *me* that I am capable of writing poems that might give pleasure to others besides my own particular friends!! indeed, indeed you do not know me thoroughly; you think far better of me than I deserve—I must tell you the history of those two little things which William in his fondness read to you. I happened to be writing a letter one evening when he and my Sister were last at Park house, I laid down the pen and thinking of little Johnny (then in bed in the next room) I muttered a few lines of that address to him about the Wind,[3] and having paper before me, wrote them down, and went on till I had finished. The other lines[4] I wrote in the same way, and as William knows every thing that I do, I shewed them to him when he came home, and he was very much pleased; but this I attributed to his partiality; yet because they gave him pleasure and for the sake

[1] *Intimations of Immortality.*
[2] *The Waggoner*, publ. 1819.
[3] *Address to a Child.*
[4] Probably *The Cottager to her Infant.*

of the children I ventured to hope that I might do something more at some time or other. Do not think that I was ever bold enough to hope to compose verses for the pleasure of grown persons. Descriptions, Sentiments, or little stories for children was all I could be ambitious of doing, and I did try one story, but failed so sadly that I was completely discouraged. Believe me, since I received your letter I have made several attempts (could I do less as you requested that I would *for your sake?*) and have been obliged to give it up in despair; and looking into my mind I find nothing there, even if I had the gift of language and numbers, that I could have the vanity to suppose could be of any use beyond our own fireside, or to please, as in your case, a few partial friends; but I have no command of language, no power of expressing my ideas, and no one was ever more inapt at molding words into regular metre. I have often tried when I have been walking alone (muttering to myself as is my Brother's custom) to express my feelings in verse; feelings, and *ideas* such as they were, I have never wanted at those times; but prose and rhyme and blank verse were jumbled together and nothing ever came of it. As to those two little things which I did write, I was very unwilling to place them beside my Brother's poems, but he insisted upon it, and I was obliged to submit; and though you have been pleased with them I cannot but think that it was chiefly owing to the spirit which William gave them in the reading and to your kindness for me. I have said far more than enough on this subject, and am almost at the end of my paper without having told you that Mrs Coleridge and Hartley are at Grasmere. She desires me to say that she intends writing to you in the course of a few days. Hartley is a very interesting child, so like his Father that it is quite affecting to observe him; his temper and many of his habits are the very same. When you see my Brother pray tell him that we shall write by next Tuesday's post, that we have received his letter sent off last Tuesday, and that Johnny is well and Dorothy much better. Adieu my good and dear Friend

> Believe me affectionately yours
> D. Wordsworth.

My Brother has a copy of my Journal of our Scotch Tour which I have desired him to leave with you when it comes from the Bookbinders, but perhaps you may be too much engaged to find time to read it. My Sister begs her kind remembrances. Excuse blunders and scrawling and this torn paper. I have a very inconvenient desk to write upon for we have not got the hut put in order yet.

Tuesday morning. Dorothy has had a good night and appears to be quite well today. The weather continues mild so I hope we shall all [*torn MS.*] though I cannot say that my Sister's cough is at all [   ]

28. *To* Lady Beaumont

[Late Sept. 1806]

My dear Friend,

I have put off writing to you for many days, hoping always that the next post would bring us a letter from Coleridge himself, from which some comfort might be gathered, and a more accurate estimate formed of the state of his mind; but no letter has arrived. I have, however, the satisfaction of telling you that he is to be at home on the 29th of this month,[1] he has written to acquaint Mrs Coleridge with this, and has told her that he has some notion of giving a course of Lectures in London in the winter. This is all we know; I do not imagine he has mentioned the subject of the lectures to Mrs C. Whatever his plan may be, I confess I very much wish he may not put it in practice, and for many reasons, first, because I fear his health would suffer from late hours and being led too much into company; and in the second place, I would fain see him address the whole powers of his soul to some great work in prose or verse, of which the effect would be permanent, and not personal and transitory. I do not mean to say that much permanent good may not be produced by communicating knowledge by means of lectures, but a man is perpetually tempted to lower himself to his hearers to bring them into sympathy with him, and no one would be more likely to yield to such temptation than Coleridge; therefore at every period of his life the objection would have applied to his devoting himself to

[1] S. T. C. arrived back in England from Italy on 17 Aug., but delayed his return to Greta Hall until 30 Oct. in order to see S. H. first.

this employment; but at this present time it seems almost necessary that he should have one grand object before him which would turn his thoughts away in a steady course from his own unhappy lot, and so prevent petty irritations and distresses, and in the end produce a habit of reconcilement and submission.—My dear friend, you will judge how much we have suffered from anxiety and distress within the few last weeks. We have long known how unfit Coleridge and his wife were for each other; but we had hoped that his ill-health, and the present need his children have of his care and fatherly instructions, and the reflections of his own mind during this long absence would have so wrought upon him that he might have returned home with comfort, ready to partake of the blessings of friendship, which he surely has in an abundant degree, and to devote himself to his studies and his children. I now trust he has brought himself into this state of mind; but as we have had no letters from him since that miserable one which we received a short time before my Brother mentioned the subject to Sir George, I do not know what his views are. Poor Soul! he had a struggle of many years, striving to bring Mrs C. to a change of temper, and something like communion with him in his enjoyments; he is now, I trust, effectually convinced that he has no power of this sort, and he has had so long a time to know and feel this that I would gladly hope things will not be so bad as he imagines when he finds himself once again with his Children under his own roof. If he *can* make use of the knowledge which he has of the utter impossibility of producing powers and qualities of mind which are not in her, or of much changing what is unsuitable to his disposition, I do not think he will be unhappy; I am sure I think he ought not to be *miserable*. While he imagined he had anything to hope for no wonder that his perpetual disappointments made him so! But suppose him once reconciled to that one great want, an utter want of sympathy, I believe he may live in peace and quiet. Mrs C. has many excellent properties; as you observe she is unremitting in her attentions as a nurse to her Children, and indeed, I believe she would have made an excellent wife to many persons. Coleridge is as little fitted for her as she for him, and I am truly sorry for her. When we meet you at Coleorton I trust we shall have been with Coleridge long enough to know what comfort he is likely to have. In the meantime I will say no more on this distressing subject unless some change should happen much for the better or the worse. I hope everything from the effect of my Brother's conversation upon Coleridge's mind; and bitterly do I regret that he did not at first go to London to meet him, as I think he might have rouzed him up and preserved him from much of the misery that he has endured. Now I must speak of the delight with which we look forward to seeing you. We think that nothing will prevent our accepting your kind offer;[1] for it is plain that Coleridge does not wish us to go to Keswick as he has not replied to that part of William's letter in which he spoke of our plans for the winter. We shall therefore prepare ourselves to be ready to set off at any time that you shall appoint, so as to be with you a few days before your departure from Coleorton; and happy indeed shall we be to turn our faces [*MS. incomplete*].

29. *To* Lady Beaumont

Coleorton Tuesday 23rd [Dec. 1806]

Coleridge and his son Hartley arrived on Sunday afternoon. My dear Lady Beaumont, the pleasure of welcoming him to your house mingled with our joy, and I think I never was more happy in my life than when we had had him an hour by the fireside; for his looks were much more like his own old self, and, though we only talked of common things, and of our Friends, we perceived that he was contented in his mind and had settled his affairs at home to his satisfaction. He has been tolerably well and chearful ever since: and has begun with his Books. Hartley, poor Boy! is very happy, and looks uncommonly well; but we are afraid of the hooping-cough; for there is now no doubt that the cough which our young ones have *is* the hooping-cough. Thomas[2] is better than when I wrote on Saturday. I long to know your opinion and Sir George's of my Brother's plan of the winter garden. Coleridge (as we females

---

[1] i.e. of the loan of Hall Farm, Coleorton.
[2] W. W.'s third child, b. the previous June.

are also) is much delighted with it, only he *doubts* about the fountain, and he thinks it is possible that an intermingling of Birch trees somewhere, on account of the richness of the colour of the naked twigs in winter, might be an advantage; I may add also from myself, that we have often stood for half an hour together at Grasmere, on a still morning, to look at the rain-drops or hoar-frost glittering in sunshine upon the birch twigs; the purple colour and the sparkling drops produce a most enchanting effect. All our family except the three children (for Dorothy is of their party) are gone to Grace Dieu[1] with one ass to help Miss H and my sister over dirty places. The fineness of the morning tempted them and I hope they will not be much fatigued as they will take a much shorter road than my Brother and I had the luck to find. Thomas is my little charge during his mother's absence; for we dare not both leave home at once, not venturing to entrust him entirely to Peggy's care: he being so very apt to catch cold if he is not managed with the utmost watchfulness and regularity. Be so good as to let us know as soon as you can where you think it best to put up the new bed as we wish to have it done as soon after we know as possible, as there must be some other beds removed to make room for it. Betty tells us that Mr Dance[2] formerly brought a woman Servant to cook with him; most likely as Betty is here he would not think of this: but I ought to have remembered to mention to you in my last that if it be agreeable to him we shall be very happy if he will take his dinner with us: you know we have your wine to set before him. Excuse this scrawl. Thomas is wanting me and I write in a hurry. God bless you my kind good Friend—we shall drink a health to you on Christmas Day in a bottle of port wine. You may remember that it is my Birthday; but in my inner heart it is never a day of jollity. Believe me ever yours

D. Wordsworth

Coleridge had intended writing to you or Sir George today, or to both, [if he h]ad not go[ne to] Grace Dieu.

---

[1] The neighbouring priory ruins.
[2] George Dance, R.A. (1741–1825), architect of the new Coleorton Hall.

30. *To* Lady Beaumont

Coleorton, Sunday Evening.
[15 Feb. 1807]

My dear Friend,

You were very kind in going through the melancholy tale of your dear Sister's sufferings in her own affecting words, yet if you had not, at the time of writing to me, been comforted by more hopeful tidings, I should have been grieved that you had done so.—I trust, as the communication by letters is not closed that you will continue to hear from her regularly till the time of her release; for a state of uncertainty is of all others the most unendurable—we had full experience of that when poor Coleridge was away from us. Oh! what reason have we not to bless the Poets, our Friends and companions in solitude or sorrow, who elevate our thoughts beyond our poor weak selves and him chiefly who was your Sister's consolation that holy Bard and greatest of men.[1]—I often think of the happy evening when, by your fireside, my Brother read to us the first book of the Paradise lost; and not without many hopes that we may again have the same pleasure together. We received the Books a week ago, all but Parke's Travels,[2] which, the Bookseller informs us are out of print, adding that a new Edition would be out in a fortnight. We have all already to thank you for a great deal of delight which we have received from them. In the first place my Brother and Sister have read the Life of Colonel Hutchinson,[3] which is a most valuable and interesting Book.—My Brother speaks of it with unqualified approbation, and he intends to read it over again. I wait for the time when the reading this work is to fall to my share with great patience for I shall next begin with Barrow's Travels,[4] and I have not quite finished the anecdotes of Frederick[5] which I find exceedingly amusing; and instructive also, as giving a lively portrait of the hardheartedness and selfishness, and servility of the Courtiers of a tyrant, and of the unsatisfactoriness of such a life.—For more than a week

[1] Milton.
[2] Mungo Park, *Travels in the Interior Districts of Africa*, 1799.
[3] *Memoirs of the Life of Colonel Hutchinson*, by his wife, 1806.
[4] Sir John Barrow, *Travels in China*, 1804.
[5] D. Thiébault, *Original Anecdotes of Frederick the Second, King of Prussia...*, trans. 1805.

we have had the most delightful weather; if William had but waited a few days, it would have been no anticipation when he said to you the "songs of spring were in the grove" for all this week the birds have chaunted from morn till evenings—Larks, blackbirds, thrushes, and far more than I can name, and the busy rooks have joined their happy voices. As soon as dinner was over today, Coleridge, Miss H, my Brother and I set forward upon a ramble, through Spring Wood, then we came to a cottage at the edge of another wood, which I believe does not belong to Sir George (I have forgotten the name of the wood) but I dare say you will recollect the spot. The cottage stands so sweetly in a sloping green field which is enclosed and sheltered by the woods in a semicircle.—We went still further and saw many traces of the coming spring; two or three primroses amongst the withered leaves, the hazels in full pride, palms, and budding honeysuckles, but what was most pleasant of all to us the paths were in most places perfectly dry and we hope that we shall henceforth be able frequently to wander in the woods. I must not forget to tell you that we have discovered a favourite cottage of yours, within this fortnight, and visited it several times; the little dwelling under two holly trees, about a hundred yards from the wayside, going to Mr Bailey's.[1] The situation of the cottage is beautiful; the peep of the Lake (Lake I will call it here for it looks exactly like one) is very sweet, and the village, when you turn your eyes to the other side, has a very chearful appearance. It gave us great satisfaction when we were sitting with the old man and his wife by their fireside to hear them let out the history of their love for the holly-trees; he told us how long ago he had planted them ("when he was a *young youth* going to service,") and that they were now a shelter for his house and nothing could prevail upon him to part with them. You can hardly conceive with what pride he direc- ted our attention to the richness of the berries, and at the same time lamented that some idle Boys had "robbed" one tree of its prettiest branches which arched over and almost touched the cottage window,—he would not have had it "cut away for half a guinea". We longed not for *those* trees; but for half a score as beautiful in the winter garden. Such a sight neither you nor we can hope to see

[1] The bailiff.

there; but a very few years will, I doubt not make it a delicious winter retreat: when the shrubs and trees once get forward they will begin to look pretty, and the situation and the form of the ground is such that it is already sheltered and warm without the help of trees. The men work industriously I am sure; for we never find them idle; but little seems yet to be done, the labour having been all employed in clearing away, removing rubbish and digging soil out for the border. My Brother thinks that, by all means, the terrace should be terminated by another tower. He is very happy in his employment, and I assure you that you need not give yourself a moment's care about interrupting him in his poetical labours; for those will and must go on when he begins, and any interruption, such as attending to the progress of the workmen and planning the garden, is of the greatest use to him; for after a certain time the progress is by no means proportioned to the labour in composition, and if he is called from it by other thoughts, he returns to it with ten times the pleasure, and his work goes on proportionally more rapidly.—He and Mr Craig[1] intend to visit the Nursery at Nottingham next week, or the week following.—It was a most kind and friendly deed when Sir George wrote to Coleridge—he had begun to write several days before he received Sir George's letter; but I do not know how long it might have been before he would have been able to finish the letter. At some future time my Brother hopes to have it in his power to profit from Sir George's kindness; he is very proud of such mutual records of their friendship; and I need not say what a grace and value one of Sir George's beautiful sketches would add to any volume of poems;[2] nor (what would be of more importance in Sir George's feelings) the great delight that we all in common by our own fireside should receive from it. Adieu, my dear Lady Beaumont, believe me with sincerest gratitude your affectionate Friend D Wordsworth.

My Sister intends to wean Thomas at the end of March or the beginning of April. She is well though not strong. She begs her Love to you. Do not think that we have suffered the least inconvenience

---

[1] The gardener.
[2] Engravings from paintings by Beaumont later appeared as frontispieces to *The White Doe of Rylstone* and *Peter Bell*.

from the cold situation of this house. Thanks to the good fires we have had no cold to complain of within doors.—and we have had every other comfort about us.

31. *To* Mrs John Marshall

Grasmere. September 19th [1807]

My dear Friend,

If I had ever been inclined to blame your silence the letter which I received a few days ago would have completely justified you and satisfied all my wishes; but, in truth, I hardly even expected to hear from you before your arrival at home; and, believe me, I feel very grateful for your kindness. We were all exceedingly interested with your account of your travels; the more so as it was somewhat flattering to find that you were in general most pleased with what most pleased my Brother and me.[1] I am sorry that our host, Macgregor, has left the Ferryhouse at Loch Ketterine, and I do not regret as he was not there that you did not go up the Lake. We did not ascend Ben Lomond; but I should have liked to have done it very much; for though it is not particularly a pleasure to me to see those places with which I am familiar below me reduced as in a map I think there is no sensation more elevating to the heart and the imagination than what we take in, on viewing distant mountains, plains, hills, vallies, towns and seas from some superior eminence. I do not wonder that you were disappointed with Glen Croe, passing it on a sunny morning and with expectations of something tremendous or terrible. It may be *sublime* under certain accidents of weather, but can never, I think be tremendous or terrible; and I think the Glen itself is unjustly treated when such epithets are used in describing it. It is a wild and solitary spot—where you feel that you are in *Scotland*—black cattle were the only living things except birds and sheep that we saw in travelling through it. I think if you had perfectly recollected what I said of Glen Croe (allowing for the difference in the time of day and the weather) you would not have been disappointed. The *Town* of Inverary is a miserable place when you

---

[1] During their Scottish tour in 1803.

are in it—dirt and [? finery,] but I think the effect of the first view of it (in combination with the broad expanse of water, fishing-boats, hills and distant mountains, and afterwards with the castle and bridges) is very impressive and beautiful. The sun was shining on the water when we first came in view of this prospect and it made a distinct impression upon my mind of festive gaiety which I shall never forget. Loch Tay, though a very pretty place to live beside, is, except at Killin and Taymouth, an insipid scene to visit by way of a sight. It is greatly inferior in beauty to all our Lakes, and not equal in grandeur I think to the most insignificant of them. You had greatly the advantage of us at Edinburgh—we were only there one day, and that was a very rainy one. I cannot agree with you in admiring the Cathedral[1] at Melrose more than the Chapel of Roslin. As far as it goes, as a whole, the Chapel of Roslin appeared to me to be *perfection*, the most beautiful in form, and of entire simplicity. Melrose has no doubt been a much grander place; but *as a whole* at present it produces little effect—the minute sculpture is excessively beautiful; but oh! how much more delight have I in the remembrance of Bolton in its retired valley, and the venerable Kirkstall![2] I hope, my dear Friend, that you will write again very soon; for we are anxious to know that the termination of your tour corresponded with the course of it, that your Mother, and Sisters and the Children were in perfect health, and that you had in every other respect a happy return to New Grange. I hope Mary Anne does not forget us, and that honest James would be ready to shake his Friend John by the hand if they were to meet again. I have no doubt that Ellen can run about by herself, and you will be glad to hear that our little Thomas is not far behind; he has gone on improving rapidly, and can go by the help of chairs, window-seats, etc. John and Dorothy were much delighted with your presents from Keswick. I cannot say that the drum survived the heavy blows which were given it many days; but the tea-things are preserved with care in Granny's cupboard, and brought out upon particular occasions as a great treat. Our new house[3] will not be ready before

---

[1] i.e. Abbey.

[2] D. W. had visited Bolton and Kirkstall in July while staying with Mrs Marshall at New Grange.

[3] Allan Bank.

Martinmas, a bad time for removing. I have been fully employed of late; for William and Mary spent 12 days at Ulswater, and returned with Sir George and Lady Beaumont, who stayed a week at Grasmere, and two days after their departure Wm and M. set forward again upon a tour, to Wasdale, Ennerdale, Whitehaven, Cockermouth etc. I expect them at home today—they have had delightful weather; and I hope I shall have a most entertaining account of their travels. Mary, you see, has been disposed to make use [of] her liberty while she has it. I am happy to say that her health is much improved though she looks thin. My Brother was exceedingly obliged to Mr. Marshall for his letter. I have just been taking a copy of it to send to Lord Lonsdale,[1] who had some talk with my Brother (when he was at Lowther with the Beaumonts) about planting, and William thinks Mr Marshall's observations so valuable, that he will take the liberty of sending them to Lord L. I must not close my letter as I should wish to add to it after Wm and M. return. I am in daily expectation of a letter from Mrs. Rawson. I have been all the morning [with] Dorothy gathering mosses and this after[noon] [   ] and little Sally and Thomas are gone a nut[ting]. [be]autiful at present, being in perfect health.

Saturday morning. My Brother and Sister returned yesterday night after a most delightful Tour. They were at Cockermouth, our native place, you know, saw the terrace walk[2] that you have heard me speak of many a time, with the privet hedge still full of roses as it used to be 30 years ago. Yes *I* remember it for *more* than 30 years.

Oh! Jane how the time rolls along! yet if it were not for dates and other artificial helps to memory I should forget that I was not as young as when you were married; for I feel no bodily difference. They saw my old nurse, and my Father's housekeeper and some of our relations. I have kept my letter back one post in the hope of getting two Whitehaven notes exchanged for two of some Bank nearer to you, that I might enclose them, and I have been at 4 or 5 houses this morning, but cannot get them changed, therefore I will send my letter without and perhaps you will not regret it, as you will probably hear from me again the sooner. My Brother and Sister

---

[1] Viscount Lowther had just been created Earl of Lonsdale.
[2] Behind Wordsworth House, overlooking the Derwent.

beg to be affectionately remembered to you all, including the family at North Hall. We often talk with pleasure of the time we spent with you. Do write soon and believe me, dear Jane, [*signature cut away*]

32. *To* William Wordsworth

Grasmere Wednesday March 23 [1808]

I trust my dearest Love, that this is the last letter we shall have to send to you further than Kendal, for at Kendal we will meet you with one—God be thanked we are all well. Mary looks better today, and seems pretty strong and dear Sara for these two days has had no tickling cough and is in other respects without cause of complaint. But we have been, and the whole vale—since Monday afternoon in the greatest consternation. If you did not leave before Saturday you must have heard the cause of it from Coleridge for I have recounted to him the melancholy history.[1]

George Green and his wife, our Sally's Father and Mother, went to Langdale on Saturday to a Sale, the morning was very cold and about noon it began to snow, though not heavily but enough to cover the ground. They left Langdale between 5 and 6 o'clock in the evening and made their way right up the Fells, intending to drop down just above their own cottage, in Easedale—(Blenkrigg Gill under Miles Holmes's Intack).[2] They came to the highest ridge of the hill that can be seen from Langdale in good time, for they were seen there by some people in Langdale: but alas! they never reached home. They were probably bewildered by a mist before daylight was gone, and may have either fallen down a precipice or perished with cold—six children had been left in the house, all younger than Sally, and the youngest an infant at the breast. Poor things they sate up till 11 o'clock on Saturday night, expecting their parents, and then went to bed, satisfied that they had stopped all night in Langdale on account of the bad weather; the next day they felt no alarm; but stayed in the house quietly and saw none of the neighbours,

---

[1] D. W.'s full account of the tragic death of the Greens was first published in 1936 as *George and Sarah Green, A Narrative*. The Wordsworths helped to organize a fund for the orphans.

[2] An enclosed piece of fell-side pasture.

therefore it was not known that their Father and Mother had not come back till Monday noon, when that pretty little Girl, the eldest of the household (whom you will remember, having admired the exquisite simplicity and beauty of her Figure one day when you were walking with Mary in Easedale)—this Girl went to George Rowlandson's to borrow a cloak. They asked why, and she told them she was going to *lait*[1] their folk who were not come home. George Rowlandson immediately concluded that they were lost and many men went out to search upon the Fells. Yesterday between 50 and 60 were out, and to-day almost as many, but all in vain. It is very unfortunate that there should be so much snow on the Fells. Mary and I have been up at the house this morning, two of the elder daughters are come home, and all wait with trembling and fear, yet with most earnest wishes, the time when the poor creatures may be brought home and carried to their graves. It is a heart-rending sight—so many little, *little* creatures. The Infant was sleeping in the cradle, a delicate creature the image of Sara Coleridge. Poor Sally is in great distress. We have told her that we will keep her till we can find a nice place for her, and in the mean time instruct her in reading, sewing etc. We hope she will continue to be a good girl.

We do not intend her to have anything to do with the children after our new servant comes. We have hired little Mary, the young woman who lived at Mrs Havill's,[2] and who has been so long desirous to come to us. This very moment three, nay four of the poor orphans (for Sally was with them) have left the room, The three had been at Mrs North's who has sent them home with a basket of provisions, and will visit them herself with clothes for all the younger, being very ragged. That sweet Girl looks so interesting, has such an intelligent, yet so innocent a countenance that she would win any heart. She is a far nicer Girl than Sally and one that we could not but have more pleasure from; but poor Sally has fallen to us, and we cannot cast her off for her Sister; but we hope that Mrs North will take *her*, or at least send her to school.

Old Molly's[3] legs are much swoln and she grows daily weaker. I

[1] seek.
[2] Wife of William Havell (1782–1857), the watercolourist.
[3] Molly Fisher, their first servant at Dove Cottage.

hope her sufferings will soon be at an end. She talks with chearfulness of dying except when she turns to poor John's desolate condition. I really think I have nothing more to say for I have not heart
to talk of our own little concerns, all being well with us. We have
been strangely unsettled for these three days. Pray bring Sally a new
Testament—you can buy it at Kendal. The children are at School.
I hope you will think Thomas looks better than when you went
away—he is very healthy.

Remember me affectionately to Mr De Quincey[1] and tell him
that we hope to hear that he intends coming into the North this
summer. We had a letter from Coleridge on Monday, written just
after you set off for Dunmow. We were much disappointed that
there was no letter from you. We hope for one from Dunmow
tonight.

God bless thee my dearest William and grant that we may see
thee again in good health and soon—thine evermore

Dorothy Wordsworth.

I open my letter to tell you that we are at ease—the poor lost
creatures are found. John Fisher has called at the window to tell
us—he says they had rolled a great way—and were found just above
Benson's, Where that is I cannot tell; but it must have been low
down. She was near a wall—and he lying a little above her.

33. *To* S. T. Coleridge[2]

May 1. 1808.

We are very anxious that 'the White Doe'[3] should be published *as
soon as possible*—if you would simply mention the passages, to which
you object, without attempting to alter them, it would be better. . . .
Our main reason (I speak in the name of the Females) for wishing
that the Poem may be *speedily* published, is that William may get
it out of his head; but further we think that it is of the *utmost*

---

[1] See List of Correspondents. De Quincey had spent a week at Dove Cottage in
Nov. 1807.

[2] Part of a letter quoted by S. T. C. in his reply to W. W.

[3] *The White Doe of Rylstone.*

importance, that it should come out before the Buz of your Lectures[1] is settled. The alterations, we trust, will not be of a difficult or troublesome kind.

34. *To* Mrs Thomas Clarkson

Sunday June 5th [1808]

We live at Allan Bank but I shall always date

Grasmere.

My dear Friend,

A short letter will be worth the postage as it will tell you good news of dearest Sara, which, if bad has reached you, will set you at ease. The fact is, that in the beginning of last week she was worse than usual, but she is now greatly better; to-day perfectly well, and I hope that the increased pain might be attributed solely to the uncertain weather, and to the bustle of removing. She did not take part in the bustle, but it was impossible that she should have perfect quiet. We are now, however, tolerably settled; though there is much to do for Henry[2] and me, who are the only able-bodied people in the house except the servant and *William*, who you know is not expected to do anything. Henry is the most useful creature in the world, and, being very poor, we are determined to make the Carpets and do everything ourselves, for he is as good as a tailor, and at the time a very pleasant companion, and fellow-labourer. Judge how busy I must have been for this fortnight past—papers, linen, books, everything to look over in the old house and put by in the new—besides curtains to make etc. etc. etc—In another fortnight all will be over we hope; for Henry and I work body and soul, and with less we should never be done. Sara sews a little, but we suffer nothing that can fatigue her, and Dearest Mary sprained her right arm three weeks ago and cannot yet use it even to write a letter. We are very thankful it is no worse; she fell over some planks and her whole Frame might have been terribly shaken. Her health is on the whole as good as could be expected in her present situation, yet she does not look as well as she has done, and is not so

[1] On Shakespeare, at the Royal Institution.
[2] M. W.'s sailor brother.

fat, or more properly speaking is *thinner*. We have been miserably anxious about dearest Coleridge, having had bad accounts of him from two quarters, but a letter from Lady Beaumont to-day tells us he is better. We expect one from himself to-night. Sara and I have a delicious view from our several room windows—both look to the East—the mighty mountains of Fairfield and Seat Sandal, now green to their very summits. Oh! that you could see that mass of clouds now resting on the Pass which we used to traverse in our visits to you, that Pass where William and I were near being lost for ever.[1] Oh, that you could see the bonny cottages and their tufts of trees and the sweet green fields! It is a soothing scene, and I trust you will one day behold it, and sit with me in this my little Castle, where I now write. We already feel the comfort of having each a room of our own, and begin to love them—but the dear cottage! I will not talk of it. To-day the loveliness of the outside, the laburnums being in the freshness of their beauty, made me quite sad—and all within, how desolate! The poem[2] is not to be published till next winter. To-day has been a day of letter writing with me. I shall have no more time till next Sunday. Do write to us, and a long letter. Why did we not get Mr Clarkson's book[3] by the same conveyance which brought it to Luff? We long to see it. God bless you for ever my beloved Friend, believe me always your faithful and affectionate

Dorothy Wordsworth.

What a great fellow Tom must be!

Do not fail [to send] the first volume of the Portraiture[4] with the other *if possible*. Mr Clarkson's letter was forwarded [to] Mr T. Hutchinson.

---

[1] When overtaken by mist on 23 Jan. 1802, according to D. W.'s *Grasmere Journal*.
[2] *The White Doe of Rylstone*, eventually publ. 1815.
[3] *The History of the Rise, Progress, and Accomplishment of the Abolition of the African Slave-Trade*, 1808.
[4] *Portraiture of Quakerism*.

35. *To* Mrs Thomas Clarkson

Thursday Evening December 8th [1808]

My dear Friend,

Month after month has gone by and no word has passed between us two. Strange it may seem, but we love each other too well, to have *therefore* slackened in our thoughts. God bless you my dear and good Friend! I think of you daily, and with increasing desire to see you—but alas! troublesome things have happened which have robbed me of the confidence of hope. Sara will have explained to you some of these, in which in the main are involved the reasons of my long silence, but for a while after Coleridge came to us I did not write because he was writing so often and I was loth to put you to the expense of double postage. I will not attempt to detail the height and depth and number of our sorrows in connection with the smoky chimneys. They are in short so very bad that if they cannot be mended we must leave the house, beautiful as everything will soon be out of doors, dear as is the vale where we have so long lived. The labour of the house is literally doubled. Dishes are washed, and no sooner set into the pantry than they are covered with smoke.—Chairs—carpets—the painted ledges of the rooms, all are ready for the reception of soot and smoke, requiring endless cleaning, and are never clean. This is not certainly the worst part of the business, but the smarting of the eyes etc. etc. you may guess at, and I speak of these other discomforts as more immediately connected with myself. In fact we have seldom an hour's leisure (either Mary or I) till after 7 o'clock (when the children go to bed), for all the time that we have for sitting still in the course of the day we are obliged to employ in scouring (and many of our evenings also). We are regularly thirteen in family, and on Saturdays and Sundays 15 (for when Saturday morning is not very stormy Hartley and Derwent come).[1] I include the servants in the number, but as you may judge, in the most convenient house there would be work enough for two maids and a little Girl. In ours there is far too much. We keep a cow—the stable is two short field lengths from the house, and the cook has both to fodder, and clean after the cow. We have also two pigs, bake all our bread

---

[1] Now both at school in Ambleside.

93

at home and though we do not *wash all* our clothes, yet we wash a part every week, and mangle or iron the whole. This is a tedious tale and I should not have troubled you with it but to let you see plainly that idleness has nothing to do with my putting off to write to you. Besides all this we were nearly a week without any servants at all (at Martinmas). You will be glad to hear that we have got one very good Servant, the *Cook*; (as I have rather aristocratically called her) the other is but muddling, yet I hope, as she is strong enough, and good natured, we shall not change till Whitsuntide. Enough of these matters. Dear Coleridge is well and in good spirits, writing letters to all his Friends and acquaintances, dispatching prospectuses, and fully prepared to begin his work.[1] Nobody, surely, but himself would have ventured to send forth this prospectus, with no one essay written, no beginning made! but yet I believe it was the only way for him. I believe he could not have made the beginning unspurred by a necessity which is now created by the promises therein made. I cannot, however, be without hauntings of fear, seeing him so often obliged to lie in bed more than half of the day—often so very poorly as to be utterly unable to do anything whatever. To-day, though he came down to dinner at three perfectly well, he did not rise till near two o'clock. I am afraid this account of him may give you some alarm. I assure you, however, that there is no need to be alarmed; his health is much, *very* much better, and his looks are almost what you would wish them to be; and however ill he may have been in the mornings he seldom fails to be chearful and comfortable at night. Sara and he are sitting together in his parlour, William and Mary (alas! all involved in smoke) in William's study, where she is writing for him (he dictating). He is engaged in a work which occupies all his thoughts. It will be a pamphlet of considerable length, entitled The Convention of Cintra brought to the Test of Principles and the People of England justified from the Charge of Prejudging, or something to that effect.[2] I believe it will first appear in the *Courier* in different sections. Mr De Quincey, whom you would love dearly, as

---

[1] His periodical *The Friend*.

[2] The agreement of 30 Aug., by which the French had been allowed to evacuate Portugal and return home in British ships, was widely regarded as a humiliating defeat. W. W.'s critique developed into an indictment of Napoleonic policy in the Peninsula, and a call to the Spanish to rise against their oppressors.

I am sure I do, is beside me, quietly turning over the leaves of a Greek book—and God be praised *we* are breathing a clear air, for the night is calm, and this room (the Dining-room) only smokes very much in a high wind. Mr De Q. will stay with us, we hope, at least till the Spring. We feel often as if he were one of the Family—he is loving, gentle, and happy—a very good scholar, and an acute Logician—so much for his mind and manners. His person is *unfortunately* diminutive, but there is a sweetness in his looks, especially about the eyes, which soon overcomes the oddness of your first feeling at the sight of so very little a Man. John sleeps with him and is passionately fond of him. Oh! my dear friend! Johnny *is* a sweet Creature; so noble, bold, gentle, and beautiful—yes! he is a beautiful Boy. D. is very pretty, very kittenish, very quick, very clever, but not given to *thought*. Coleridge often repeats to her (altering a line of William's poem of *Ruth*) 'the wild cat of the wilderness was not so fair as she'.[1] To this she replies with a squall, inviting him to some fresh skirmish. C. says that John has all the virtues of a tame Dog, she the qualities of the Cat. God bless them! They are both sweet in their way; but it must be allowed that John is the finer creature. As to little Thomas he is a Darling—but he having spent much of his early time in the kitchen he is never happier than when he is among the pots and pans. Therefore he is called 'Potiphar'. To this name he lustily replies, 'Me no Potiphar, me a good boy.' Happy, however, as he is among his old Friends in the Kitchen, he is very proud of a little parlour notice, and we are all (whatever you and his jealous Godmother may think) very proud of him. He is a remarkably affectionate child, has beautiful eyes, and is very pleasant looking. Your God daughter is very stout and healthy, I think she will be like the rest of them, but they were all handsome at her age. I have not yet said a word of dearest Sara. God be praised, her side is better. She has had a Bowel complaint which we hope has been of great use to her. She looks thin and pale, but that is not to be wondered at. Her appetite is better than it has been for some time past. Mary is usually well and so am I. God bless you dear Friend.

Believe me evermore your affectionate

D. W.

[1] See *Ruth*, ll. 38–9.

Your account of Tom is very interesting. My love to him and his Father.

Do write and write immediately. Say not when you see this letter 'It is the face of a stranger'. I am sure you will scan it at the other end of the room.

36. *To* Thomas De Quincey

Grasmere, Saturday, 6th May [1809]

My dear Friend,

I cannot let Mr Jameson[1] go without a greeting from us to you, though my Brother and Miss Hutchinson wrote yesterday. I long for the carrier's return to-night, for assuredly we shall, at least, have a *letter* from you. Would that the pamphlets might come too![2] William still continues to haunt himself with fancies about Newgate and Dorchester or some other gaol, but as his mind clings to the gloomy, Newgate is his favourite theme. *We*, however, have no fears, for, even if the words be actionable (which I cannot but think they are not), in these times they would not dare to inflict such a punishment; above all, the infamy alluded to, proceeding from the *Convention of Cintra*. Though the expense of cancelling the leaf and the consequent delay would be serious evils, what I should most grieve for would be your trouble and vexation. I do not recollect that we want anything in London. Making presents is a very pleasant way of disposing of money; but, alas! that is a commodity in which we do not much abound, and whatever wishes we might have of that sort we are forced to suppress. Another week is gone by, and *The Friend* does not appear. Coleridge at first talked of printing upon *un*stamped paper, in case the stamped should not arrive in time; but in the last letter we had from him he says that is impossible. I suppose he has had some fresh information on the subject since he talked of the unstamped paper. The Paper was sent off from London some weeks ago, and has not yet arrived, and this is certainly an undeniable cause of delay; but I much fear that there is little

[1] An Ambleside friend.
[2] De Quincey was superintending the publication of W. W.'s pamphlet in London.

done on Coleridge's part, and that he himself is not sorry that there should be an excuse in which he has no concern. He has written to London to desire that a sufficient quantity of paper for one Number may be sent by the Coach, and it is his intention to go to Penrith next week to superintend the Press.

Miss Hutchinson has told you that we are busy with the cottage.[1] I hope it will be a very nice place before you come to it, though the poor Laurels in the garden have been so cruelly mauled by Atkinson that I fear they will never look like anything but dismembered creatures. John Fisher is very proud of his Post; he is gardener and steward, that is, overseer of the other workmen.

The weather is now very delightful, and it is quite a pleasure to us to go down to the old spot and linger about as if we were again at home there. Yesterday I sat half an hour musing by myself in the moss-hut, and for the first time this season I heard the cuckow there. The little Birds too, our old companions, I could have half fancied were glad that we were come back again, for it seemed I had never before seen them so joyous on the branches of the naked apple trees. Pleasant indeed it is to think of that little orchard which for one seven years at least will be a secure covert for the Birds, and undisturbed by the woodman's ax. There is no other spot which we may have prized year after year that we can ever look upon without apprehension that next year, next month, or even to-morrow it may be deformed and ravaged. You have walked to Rydale under Nab Scar? Surely you have? If not, it will be forever to be regretted, as there is not anywhere in this country such a scene of ancient trees and Rocks as you might have there beheld—trees of centuries growth inrooted among and overhanging the mighty crags. These trees you would have thought could have had no enemy to contend with but the mountain winds, for they seemed to set all human avarice at defiance; and indeed if the owners had had no other passion but avarice they might have remained till the last stump was mouldered away, but *malice* has done the work, and the trees are levelled.

A hundred Labourers—more or less—Men, Women, and Children, have been employed for more than a week in hewing, peeling Bark, gathering sticks, etc., etc., etc., and the mountain echoes with

[1] Dove Cottage, which De Quincey was to lease.

the riotous sound of their voices. You must know that these trees upon Nab Scar grow on unenclosed ground, and Mr North[1] claims the Right of *topping* and *lopping* them, a Right which Lady Fleming[2] as Lady of the Manor claims also. Now Mr North allows (with everybody else) that she has a right to fell the trees themselves, and he only claims the Boughs. Accordingly he sent one or two workmen to lop some of the Trees on Nab Scar; Lady F.'s Steward forbade him to go on; and in consequence he offered 5/– per day to any Labourers who would go and work for him. At the same time Lady F.'s Steward procured all the Labourers he could also at great wages, and the opposite parties have had a sort of warfare upon the crags, Mr North's men seizing the finest trees to lop off the Branches, and drag them upon Mr N.'s ground, and Lady Fleming's men being also in an equal hurry to choose the very finest, which *they* felled with the branches on their heads, to prevent Mr N. from getting them; and, not content with this, they fell those also which Mr N. has been beforehand with them in lopping, to prevent him from receiving any benefit from them in future. Oh, my dear Friend! is not this an impious strife? Can we call it by a milder name? I cannot express how deeply we have been affected by the loss of the trees (many and many a happy hour have we passed under their shade), but we have been more troubled to think that such wicked passions should have been let loose among them. The profits of the wood will not pay the expenses of the workmen on either side!!!

A law-suit will no doubt be the consequence, and I hope that both parties will have to pay severely for their folly, malice, and other bad feelings. Mr. North is a native of Liverpool. I daresay you may have often heard us mention him as a Man hated by all his Neighbours. Mr N. has taken an active part in the business. But to turn to pleasanter thoughts. You inquired after dear little Dorothy. She is now at Appleby with Miss Weir who keeps a boarding-school, and I have no doubt is as happy as the day is long. Her uncle Hutchinson,[3] who has been here, saw her at Penrith, and he said she was very merry, very entertaining, very pretty, and the greatest chatterer in the world. She was very proud of the notion of going to Appleby and said she

[1] Occupant of Rydal Mount before the Wordsworths.
[2] Owner of Rydal Hall.
[3] Thomas, now farming at Hindwell, Radnor.

would travel in the Coach by herself, 'nobody should go with her'. Accordingly she was to be entrusted to the Guard, and Miss Weir would meet her at the Inn. Her uncle says she spells very well, and will soon learn to read. She is not to come home till midsummer. I hope when she *does* come that it will be long before we part with her again, though I must say that Tom has almost supplied her place in the way of furnishing Entertainment for the house.

My dear Friend, I am ashamed of this blotted letter. You will say I always write in a hurry, and indeed I plead guilty; but you must take it as a proof of my affection that my penmanship is so bad, for in proportion as my Friends have become more near and dear to me I have always been unable to keep my pen in such order as to make it write decently. When I wrote the first page of this letter Tom was plaguing me, and I hardly knew what I was doing. That is the cause of the superabundance of mistakes and blots; and latterly I have been expecting every moment to be called down to tea. After tea I shall walk to Ambleside with my letter. Mr Jameson goes off to morrow. Wm and I walked to A. last night, and were somewhat disappointed at not receiving a letter from you. Adieu. God bless you!

Believe me, ever your affectionate friend,
Dorothy Wordsworth

We have not seen the Proclamation, or Address, or whatever it is, of the Juntas respecting Saragossa.[1] The Carpet is not yet arrived.

37. *To* Mrs Thomas Clarkson

Grasmere, Wednesday, 15th June [1809]

My dear Friend,

At ten o'clock yesterday morning Coleridge arrived. He had slept at Luff's, and came over the Hawes, and was not fatigued. This you will say is a proof of his bodily *strength*, but such proofs we do not need; for what human body but one of extraordinary strength could

---

[1] Saragossa had fallen to the French on 20 Feb.

have stood out against the trials which he has put his to? You will have seen from his second number[1] that he intends to have one week's respite. His reason for this is that many orders have been sent in from booksellers, and he wants to have the *names*, that the papers may be sent addressed to the respective persons. Whether it was absolutely necessary, or not, to wait a week I do not know. I am, however, convinced that it is a wise thing; for by this means, if he makes good use of his time, he may get beforehand, and I am assured that without that, it would be *impossible* that he should go on.

He is in good spirits, and he tells us that he has left his third number with Brown[2] who is actually printing it. At all events I am glad that he is here, for if he perseveres anywhere in well doing it will be at Grasmere; but there is one thing sadly in his way. The stamped paper must be paid for with ready money, and he has none. [*Three words erased*] Now after the first twenty weeks, the time fixed for payment to him, this will be got over—he will then have money to command, but in the meantime I know not what is to be done. He has beforehand stamped paper only for two numbers. He has, however, ordered an additional supply, which I hope will come in due time for his 5th number.

There are a few passages in the two papers published which have given us pain; and which, if he had been at Grasmere, would never have appeared. The one where he speaks of the *one* poet of his own time. This passage cannot but have wounded Southey, and I think that it was unjust to S.; besides, it is a sort of praise that can do William no good. The other passages to which I allude are contained in the notes to the second number. I think it was beneath Coleridge to justify himself against the calumnies of the Anti-Jacobin Review,[3] foolish to bring to light a thing long forgotten, and still more foolish to talk of his homesickness as a *husband*, or of anything relating to his private and domestic concerns. There are beautiful passages in both the Essays, and everywhere the power of thought and the originality of a great mind are visible, but there is wanting a happiness of manner; and the first number is certainly very obscure—in short, it is plainly shewn under what circumstances of constraint and

[1] Of *The Friend*.
[2] Printer at Penrith.
[3] It had ridiculed the Lake Poets in 1798.

compulsion he wrote; and I cannot enough admire his resolution in having written at all, or enough pity his sufferings before he began, though no doubt almost wholly proceeding from weakness; an utter want of power to govern his mind, either its wishes or its efforts. He says he rises at 6 o'clock in the morning; that is, he has done so for more than a week, nay, I believe a fortnight; and this morning, when I rung the bell to call the maid to fetch Catharine[1] away, he came all alive to my door to ask if he could do anything for me. A week's residence in Thomas Wilkinson's[2] humble cottage brought about this change, and I believe that Thomas, even at the last, was the Father of *The Friend*. C. was happy in Thomas's quiet and simple way of life, drank no spirits, and was comfortable all the time, and Thomas urged him to the work. This we heard from Luff, and C. himself speaks with delight of the time he spent under Thomas's roof. I must tell you that he has had no liquor but ale since he returned; but indeed while he has been with us, he has seldom had any kind of spirits except in water gruel, which he was always fond of taking when he had a pain in his Bowels.—

I hope you will let us know when we are likely to see Mr Clarkson and Tom. Would that you were coming with them. I do not like to anticipate evils; but I cannot help wishing that you were not entangled with a farm. I would much rather have heard that Mr C was about to engage in another literary labour; for a farm I fear will bring you many and daily cares; and if Mr C. wholly employs his mind in that way his power of being serviceable to his fellow creatures must needs be much contracted. I hope that you have ere this seen my Brother's Pamphlet. I cannot doubt but that you will have received great delight from it. What a pity that it did not come out sooner! It would have been then much plainer to all Readers (very few of whom will bear in mind *the time* at which the Tract was written) what a true prophet he has been. C. has had an interesting letter from Charles Lamb.[3] Poor Mary[4] is again in confinement. They have changed their chambers, and the fatigue and novelty of

---

[1] W. W.'s fourth child (b. 1808), Mrs Clarkson's goddaughter.

[2] Of Yanwath, a Quaker.

[3] D. W. had known Charles Lamb (1775–1834) since the Alfoxden days.

[4] For Mary Lamb see List of Correspondents. In 1796 she had murdered her mother in a fit of insanity, and thereafter had occasionally to be confined.

removing were too much for her. Charles says that his new rooms are much better than the old, and the rent only £30 but he cannot take at once to anything that is new, and he looks forward to two or three months of melancholy separation, As he says, it is indeed a great cutting out from the short term of human life. Mrs Cookson[1] of Kendal is with us; she came yesterday with her Husband and one of her sons to stay a week. Mr C. is to come and fetch her and her little Boy home to meet Miss Weir and her niece and little Dorothy, who are to spend yet another week with Mrs Cookson at Kendal, and then we shall see the little Darling's sprightly face again. You cannot think how fretfully impatient I am for the happy day, now that it is so near. *Your* child, Catharine, is a sweet creature—very fair, very bonny, but not *beautiful* in spite of her blue eyes. She is exceedingly mild-tempered and a very good sleeper. This last mentioned good quality is a great comfort to me for bad nights cut me up, and we do not like to trust Babies with young servants who work hard all day. Mr De Quincey has made us promise that he is to be her sole Tutor; so we shall not dare to show her a letter in a book when she is old enough to have the wit to learn; and you may expect that she will be a very learned lady, for Mr De Q. is an excellent scholar. If, however, he fails in inspiring her with a love of learning, I am sure he cannot fail in one thing. His gentle, sweet manners must lead her to sweetness and gentle thoughts. His conversation has been of very great use to John, who is certainly now the finest boy I ever saw. His countenance is delicious, and though not bright at his book, he is far from being dull in acquiring knowledge, and is very thoughtful: but what is most delightful is his tenderness of disposition, his joyous, benignant expression of countenance, and his exceeding modesty. This makes his address awkward to strangers, but there is no awkwardness in his looks or carriage. Thomas is a pretty Boy, very entertaining in a lively Baby manner. He is a great chatterer and very loving.—Sara continues to be troubled with a pain in her side, and has a sort of *humming* cough. I wish these would go away. She has no other symptoms of consumption, and I cannot but hope that riding on horseback would cure her. We are going to get a horse for her as soon as possible. I think it is most probable that Stuart[2] will remove

[1] A local friend.
[2] Daniel Stuart (1766–1846), editor of the *Courier*.

Coleridge's uneasiness of mind respecting money for the stamped paper. It is probable that Stuart has kept back from offering on account of Coleridge's slowness to begin, and now that he has begun I have little doubt that Stuart will come forward. God bless you my dear kind Friend. Believe me evermore your affec^te.

D. W.

38. *To* Lady Beaumont

Grasmere Thursday December 28th 1809

My dear Friend,

Yesterday evening I returned with our whole family from the house of the very person whom you inquire after with so much anxiety. In our way thither on Christmas day I received your letter, and wished to have answered it from that place; but I could not find leisure to take up my pen; and now that I am at home again I am determined to make no further delay. Surely I have spoken to you (not by word of mouth but by letter) of Mr Wilson,[1] a young man of some fortune who has built a house in a very fine situation not far from Bowness. Miss Hutchinson, Johnny, and I spent a few days there last summer with his Mother and Sister, and I think I mentioned this to you. This same Mr Wilson is the Author of the letter signed Mathetes:[2] he has from his very boyhood been a passionate admirer of my Brother's writings; and before he went to Oxford he ventured to write a long letter to my Brother respecting some of his poems, and expressing his deep gratitude for the new joy and knowledge which his writings had opened out to him. Several years after this, he bought a small estate near Windermere, and began to build a house. In the mean-time, however, he fitted up a room in a cottage near the new building, and by degrees made little improvements in the cottage, till it is become so comfortable that, though the large house is finished, he has no wish to remove, and seems, indeed, to have no motive, as the Cottage is large enough to accommodate

[1] John Wilson (1785–1854), 'Christopher North' of *Blackwood's Magazine*, now living at Elleray on Windermere.

[2] In *The Friend*. It drew from W. W. his *Reply to 'Mathetes'*, publ. 14 Dec. 1809 and 4 Jan. 1810.

himself and his mother and sister and two or three friends, and as they are all pleased with the snugness and comfort of their present modest dwelling—indeed, he often regrets that he built the larger house; if, however, he should marry (which is very likely) he will find it necessary. His Mother and Sister are at present at Edinburgh (where, in fact, their home is, but they are so much pleased with this country that for the last two years they have spent more than half their time here) and we all, including Mr de Quincey and Coleridge, have been to pay the Bachelor a Christmas visit, and we enjoyed ourselves very much, in a pleasant mixture of merriment and thoughtful discourse. He is a very interesting young Man, of noble dispositions, and pure ingenuous feelings; but, having lost his Father in early youth, and having had a command of money to procure pleasures at a cheap rate, and having that yielding disposition of which he speaks, which makes him ready to discover virtues that do not really exist in minds greatly inferior to his own (which have yet a sufficient share of qualities in sympathy with his own to draw them to him at first) his time has often been idly spent in the pursuit of idle enjoyments, and dissatisfaction with himself has followed. He had been more than a year in this neighbourhood before he could resolve to call upon my Brother—this from modesty, and a fear of intruding upon him; but since that time we have had frequent intercourse with him, and are all most affectionately attached to him. He has the utmost reverence for my Brother, and has no delight superior to that of conversing with him; and he has often said that he is indebted to him for preserving the best part of his Nature, and for the most valuable knowledge that he possesses. He is now twenty three years of age. Probably before this letter reaches you, you will have received the 19th Number of the Friend, which contains the continuation of my Brother's reply to Mathetes's letter. Mr Wilson sent the letter to Coleridge, and Coleridge requested my Brother to reply to it, he being at leisure, and disposed at that time to write something for the Friend. You will be glad to hear that he is going to finish the Poem of the White Doe, and is resolved to publish it, when he has finished it to his satisfaction.—I should not have been so slow to thank you for the most interesting narrative of the life of 'an English Hermit,' if I had not been particularly engaged during the last fortnight. My Sister has been at Kendal (we met her at Mr Wilson's on her way home), and during her absence I was employed in arranging the books, and putting the house into order; we having only just got rid of workmen, who had been about the house ever since the month of July. I told you the history of the Chimneys, and Mr Crump has been throwing out a Recess with a large bow window in my Brother's study. This obliged us to have the Books stowed in the lodging-rooms in heaps; and you will guess that it was no trifling labour to put them all in their places again upon the shelves. We have had much discomfort from the workmen, but, now that it is over, we think ourselves amply repaid, the room being so much improved. The new window looks towards the Crags and wood behind the house, and a most interesting prospect it is, especially in the winter time, when the goings-on of nature are so various. Coleridge has been very well of late, and very busy, as you will judge, when I tell you that he has published a series of essays in the Courier, on the Spanish affairs. We wish very much that you should see them. They have been published within the last fortnight. I do not recollect the date of the first; but you may easily I should think, procure the Papers by applying to any Friend who takes them in, for, as Coleridge has signed his name, and as they have been so recently published, they will be easily collected together. In the 19th or 16th number of "the Friend" Coleridge has desired that the purchasers of the Friend will pay their money into the hands of Mr Ward, Bookseller in Skinner Street. I do not recollect the number—I mean of Mr Ward's shop—but you will easily find it by referring to the Friend, or if it be more convenient the money may be sent to Grasmere. We have received the Books from Coleorton. We were much affected by your account of the good old Lady Beaumont's reception of you at Dunmow. What an affecting and instructive spectacle the sight of such a woman at her years! You have not mentioned Sir George's health lately. I trust he is pretty well. May God grant you both many years of comfort and happiness! Believe me ever, with grateful affection, your faithful Friend,

D. Wordsworth.

I ought to have said more of the pleasure we received from the interesting history of the Hermit, but I have not room for it—Coleridge wishes it could be published in the Friend—but perhaps this cannot be allowed.

I was mistaken. The answer to Mathetes' letter does not come out in the next Friend, but the next but one.

39. *To* William Wordsworth and Sara Hutchinson

Bury St Edmunds[1] August 14, 1810.

My dearest William,

After I had parted from you I was so low spirited that I hardly knew what to do with myself, so I went to Ashby to put aside my thoughts. In the afternoon we looked over half the drawings from Chaucer, and read as much of the prologue, and walked in the evening—the next day looked over the rest of the drawings to my great delight, and read the Knight's Tale. On Wednesday Sir George arrived to dinner with good accounts of you, and he himself delighted with his journey, and not at all the worse for it.—Just as I wrote the last word the Cook brought me in your letter, dearest Sara and dear William—I have been at least an hour in reading it, first to myself and then to Mrs Clarkson who is in bed and will remain there till between 12 and 1 o'clock. First I must tell you that when I saw her at first without a perfect light she seemed to me not to look better than when I last parted from her—Perhaps having heard that she was fatter I had expected to have perceived a great difference, and she looked shrunken and thin; but when I got to the kitchen fire-side with her she really appeared quite beautiful, her cheeks being flushed and her countenance animated, and I then saw that she was much fatter than when at Grasmere. The next morning however she did not look so well—this owing to the setting-off which candle-light gives to the complexion—Now for my journey—Friday was a beautiful day—I went down alone after breakfast to visit the blind man of whom William will tell you—I carried him some snuff and tobacco, and talked with him awhile. Feeble, blind, paralytic, he takes more delight in talking of the blessings which have been showered upon him, than a sickly fine Lady in recounting her miseries. His wife, who he told me, 'was as kind to him as if he was a child', said to me when I was speaking of his blindness 'he does not

[1] D. W. had been at Coleorton, and was now visiting the Clarksons. W. W. and S. H. had gone on to Hindwell.

lament over it.' 'Why no' said he 'I enjoyed my sight a long time, seventy four years it is but ten years since I lost it.' I asked him if he could perceive any light from the midday sun—'No' he answered 'nothing but heat no light but I have an inward light and am happy in thinking that through the merits of my Saviour I shall be blessed hereafter'—I then repeated to him those lines of Milton 'Hail! holy light!' and the poor old man was much affected and shook me by the hand very feelingly at parting. After this I went to the Holly Cottage. The old man was thatching his haystack and his wife reaching up the straw to him; for when he is on the ladder he cannot stir without her help—She went half way up the hill with me homewards.—I then visited Betty and went with Lady Beaumont to Miss Tone's at the Farmouse, and drank a glass of her homemade wine. Lady B. by way of talk said that Mr Taylor[1] was much of a Gentleman and a very good farmer—'Why' replied Miss Tone smiling significantly 'he *may* be and I have no doubt is quite a Gentleman but as to his farming, I cannot think much of that for he did not know what white clover is; he saw a field of white clover and asked what it was, if it was honeysuckle'—Sir George gives Miss Tone's Man the credit of this invention, and he says that he does not doubt that Mr Shirman has made a much better lie about him, and Mr Harris still better—the best of all. After dinner we all went into the winter garden, where the gardener has been making an arched bower or berceau (his own contrivance) over the doorway. He has trained the honeysuckles etc over the willow wands, and it is hereafter to have evergreens—This is a great improvement—dearest William I wish you had seen it—The door is by this means thrown into shade and to a greater distance and is converted from an ugly object into a pretty one. After tea we sat in the Library till my departure at 8 o'clock—I was very sorry to go away and had some difficulty in keeping up my spirits all day—I left Colly[2] to follow me to the Farm-house, and was glad to be by myself for I cried bitterly and eased my heart in this way—but poor Betty was so much affected at parting with me that I was no better when I got to the Farmhouse. The sun was just gone down, and the place looked so chearful, yet so quiet and beautiful, that I

---

[1] Beaumont's agent.
[2] Beaumont's valet.

could not but grieve to part from it as well as from my kind Friends.—

In my way to Ashby I cheared up and Colly and I had some friendly talk—He left me in the snug parlour with one small candle; this will give you a notion that it was but a 3rd rate Inn—it suited me however the better, for the woman was very civil. I took my Book out, but could not attend to it—so after writing a few lines to Lady B. I went to bed, but did not take off my clothes—I found myself much refreshed when I was called at 12 o'clock, tho' I had not slept—but what was my disappointment on finding that there was no inside place—I must either mount the Coach or take a Chaise—I chose the former, but alas! the Landlady had no cloak to lend me, so I wrapped myself up as well as I could in Mary's thin blue coat and my shawl, and seated myself in the front between a quiet old man and a civil young gentleman-like man from Liverpool. It was a beautiful night and mild at Ashby, but very cold upon the Forest. We reached Leicester at $\frac{1}{2}$ past 3, and after warming myself by the Kitchen fire I went to bed again in my clothes and dropped asleep a little before 6—when I was called again. Breakfasted with a Gentleman who was going on to Cambridge, and the morning was so fine that I resolved to go on the outside, as he promised to protect me. A Gentleman's servant with 3 dogs, two in a hamper, and one who served to keep my legs warm were my other companions. The Servant was very pleasant and very polite—and both most delicate in their attentions to me—If they had been my Brothers they could not have been more kindly attentive and delicate in helping me up to and down from my seat. Afterwards we took up two well-behaved young women—better dressed than I was—and very modest. I breakfasted again with the Passengers being determined to take care of myself—we changed coaches at Stamford, and I shared my sandwiches with one of the women and she gave me of her cakes—so I saved a dinner—and did not drink tea at Huntingdon where the rest had Tea.

I was pleased to find at Stamford so many new pleasures in Store for our latter years. I used to think it an ugly town—and wherever I looked I saw something to admire—the churches—the old houses—the forms of the streets—In short it seems to me a very fine town for a Painter—To be sure the sunshine and the cleanliness of the streets set it off to the best advantage—I got into the coach at Huntingdon, for the evening was cold. By the bye I must not forget the Coachman who is one of the nicest men I ever met with; I might have ridden in the inside whenever I liked—Dear William we stopped at the gate of St John to set down the Professor of Arabic, who, I afterwards learned, was a Cockermouth man[1]—I was awe-stricken with the venerable appearance of the gateway, and the light from a distance streaming along the level pavement—Thy Fresh-man's days came into my mind and I could have burst into tears—I found dear Mr C.[2] at the door of the Inn—the same where you were, Sara—I was sick and giddy when I got out (it was half past 9); this I had never been when I was on the outside—supped upon a Lamb chop—Mr Tilbrook[3] came in to invite us to breakfast; This we declined—rose at a quarter before 8, and went to Trinity Chapel, and I stood in silence while the organ was playing for many minutes before the statue of Newton.[4] It is the most beautiful statue I ever beheld, and before this time I had comparatively, viewed it with indifference. The silent face[5] gave me feelings that were I am sure sublime—though dear Mr Clarkson did now and then disturb me by pointing out the wrinkles in the silk stockings, the buckles etc etc—all which etceteras are in truth worthy of admiration. I was charmed with the walks, found out William's ashtree,[6] the fine willow is dying—dined with Mr Tilbrook—visited King's Chapel after dinner—set off at ¼ past 4—drank tea at Newmarket—reached Bury at 9 o'clock—lay in bed yesterday till 12—wrote to Mary after dinner—Mrs C. rode to that nice old fashioned place with the gar-den near a heath, and I walked by her side. This all I have seen—except the churchyard by moonlight—I like this house very much; it is just the same as being in a Village. I could not write to you yesterday rising so late. Mrs Clarkson never [   ] but is well. I will write again before the end of the week and on larger paper—I am going now to write to Lady B, I will copy a part of what you say of Mr Taylor. You were very good, Sara, in writing so long a letter

[1] John Palmer (1769–1840), a benefactor of St John's College.
[2] Mr Clarkson.
[3] Fellow of Peterhouse, a summer visitor to Rydal.
[4] By Roubiliac.
[5] Cf. *Prelude* (1805), iii. 59.
[6] *Ibid.*, vi. 90–102.

to me. We were delighted with the news of Sara's good looks.

God bless thee dearest William and dear Sara—write often I pray you—I have yet a hundred things to say—Why did not Christ[r] come to Coleorton? Priscilla and Christ[r] did very wrong in not writing if only in common courtesy to Sir G. and Lady B. I think that surely Priscilla would not let him come to see us.

[*Unsigned*]

40. *To* Henry Crabb Robinson

Grasmere near Kendal.
November 6th 1810.

My dear Sir,

I am very proud of a commission which my Brother has given me as it affords me an opportunity of expressing the pleasure with which I think of you and of our long journey side by side in the pleasant sunshine, our splendid entrance into the great city and our rambles together in the crowded streets. I assure you I am not ungrateful for even the least of your kind attentions, and shall be happy in return to be your guide amongst these mountains, where, if you bring a mind free from care, I can promise you rich store of noble enjoyment. My Brother and Sister too will be exceedingly happy to see you; and if you will tell him stories from Spain of enthusiasm, patriotism, and. detestation of the Usurper[1] my Brother will be a ready listener and in presence of these grand Works of Nature you may feed each other's lofty hopes. We are waiting with the utmost anxiety for the Issue of that Battle which you arranged so nicely by Charles Lamb's fireside. My Brother goes to seek the newspapers whenever it is possible to get a sight of one, and he is almost out of patience that the tidings are delayed so long.

We had this morning a letter from Mrs Montagu with alarming accounts of the state of the King's health. We are loyal subjects, wishing him a long life, and, if he die at this time, shall sincerely grieve for his death. No doubt you have heard that our Friend Coleridge accompanied the Montagus to London, and possibly you may even

[1] Napoleon.

have seen him. They and I were travelling at the same time; but we took different Roads; otherwise we might have had a mortifying glimpse of each other's faces, or a three minutes' Talk at some Inn; for on your side of Manchester the people are never more than three minutes in changing horses for the Mail. I am much afraid that Miss Lamb is very poorly.—I have had a letter from Charles, written in miserably bad spirits. I had thoughtlessly (and you cannot imagine how bitterly I reproach myself for it) I had thoughtlessly requested her to execute some commissions for me; and her Brother writes to beg that I will hold her excused from every office of that sort at present, she being utterly unable to support herself under any fatigue either of body or mind—Why had not I the sense to perceive this truth in its full extent? I have caused them great pain by forcing them to a refusal, and myself many inward pangs. I feel as if I *ought* to have perceived that everything out of the common course of her own daily life caused excitement and agitation equally injurious to her—Charles speaks of the necessity of absolute quiet and at the same time of being obliged sometimes to have company that they would be better without. Surely in such a case as theirs it would be right to select whom they will admit, admit those only when they are likely to be bettered by society; and to exclude *all* others! They [have not] one true Friend who would not take it the more kindly of them to be so treated. Pray, as you most likely see *Charles* at least from time to time, tell me how they are going on. There is nobody in the world out of our own house for whom I am more deeply interested. . . . You will, I know, be happy to hear that our little ones are all going on well—the little delicate Catharine, the only one for whom we had any serious alarm gains ground daily; yet it will be long before she can be, or have the appearance of, a stout Child. There was great joy in the house at my return, which each shewed in a different way. They are sweet wild Creatures, and I think you would love them all.—John is thoughtful with *his* wildness, Dorothy alive, active, and quick, Thomas innocent and simple as a newborn Babe. John had no feeling but of bursting joy when he saw me. Dorothy's first question was, 'Where is my Doll?' We had delightful weather when I first got home; but on the fourth morning Dorothy roused me from my sleep with, 'It is time to get up, Aunt, it is a *blasty* morning, it *does blast* so' and the next morning—Not more encouraging to me,—she says, 'It is a *haily* morning it hails so hard!' ... You must know our house stands on a hill, exposed to all *hails* and *blasts*, and the cold seemed to cut me through and through. I did really think, with the good people of Bury who used to try to persuade me that we must be starved to death in the North among these mountains, that it really would be so in my case, and that Grasmere was colder than any place in the world—but it is time to deliver my Brother's message. Can you procure any Spanish, Portuguese or French papers for Mr Southey? He writes the historical part of the Edinburgh Annual Register and they would be of great use to him. Pray let us know if you can, and how they may be sent and upon what terms. My Brother begs to be most kindly remembered to you. Pray make my respectful compliments to Mrs Collier[1] and believe me, my dear Sir,

Yours affectionate Friend

D. Wordsworth

My Brother is much interested about Madame La Vachi[2] you know who I mean—the Spanish Lady, but the above letters may make a word as like any other person's name as her's—are you likely to have a journey into Spain?

41. *To* Mrs Thomas Clarkson

Kendal Sunday [9 Dec. 1810]

My dear Friend,

I began to write to you two days after I received your last letter, was prevented from going on, and never found an opportunity to mind to begin again till Thursday arrived, the day I had fixed for coming to see Mrs Cookson at Kendal. I then thought I should find opportunity at Kendal for writing the long letter which I intended, for I have a hundred things to say, or rather talk about, but at Kendal I find I have less leisure than at home. The day goes on I know not how. I came hither last Thursday, and shall return to Elleray on

---

[1] Robinson's landlady.

[2] A refugee, whom Robinson had helped to escape to England with her husband, the Treasurer of Galicia.

Tuesday, and about the Monday following we shall, I daresay, proceed to Grasmere, for the fever has not broken out afresh for several weeks, and all the Patients look upon themselves as fit to go about among their neighbours.

My dear Friend I cannot express what pain I feel in refusing to grant any request of yours, and above all one in which dear Mr Clarkson joins so earnestly, but indeed I cannot have that narrative[1] published. My reasons are entirely disconnected with myself, much as I should detest the idea of setting myself up as an Author. I should not object on that score as if it had been an invention of my own it might have been published without a name, and nobody would have thought of me. But on account of the Family of the Greens I cannot consent. Their story was only represented to the world in that narrative which was drawn up for the collecting of the subscription, so far as might tend to produce the end desired, but by publishing this narrative of mine I should bring the children forward to notice as Individuals, and we know not what injurious effect this might have upon them. Besides it appears to me that the events are too recent to be published in delicacy to others as well as to the children. I should be the more hurt at having to return such an answer to your request, if I could believe that the story would be of that service to the work which Mr Clarkson imagines. I cannot believe that it would do much for it. Thirty or forty years hence when the Characters of the children are formed and they can be no longer objects of curiosity, if it should be thought that any service would be done, it is my present wish that it should then be published whether I am alive or dead. I left all well at Elleray—Catharine is completely transformed into a jolly healthy looking lively [child], yet she coughs very often and her lameness is very visible. William[2] has begun to thrive again though *he* coughs seriously. No children in the neighbourhood have had the disease half so bad as ours. Catharine was as near gone as possible. Poor Mrs Kitchener![3] give my love to her. I fear hers will not escape. We have not heard from Coleridge therefore I know nothing of the schemes respecting the Courier or anything else, but knowing he must get somewhere I am

[1] *George and Sarah Green.*
[2] W. W.'s fifth child, b. the previous May.
[3] Mrs Clarkson's housekeeper.

going to write to him on business before I leave Kendal. All agree that he looked well and was in good spirits, but Mary says they do not understand his looks; for when he passed through Grasmere he appeared bloated and swollen up with fat and to her mind looked very ill. As soon as we reach home I will write to you a letter more to my own satisfaction—I am grieved to send off this. God bless you. I think of you and Bury, and speak of you every hour of the day when I am at home. I hope my name does not sleep by your fireside, and my dearest friend that you think of me in your solitary hours—how happy I should be by your side—happy as I am in the company of my beloved friends and the dearest of children. We had a sweet letter from Sara lately.[1] Poor thing, she longs to be with us again—but money! money! I am determined however when it is possible to go into Wales. What if I should meet you there next year! My kindest love to Mr Clarkson and Tom and your Father and Mother. Believe me ever more

yours affectionately
D. W.

I am called to dinner.

42. *To* Mrs Thomas Clarkson

Finished at 12 o'clock Sunday night May 12th [1811]

My dear Friend,

My idle scribbling wandering way of using my pen tempts me to take this large sheet of paper which I think I shall hardly have leisure to fill; but I do not like to be stopped for want of room. I wished to write to you directly after I received your last letter but one, longing to express my joy at the chearing accounts which it brought us of the state of your health. Your last says nothing about it but from what you say of your goings on I gather that you have continued to be as well as when you wrote before. I am very glad that Miss Smith[2] has been so long with you, and that you have had so much comfort in her society, you will feel yourself lonely till your sisters return. When is

---

[1] S. H. was still at Hindwell.
[2] Daughter of William Smith, M.P. for Norwich.

that to be? You have not mentioned your Father's Asthma lately. I hope therefore that he is better. I am very glad that Mr Clarkson is at work with the Life of William Penn[1] and that matters go on well at the Farm. I only grieve that you do not talk of a time for coming into the North. Yet what can you do till Tom leaves school? for you ought not to come for a short season to be hurried away before you know whether the country agrees with you or not. I should wish you to be loose, unencumbered with a house elsewhere when you do come, so that you might stay a whole year. I wish I could afford (in my affording I include both money and time) to spend one month with you at Bury next winter or the winter after that if one might dare to look forward so far. A long way that is indeed to look before us, but how short when the time is gone! It is almost a year since I set forward upon my last journey (it was on the 1st of July) and it seems now but as long as three or four months used formerly to be. So it is with every person after thirty who is not utterly thoughtless. The longest period of the year to my memory is the time of my absence from home; for the many [?] and the business and bustle which we have had of late more than anything tend to make the time pass away without leaving its due record on the mind. We have had no leisure for reading. I have not opened a Book except on a Sunday, and when the rest of the family were in bed, since my return to Grasmere, and the only book which I have read through has been Beaver's account of the disastrous Expedition to Bulama.[2] I suppose you have read his book as it concerns Africa and the Slave Trade. I admire Beaver's character more than any character of modern times that I have heard of. I could not help wishing to see him at the head of a large army in Spain. God be thanked the tide is turned against Buonaparte and we shall see, I trust, the delusion speedily vanish which even in England has spread too widely, that he was a great genius and a great Hero.

½ past 7 o'clock—I wrote this far before afternoon church. I now take up the pen in the midst of a storm of thunder, lightning and rain. It was preceded by the most awful darkness I ever beheld and accompanied by every accident that could add to the grandeur of a thunder-storm. The most vivid sunbeams intermingled with dark-

---

[1] Pub. 1813.
[2] Philip Beaver, *African Memoranda: relative to an Attempt to establish a British Settlement . . . on the Western Coast of Africa in the Year 1792,* 1805.

ness, and a Rainbow, a perfect arch spanning the vale slantways. The storm began an hour ago, and upon the sky clearing we suffered Hartley, Derwent and Algernon Montagu (M's eldest son by his second wife) to set off to Ambleside, and poor things! it now rains dreadfully and the thunder is very loud and frequent. These three boys came yesterday morning for the last time of staying all night this summer as we shall have no beds for them. H and D have hither-to come every week, but Algernon only occasionally; for the noise of our own five with H and D was so much that we could not every week have all three; but Algernon has come in the short holidays when H and D were at Keswick. Mary went with the troop to church in the morning, and I in the afternoon, and a pretty show we make. I assure you we are become regular church-goers (we take it in turn) for the sake of the children, and indeed Mr Johnson,[1] our present curate, appears to be so much in earnest, and is so unassuming and amiable a man that I think we should often go even if we had not the children, who seem to make it a duty to us. Joanna[2] left us yesterday, we shall find a great loss of her in the busy time which is at hand; for she was a good nurse and always ready to be useful. We took advan-tage of her services in nursing etc. to piece up some old gowns and other things which we had no value for into bed quilts, amongst these is old Molly's legacy to me—her best gown, and during the last ten days Mary and I have with our own hands without any help quilted two of them. We had intended to do the third next week, but as Joanna is gone and as we must move the [? week] after we give up this point and shall set up the quilting frames during our discomfort in the parsonage house[3]—for much discomfort we may expect at first. Mrs Rowlandson[4] quits it to-morrow but it is unpainted—the kitchen chimney is to be pulled down and chimney pieces put up in all the rooms except two—and many more little jobs—and the Crumps (though they desire us not to put ourselves to incon-venience) are, we know, so very anxious to be home that we think we ought not to remain longer than till the end of the week after next—rather next week, for this is the first day of this present

---

[1] The Revd William Johnson (see List of Correspondents).
[2] Joanna Hutchinson.
[3] Their new home in Grasmere.
[4] Widow of the previous curate.

week—little William's birthday—old May-day—We must be dispersed at different places in the Vale—or I must go to Keswick with Catharine if we cannot have Robt Newton's lodgings[1] which we have some hope of getting, as a family who are now there are likely to remove next week—I will tell you nothing about the new house until I can say more good of it—at present it makes me sick to look at it, and the workmen are so dilatory that it is nothing but plague to us. It is however capable of being made a very canny spot, and the house if finished according to our desires will be much more like a home of ours than our present house. It will be a large cottage. Oh! may we even live to see your chearful face by the fire-side! We have had two letters from Charles Lamb lately—His dear sister shews signs of amendment, but is still far from well. Lamb's last letter was written to desire us to forward all Coleridge's Manuscripts—He has sold all his work to Longman (among the rest his Tragedy[2]) and they are to be published immediately. Coleridge himself tells Mrs C that by the advice of Stuart he is going to begin the Friend again.

We find that C is offended with William. I do not like to begin with such stories nor should I have mentioned it at all, if I had not thought that perhaps Henry Robinson may have heard something of it, and a mutilated tale might so come to your ears. In few words I will tell you, though I am sure you would not be inclined to blame my Brother whatever you might hear from other quarters. You know that C went to London with the Montagus, and that their plan was, to lodge him in their own house, and no doubt M. expected to have so much influence over him as to lead him into the way of following up his schemes with industry. Montagu himself is the most industrious creature in the world, rises early and works late, but his health is by no means good and when he goes from his labours rest of Body and Mind is absolutely necessary to him; and William perceived clearly that any interruption of his tranquility would be a serious injury to him, and if to him consequently to his Family. Further he was convinced that if Coleridge took up his abode in M's house they would soon part with mutual dissatisfaction, Montagu being the last man in the world to tolerate in another person (and that person an inmate with him) habits utterly discordant with his

---

[1] In Grasmere.
[2] *Osorio*, written 1797.

own. Convinced of these truths William used many arguments to persuade M. that his purpose of keeping Coleridge comfortable could not be answered by their being in the same house together—but in vain. Montagu was resolved. 'He would do all that could be done for him and would have him at his house.' After this William spoke out and told M the nature of C's habits (nothing in fact which everybody in whose house he has been for two days has [not] seen of themselves) and Montagu then perceived that it would be better for C to have lodgings near him. William intended giving C advice to the same effect; but he had no opportunity of talking with him when C passed through Grasmere on his way to London. Soon after they got to London Montagu wrote to William that on their road he had seen so much of C's habits that he was convinced he should be miserable under the same roof with him, and that he had repeated to C what William had said to him and that C had been very angry. Now what could be so absurd as M's bringing forward William's communications as his reason for not wishing to have C in the house with him, when he had himself as he says 'seen a confirmation of all that W. had said' in the very short time that they were together. So however he did, and William contented himself with telling M that he thought he had done unwisely—and he gave him his reasons for thinking so. We heard no more of this, or of C in any way except soon after his arrival in Town, by Mrs Montagu, that he was well in health, powdered etc. and talked of being busy—from Lamb that he was 'in good spirits and resolved to be orderly'—and from other quarters to the like effect. But in a letter written by poor dear Mary Lamb a few days before her last confinement she says she 'knows there is a coolness between my Brother and C'. In consequence of this I told her what had passed between M and Wm and assured her of the truth that there was no coolness on William's part. I of course received no answer to this letter for she was taken away before it reached London, and we heard no more of the matter till the other day when Mrs C received a letter from Coleridge about his MSS. in which he says as an excuse for having written to no-one and having done nothing, that he had endured a series of injuries during the first month of his stay in London—but I will give you his own words as reported to us by Mrs C. She says 'He writes as one who had been cruelly injured—He says "If you knew in detail of my most unprovoked sufferings for the first month after I left Keswick and with what a thunder-clap that *part* came upon me which gave the whole power of the anguish to all the rest—you would pity, you would less wonder at my conduct, or rather my suspension of all conduct—in short that a frenzy of the heart should produce some of the effects of a derangement of the brain etc. etc." '—so I suppose there is a good deal more of this, but she says he mentions no names except Mr and Mrs Morgan's.[1] He says 'I leave it to Mrs Morgan to inform you of my health and habits' adding that it is to hers and her husband's kindness he owes it that he is now in his senses—in short that he is alive. I must own that at first when I read all this my soul burned with indignation that William should thus (by implication) be charged with having caused disarrangement in his Friend's mind. A pretty story to be told. 'Coleridge has been driven to madness by Wordsworth's cruel or unjust conduct towards him.' Would not anybody suppose that he had been guilty of the most atrocious treachery or cruelty? but what is the sum of all he did? he privately warned a common friend disposed to serve C with all his might, that C had one or two habits which might disturb his tranquility, he told him what those habits were, and a greater kindness could hardly have been done to C, for it is not fit that he should go into houses where he is not already known. If he were to be told what was said at Penrith after he had been at Anthony Harrison's, then he might be thankful to William. I am sure we suffered enough on that account and were anxious enough to get him away. I say that at first I was strong with indignation but *that* soon subsided and I was lost in pity for his miserable weakness. It is certainly very unfortunate for William that he should be the person on whom he has to charge his neglect of duty—but to Coleridge the difference is nothing, for if this had not happened there would have been somebody else on whom to cast the blame. William wrote to Mrs C immediately and wished her to transcribe his letter, or parts of it for C and told her that he would not write to C himself as he had not communicated his displeasure to him. Mrs C replies that she is afraid to do this as C did not desire her to inform us, and that it may prevent him from opening letters

---

[1] S. T. C.'s old Bristol friends, with whom he was now staying in Hammersmith.

in future etc etc. I ought to have told you that C had a violent quarrel with Carlyle[1] who refused to attend him as a surgeon after C had slighted his prescriptions. My dear friend you cannot imagine what an irksome task it has been to me to write the above. I would wish it to rest for ever. Time will remove the cloud from his mind as far as the right view of our conduct is obscured, and having deserved no blame we are easy on that score. If he seek an explanation William will be ready to give it, but I think it is more likely that his fancies will die away of themselves—Poor creature! unhappy as he makes others how much more unhappy is he himself! Do not mention this subject I entreat you to Mr Clarkson or any other person (of course when I exclude him)—

William has begun to work at his great poem.[2] I wish you could hear him read it. We are all well but Catharine's lameness does not go away. You forgot Dr Beddoes's[3] prescription for the warm bath, pray send it to us. Charles Lloyd has been very ill in a nervous fever. He and Mrs L called yesterday for the first time since his illness. Mrs L has had a good account of Priscilla for herself within the last ten days. You mentioned her having 'fallen into a sad state' and immediately followed it with speaking of that Lady's derangement and Mary Lamb's illness. This added to my alarm and I was made very uneasy, fancying that Priscilla's disorder was connected in your mind with madness. I fear, though she is better now, that Christopher will have little comfort with her and much anxiety. I cannot but think it unfortunate that Miss Dolben's[4] mind should have taken such a decided turn towards religious contemplation. She has honesty and sensibility enough to have been good and happy in another way and I should indeed fear with you, as there is a tendency towards melancholy in the family, that she may overstrain her mind. If she or Miss Harriet ever enquire after me pray tell them I remember them with pleasure. You do not mention Georgiana and Sara Gower and the Mapletofts.[4] I wish to be forgotten by people who cannot remember their own sisters. It is long since you mentioned Mrs Kitchener and her sweet Boys, give my

[1] Montagu's doctor.
[2] *The Excursion*, publ. 1814.
[3] The famous Bristol specialist.
[4] Acquaintances at Bury St Edmunds.

love to them. My kind love to Tom who I hope will profit by all the good advice he gets. God bless you my dearest friend do write soon and believe me yours ever more

D. W.

John was very smart today in Tom's nankeen trousers and waistcoat. I made a pair of trousers for him out of the back parts of the two pairs and another pair for Thomas out of the fore-parts. Tom is very proud of his. John cares nothing about dress. Remember me to Betsy. Think of you at the Installation![1] Well! it is a good sign that you can bear the notion of it. Do write and comfort us in our discomforts. Poor Frederick Malkin.[2] I am very sorry for him and his mother.

43. *To* Thomas De Quincey

[5 June 1812]

My dear Friend,

I am grieved to the heart when I write to you—but you must bear the sad tidings—Our sweet little Catharine was seized with convulsions on Wednesday night at $\frac{1}{2}$ before ten or $\frac{1}{2}$ past 9 o'clock. The fits continued till $\frac{1}{4}$ after 5 in the morning, when she breathed her last. She had been in perfect health, and looked unusually well—her leg and arm had gained strength[3]—and we were full of hope. In short, we had sent the most delightful accounts to her poor Mother. It is a great addition to our affliction that her Father and Mother were not here to witness her last struggles, and to see her in the last happy weeks of her short life — She never forgot Quincey—dear Innocent, she now lies upon her Mother's Bed, a perfect image of peace—this to me was a soothing spectacle after having beheld her struggles. It is an unspeakable consolation to us that we are assured that no foresight could have prevented the disease in this last instance, and that it was not occasioned by any negligence, or improper food. This was proved by her evacuations:

[1] Of the Duke of Gloucester as Chancellor of Cambridge.
[2] Son of the headmaster of Bury G.S.
[3] She had been partially paralysed, following a seizure in 1810.

but we were almost confident it could not be so before we had demonstration of this. The disease lay in the Brain, and if it had been possible for her to recover, it is much to be feared that she would not have retained the Faculties of her Mind. God bless you!

Yours affectionately,

D. Wordsworth

We have written to my Brother,[1] and he will proceed immediately into Wales to impart the sad intelligence to my Sister. You will be pleased to hear that Mary Dawson[2] has been very kind in her attentions to us—we are all pretty well. John has been greatly afflicted, but he has begun to admit consolation. The Funeral will be on Monday afternoon—I wish you had been here to follow your Darling to her Grave.

44. *To* Richard Wordsworth

Grasmere 11th January 1813.

My dear Brother,

William has intended writing to you for some time past; but the Task was so painful to him that he has put it off from day to day, and I have therefore taken it upon myself, being unwilling that any event which has had so material an effect upon our happiness should longer remain unknown to you. On the 1st of last month William's second Son, Thomas, died of an inflammation on the lungs, while the eruption of the measles was upon him. He had been carried on as favorably as possible; and but half an hour before the inflammation began, the Apothecary had seen him and pronounced him in a fair way of speedy recovery. In fact there had never been a moment's apprehension about him till the change took place, at once—and he was dead in five hours afterwards. This shock has been a dreadful one, coming so soon after the other which was equally sudden; and to add to the former affliction both the

[1] W. W. was in London trying to clear up the misunderstanding with S. T. C. M. W. was at Hindwell.

[2] De Quincey's housekeeper at Dove Cottage.

Father and Mother were absent, and could not be summoned to the Funeral. I was at Watermillock when Thomas died, but I had the comfort of following him to his grave. He was the darling of the whole house and beloved by every body who knew him. His dispositions were affectionate and good—he was fond of his Book and was in all respects as promising a Child as ever breathed. God's will must be submitted to, and I hope his poor Mother and all of us will be enabled to submit as we ought; but it has been a hard stroke for her; and has shattered her very much. The Boy was six years and a half old. There are now but three left—John—Dorothy, and William—aged 9—8—and two and a half years. Our present Residence, which is close to the Churchyard and the school which was our darling's Daily pride and pleasure is become so melancholy that we have resolved to remove from it, and Wm has taken a house at Rydale which is very pleasantly situated: thither we shall remove at May-day, or before, if the present Tenant quits it before that time, which is expected. I hope you will come to see us as soon as possible after your return to Sockbridge—I was much disappointed that I did not see you when I was in that neighbourhood, and I do not think I can have the heart to make the same journey next summer—therefore I hope you will come to us.

We are much obliged to you for the account of the money that we have drawn for; but pray be so kind as to send an exact account of what we possess on the other side. I hope that there was enough remaining of the Remnant of my Father's property with what we had from my Uncle William[1] to cover the debt to my Aunt Wordsworth;[2] but how this is pray let us know—and whether you have made any settlement with the Executors of my Uncle Crackenthorpe. Do be so good as let this statement be sent to us without delay. We wish to shape our expences accordingly.

William will draw upon you in the course of a week for 19£ in favour of Mr Edward Partridge at one month after date.

Again I entreat you to come and see us. Human life is short—year passes on after year and we do not meet, and I wish you to see and know your Nephews and Niece. The late warnings make us feel

---

[1] Canon Cookson.

[2] Money advanced for W. W.'s education by his uncle Richard (d. 1794), of Whitehaven, was still owed to the estate of the widow (d. 1809).

daily, the uncertainty of their life, and ours—May God bless you, my dear Brother

> Believe me your ever affectionate Sister
>
> D Wordsworth

William and Mary send their kindest Love. I shall expect a letter from you very soon.

45. *To* Mrs John Marshall

> Rydale Mount, Thursday morning [2 May 1813].

My dear Friend,

When I tell you that we removed yesterday, you will not wonder that I write a short note. We are all well, though some of us, especially my Sister, jaded with our fatigues. The weather is delightful, and the place a paradise; but my inner thoughts *will* go back to Grasmere. I was the last person who left the House yesterday evening. It seemed as quiet as the grave; and the very church-yard where our darlings lie, when I gave a last look upon it [seemed] to chear my thoughts. There I could think of life and immortality—the house only reminded me of desolation, gloom, emptiness, and chearless silence—but why do I turn to these thoughts? the morning is bright and I am more chearful today.

I write now merely to request that you will send Miss Watson's[1] Novel as soon as you have done with it—directed to Mrs Coleridge to be left at Miss Crosthwaites' Keswick; and if you have to read it pray read it immediately, for I promised Lloyd long since to procure it immediately after your return. I have been disappointed at not hearing from you before now. God bless you all.

> D. Wordsworth

The Novel may be sent by the coach from Penrith.

---

[1] Daughter of Richard Watson (1737–1816), Bishop of Llandaff, resident at Calgarth on Windermere.

46. *To* Mrs Thomas Clarkson

[*c.* 14 Sept. 1813]

My dearest Friend,

I take a large sheet of paper because I do not like to begin with my scrawling hand as if I *intended* to write you a short Letter, though as I am determined to save the post, and as I do not know when the Man goes to Ambleside or what interruptions I may have, I do not know whether the letter will turn out long or short; but I have this satisfaction that to you it will be twice over worth the postage when I tell you that there has been no unpleasant cause for my long silence. Many employments and a little bustle that perhaps we have sometimes impatiently wished to be over have been no evil to any one of us, and I hope the minds of all by these means, and by the intervention of pious thoughts (which must needs bring on Resignation to all the sorrows of this world, especially when so many blessings are left) have been strengthened and that we shall be able to enjoy the pleasures of leisure when leisure comes. Oh that you were here! or that you were coming in a fortnight for then we shall have our carpets laid down and shall be all complete. I talk lightly but you cannot think (for you have never been at this beautiful place) you cannot think with what earnestness I utter the wish. The carpets popped in after the wish was uttered and with a smile and a tear I set down the foolish thought—but now I must tell you of our grandeur. We are going to have a *Turkey*!!! carpet—in the dining-room, and a Brussels in William's study. You stare, and the simplicity of the dear Town End Cottage comes before your eyes, and you are tempted to say, 'are they changed, are they setting up for fine Folks? for making parties—giving Dinners etc etc?' No no, you do not make such a guess; but you want an explanation and I must give it to you. The Turkey carpet (it is a large Room) will cost 22 guineas, and a Scotch carpet would cost 9 or 10. The Turkey will last 4 Scotch, therefore will be the cheapest, and will never be shabby, and from this consideration we were all of one mind that the dining Room carpet should be a Turkey one; but Mary and I were rather ashamed of the thought of a Brussels, and inclined to the Scotch as looking less ambitious and less like setting up ourselves upon the model of our neighbours—the Ambleside gentry, who all intend calling upon us, though happily most of them considered it would be inconvenient at present, and I assure you we take their apologies very quietly and say as few civil things in return as possible. Our Master was all for the Brussels and to him we yielded—a humour took him to make his Room smart, and as we think that in the end, even that will be cheaper than a Scotch carpet we did not oppose his wish. Tom Monkhouse[1] has been the purchaser of these sumptuous wares, and has got them at the cheapest hand. The Study is furnished with a large book-case, some chairs that we had at Allan Bank painted black, and Sir George Beaumont's pictures—and looks very neat. We have got window curtains for it, and a nice writing-table—and a new bed for Sara and stair carpets and oil cloth for the passage—and these are all the new things we wanted and the house is very neat and comfortable—and most convenient—though far from being as good a house as we expected. We had never seen the inside of it till we came to live in it. We have three kitchens one of which is called the *Deep* kitchen. The grate is decked out by the Kitchen Maid with flourishing green Boughs, which are only displaced in the washing week, when this same kitchen is used as a laundry. At other times the clock lives there in perfect solitude, except that it has the company of two nice white tables and other appropriate furniture

You cannot imagine what a deal of work removing from one house to another causes—there is so much unripping of curtains etc—and so much carpenter's work—but before the end of next week all will be over and would have been long since if we had not had to *wait* for what we wanted. We are all gardeners, especially Sara, who is mistress and superintendent of that concern. I am contented to work under her—and Mary does her share, and sometimes we work very hard, and this is a great amusement to us though sad thoughts often come between. Thomas was a darling in a garden—our best helper—steady to his work—always pleased. God bless his memory! I see him wherever I turn—beautiful innocent that he was—he had a slow heavenly up-turning of his large blue eyes that is never to be forgotten. Would that you had seen him! But my dear friend why have I turned to this subject? Because

[1] See List of Correspondents.

I write to you what comes uppermost the pen following the heart—but no more. You must indeed you must come next year. I never talk of *next year's* plans, but I think of Death. Come however you must if you live whether we are *all* alive or not. It is the place of all others for you—so dry that you need never have a wet foot after the heaviest shower; and the prospect so various and beautiful that an Invalid or a weakly person might be accused of discontentedness of disposition who should wish for anything else, or repine at not being able to go further than round our garden.

John Gough[1] takes Boys to prepare them in Mathematics for the University, and it has struck Sara and me as a likely plan for you to adopt to place Tom under his care for a while, and then there could be no possible objection to your coming into the North for a while—and in our house you might have every accommodation. It is large enough for both you and your Maid—and Tom occasionally, and Mr Clarkson as long as he could stay. Do come—and say in your next that you will. Often do we talk of it and have wished that you were here even in the midst of our worst bustles. You may judge how busy we have been when I tell you that we knew nothing about the Curate Bill[2] and William was not at home to explain it to us. We have had no time to read Newspapers but have been obliged to content ourselves with William's Report even of the late most important battles in Germany and all other proceedings. Murders we do read and were horror struck with that of Mr and Mrs Brown and the confession of the murderer—Good God! If the thought of murder is to come in that way into the head of a person apparently not insane, nobody seems to be safe; but it seems to us that all these murders have been commited by people of no education, and are strong arguments in favour of the early and universal instruction of the Children of the Poor. Blessed be your Father and all good people who labour in this holy work! Pray tell us anything further that you know, which is not in the papers, respecting Mr and Mrs Brown their family and the Murderer. What you have told us, affected us very much. William is decidedly against the Catholics, and I think he would convince you if you had an hour's talk with him and you *shall*, and you *must* have it next summer. We have

---

[1] The blind mathematician and naturalist of Kendal.
[2] To increase their minimum stipends.

such a Terrace for you to walk upon and such a nice seat at the end
of it. Oh my dearest Friend that you were here.—We have not
received Mr Clarkson's Book[1] which vexes us much. Pray how is it
sent that we may inquire after it. I do not think that a copy has
reached this neighbourhood, or we should have heard of it. I long
to see it; most of it must be new to *me* at least and the subject is a very
interesting one. Of course I need not ask you to inquire the reason
why the Book has not reached us if by so doing you can forward it
to us. I am glad that your Brother Robert is going on so well—why
does not he fix upon a wife to grace his pretty dwelling?—Sam is my
favourite of all your brothers and I should much rejoice to hear that
he had his Farm on good terms—nicely fitted up and had a good
Wife to make him as happy as he deserves to be. Remember me to
them all and to your dear Father whom I hope before I die to
see again. We have had a letter from Luff dated January. They
were only just arrived at the Mauritius. You may judge what a
tedious passage they had had, for a Friend of Miss Dowling's[2] who
sailed 4 months after them had arrived before them. They give a
wretched account of the place, overrun with insects continually
biting—provisions and everything else enormously dear—and the
country without fertility or Beauty. They hoped to be removed to
Java—or possibly to Lisbon which would be far better, but what a
voyage! Poor Mrs Luff! I pity her the most for she must have the
Pangs of Remorse. He went chiefly to satisfy her, and the Remembrance of his Motives may bear him up. Luff mentioned you and
all his friends but his letter was very short. Mrs L. has written to
others in the same style of regret. Mary is well in health, though
weak and miserably thin, yet it is amazing what exertions she can
go through. Sara has been poorly but is better. We expect Miss
Barker tomorrow, Sara has been with her at Keswick. William is at
Penrith on Stamp business.[3] Till the end of this Month he will be
entirely engaged with it. He has done nothing else for weeks and
been from home 2 thirds of his time. Afterwards all will be easy, little
for him to do. He has got a clerk who promises well. He is to work

[1] *Memoirs of the Private and Public Life of William Penn*, 1813.

[2] Schoolmistress at Ambleside.

[3] W. W. had recently been appointed Distributor of Stamps for Westmorland on
Lord Lonsdale's recommendation.

in the garden also.—Do write very soon, tell us about the Book. This is a reason for your writing immediately and pray do—May God bless you my dear Friend. ever yours

D. W.

My kindest love to [Mr C.] and to Tom.

No news of Coleridge! Charles Lloyd is pretty well at present, but poor soul he is often *dreadfully* ill.

47. *To* Josiah Wade

Keswick 27th March 1814
Miss Wordsworth

My dear Sir,

I am sure that you will at once recognise the name of an old Friend though the hand-writing will appear to you like that of a Stranger, so many years have elapsed since we have seen each other or heard any tidings except through the medium of mutual acquaintances.

I write at the request of Mrs Coleridge, who is in an anxious and unhappy state of mind, not having had letters from Coleridge or any direct intelligence concerning him for a long time, and as he is at Bristol[1] she and I hope that through your means her wishes may be communicated to him. She wrote to him many weeks ago to remind him of the Insurance upon his Life which ought to be paid about this time, and she would take it very kindly if you would ask him if it has been paid. Her letter touched upon several other important points, especially the completion of Hartley's education, she being now most anxious (for he is now 17 years old) that some plan should be settled and the means pointed out for the execution of it. I hope you may be able to learn from his Father what his views are respecting Hartley, and I should be exceedingly happy and most grateful to you if you could communicate to me any thing satisfactory on this head: but, at all events, I beg you will not fail, without delay, to put the question to him respecting the Insurance;

---

[1] S. T. C. had recently been prostrated by ill-health and the opium habit, but was now about to give a new course of lectures.

and all all other information which you can give us concerning Coleridge will be very acceptable. Many Months ago he gave Mrs Coleridge and his Friends reason to expect that he would be coming into the North; and I hope that the Spring or Summer may tempt him down, provided he can go on with such labours as he may have planned, which I should think might be better done in the Country than in London, Bristol, or any large town.——. I have been staying nine weeks at Keswick with a Miss Barker, Mr Southey's next door Neighbour, at whose house, Basil Montagu,[1] whom you were so kind to at Bristol, was taken dangerously ill three months since. I came hither to assist her in attending upon him. His disorder was a violent Haemorrage, which brought him to the last state of weakness; but he is now recovering, though I fear that his Life will not be long. There is great cause to apprehend a Consumption. I hope to be able to return home in about three weeks. We now live at Rydale, fifteen miles from Keswick. Coleridge's Boys are at School within two miles of us, and we frequently see them. They are fine Lads—both good and clever—favorites with their School-master, and approved of by every Body else who knows them. Sara Coleridge is also very clever, and a good Girl; but poor thing! her health is not strong; and she has at present unfortunately sprained her ancle which hinders her from using as much exercise as is desirable. Mrs Coleridge is well in health, and desires to be kindly remembered to you.

My Brother and his Wife and Children are well. He has now only three Children, having suddenly lost two in the course of one short half a year, an interesting Girl almost four years old, and a lovely and most promising Boy of six years and a half. These were heavy afflictions.——

I have now only to beg that you will favor me with a letter as soon as possible—directing to me at Miss Barker's Keswick. I am aware that on a first interview with Coleridge you may probably not be able to touch upon some of the subjects of inquiry which I have proposed to you: but I beg that you will not fail in the first instance, and *immediately*, to ask him concerning the Insurance; and for Mrs Coleridge's satisfaction pray write as soon as you can give an answer

[1] i.e. Basil Montagu jnr.

on that head; and any further information hereafter will much oblige me.

I beg you will inform me of the state of your own health, and any other particulars respecting your own prospects or way of life will be very acceptable. If my Brother were here he would join with me in kind Remembrances and good wishes.

I am dear Sir with lively recollections of kindnesses received from you long ago. Yours sincerely

Dorothy Wordsworth

48. *To* Mrs Thomas Clarkson

[The Stowe, nr Hindwell] November 11th [1814]

My conscience has long been busy prompting me to write to you, and if I could have done so unknown to Sara I would have written; but as she had determined to write tho' she put it off from day to day, I was unwilling to take the pen, being well assured that she would so satisfy her mind saying 'There is no need for me to write as you have written'. I rode over to the Stowe[1] yesterday with Joanna Hutchinson, and while she and John Monkhouse are walking through the fields I think I cannot do better than thank you for your last most satisfactory letter, briefly tell you that we are all well, and transcribe a poem which we have received from William—you will have an opportunity of reading it very soon in the Octavo Edition of his poems, which is now printing and speedily will be published; but I think you will not say my time is mis-spent in giving you a pleasure beforehand which would only have been half a pleasure when at the same time you should have seen many other poems that are new to you; for he is printing considerable additions to the old stock. He wrote to me from Lowther Castle on the 4th and intended to return to Rydale on the 7th. he was unlucky in not arriving at L. a few days earlier as the Duke of Devonshire had been there and expressed a great desire to see him. He had just returned from Ireland, where he had made 'the Excursion' the Companion of his tour and had been greatly pleased with it. I say he was

---

[1] Residence of John Monkhouse, M. W.'s cousin.

unfortunate because his enemies will be busy enough in the Reviews and elsewhere, and it is really of no little importance to us that the Work should sell—and for another reason. He intends publishing the 'White Doe' in the spring, and the scene of that Poem is Bolton Abbey, the favorite and much admired by him property of the Duke of Devonshire. Perhaps you may not guess for I have but half explained myself why I am sorry that William did not see the Duke on account of the sale of the Excursion. I think the more Friends he has either of Rank or Talents or notoriety the better, that they may *talk* against the Writers, for the more that is said of the work the better; none deny that he has talents and poetic Genius. I saw two sections of Hazlitt's Review[1] at Rydale, and did not think them nearly so well written as I should have expected from him—though he praised *more* than I should have expected. His opinion that all the Characters are but one character, I cannot but think utterly false—there seems to me to be an astonishing difference considering that the primary elements are the same—fine Talents and strong imagination. He says that the narratives[2] are a Clog upon the poem. I was not sorry to hear that for I am sure with common Readers those parts of the poem will be by far the most interesting. Mary tells me that they have seen the last part of Hazlitt's Review which is more a Criticism upon Country Life and its effects than upon the poem, and amongst other evils he has the audacity to complain that there are no Courtesans to be found in the country. He makes another bold assertion that all people living in retirement hate each other. Mary tells me that William has a plan for going up to London with me when we go to France[3] in April. Sara will remain here and I shall go home before the December moon is at the full—probably about the 18th. I wish you may be in London either when we go to France or return; but if we have not that good fortune I would fain return by Bury. This if all goes well we certainly shall do; but I have a depressing timidity when I speak of plans for any distant time. Thank God! all goes well at home. I left home on the 16th September

---

[1] In *The Examiner*.

[2] i.e. the life-stories of villagers in Bks. v and vi.

[3] Caroline, W. W.'s 'French' daughter, was now engaged to be married, and D. W. was hoping to attend the wedding in Paris; but it was postponed following Napoleon's escape from Elba, and when it finally took place in 1816 she was unable to go.

so I shall have been more than three months absent when I return. I have been very happy at Hindwell. The country is beautiful, and we have been so fortunate in weather as not to have been confined to the house a single day. By little and little I have become a tolerable horse-woman. I have no fears and that is a great point—but I cannot attain the power of managing my horse; I can however ride for four of five hours without fatigue, at a pace which was torture to me when I first began. To-morrow I am going to Hereford with John Monkhouse, a distance of 16 miles and we shall return in the evening. I often think of your rides when I used to walk by your side. They were very pleasant but would have been still more pleasant if we could have ridden side by side, and if I had been mistress of my present skill I should certainly have endeavoured to procure a horse. We shall return to Hindwell on Sunday or Monday. We came unexpectedly upon John Monkhouse, to his great joy; for he leads a solitary life; but his temper is so happy and his mind so busy that he is never dull. He is a thoroughly amiable man; of such kindly affections, and so happy in communicating his sentiments on Books (he is a great Reader) and everything else that I cannot but more than ever regret that his wife was taken from him, or that he has not been fortunate enough to fix his affections upon another amiable woman to supply her place. His sister[1] is very happy, and a sweet creature, and her husband is most truly sensible of her worth. I only regret that she should live where her merits are hardly seen or felt except by her own family. They are however those of the most importance and she is very contented and expresses her benevolent and charitable disposition towards her poor neighbours—but I am going on and shall not have Room for the poem. I shall put my letter into the Post Office at Hereford, and shall not tell Sara that I have written that I may not prevent her fulfilling her intentions.—Now for the poem it is printed after 'Yarrow unvisited'—

[*Here follows* Yarrow Visited][2]

Alas! I am as bad as Sara. I have not yet written to Tillbrook, but I hope I shall very soon. In the meantime give my kind love to him

[1] Thomas Hutchinson's wife, Mary.

[2] A product of W. W.'s Scottish tour the previous summer, publ. in corrected form in *Poems*, 1815.

if you see him. Your anecdote of Tom that he sate up all night reading William's poem gave me as much pleasure as anything I have heard of the effect produced by it. I must say I think it speaks highly in favour of Tom's feeling and enthusiasm that he was so wrought upon. Do write as soon as you can. I believe Sara's letter will reach you ere long; but do not wait for it I pray you. I feel cheared now while I write to you because I seem to see before me a little way. If we are all alive I am almost confident that we shall meet somewhere before the end of next summer—at Bury—in London, or in Westmorland.

I have had one of the worst pens that ever was used—John Monkhouse cannot find his knife to mend it for me. I should not mind this if it were not for the poem; but I am afraid you will not find it easy to make it out and that will spoil the first effect of it.

Joanna Hutchinson and John M. beg their best remembrances. They are busy putting up Books and they want me to help them. We have been making ourselves merry with their unscientific way of putting them up—all by the backs.

My love to Mr Clarkson and Tom. God Bless you my dearest Friend

Yours evermore
D. W.

49. *To* Priscilla Wordsworth

[27 Feb. 1815]

My dear Sister

Your letter from Hampstead arrived last night. In reply to it there is not need to enter into particulars as the situation offered would not, I am sure, suit Mr Jackson[1] under his present circumstances, nor do I think that *he* would altogether suit the situation, his religious opinions being, though orthodox, moderate, and not what are now styled (surely with no great propriety!) evangelical. Mr Jackson's employments at College are at present so lucrative, and his prospects so good that I do not think it likely the curacy at

---

[1] The Revd William Jackson (1792–1878), son of the rector of Grasmere: later, Provost of Queen's College, Oxford.

Bocking[1] would be a temptation to him, therefore my Brother had better be on the lookout, not at all considering Mr Jackson; and when he is determined on having a curate it will then be time enough to propose the matter to Mr J's consideration, provided my Brother has not met with one entirely to his satisfaction. The ground upon which I conclude that Mrs Hoare's[2] proposal would not suit Mr J. is this, that the situation of schoolmaster or Tutor to a set of Children is not what he wishes to undertake.

The day before yesterday Miss Alne dined with us, and from her we learned that Chris's sermons were just arrived at Brathay, so William walked to B. with Miss A. and borrowed one volume—It is the second. William and Mary have read several of the sermons and are very much delighted with them—I have not yet had leisure when the book has been at liberty and have only snatched a look at the subjects and the mode of treating them which appear to me to be very interesting. Pleased I was to greet that discourse upon Paul and Festus which I heard my Brother preach at Binfield,[3] a pleasure which I shall never forget; and often do I lament that you are so far distant from us that I am not likely *often* to enjoy the same pleasure. I may say to you that I never heard a preacher so exactly to my mind, and I flatter myself that my admiration of my Brother's discourse and of the manner in which it was delivered was thoroughly impartial; for my opinion was supported by that of many others, who could not be supposed to have any likings predisposing them to a partial judgment. I have not read any part of the sermon on Paul and Festus; but on looking it over it seems to me as if it had been shortened. Is it so? The only sermon of which I can say that I have *read* any part is that upon National Education and an excellent discourse it appears to be. What can be the reason that the Copy destined for us is not arrived? Your Brother's and ours might just as well have come together by the Coach. The expense would have been no more of two sets than of one. If our copy is sent off pray let us know how, and when, that we may inquire after it; and if it be not sent let Christopher order it to go to Longman's to be forwarded to Rydale with the copies of the two volumes of

[1] C. W.'s living in Essex.
[2] The Wordsworths' Hampstead friend.
[3] Canon Cookson's parish nr Windsor.

poems[1] which are nearly through the press and which we hope will
be ready to send off in less than a fortnight. William had desired
that the poems may be sent you—pray read the new preface and
the supplementary Essay with particular attention. You will find
that he speaks in a lofty tone which will no doubt surprize the blind
adorers of that ignorant Coxcomb Jeffrey.[2] We have seen none of
the Reviews. The Eclectic, we are told, is highly encomiastic, and
probably it may be of use towards promoting the sale of the Excursion amongst the serious and religious part of the reading public;
but I am convinced, notwithstanding the zeal of a whole Body of
the admirers of the Edinburgh Review that [?that] Review will do
less harm than the feeble praise of the Quarterly. An injudicious
and malignant enemy often serves the cause he means to injure; but
a feeble friend never attains that end. By the bye the history of that
same criticism in the Quarterly is very provoking. It was originally
drawn up by Charles Lamb at the request of Southey; but so
deformed by the lopping-knife of Gifford,[3] and by the substitution
of his own flat phrases that not even the skeleton of Lamb's produc-
tion remains; which Lamb says was pronounced by his sister to be
in his best style—'the best piece of prose that he ever wrote.' From
this we have learned one lesson, which I hope Christopher also will
profit by, never to employ a friend to review a Book unless he has
the full command of the Review; so that the master critic can
neither add to nor diminish. Last night's post brought two sheets
of the White Doe. William will do all he can to hurry it through the
press that it may come out in the busy time of London gaieties. I
have no anxiety about the fate of either the Excursion or the White
Doe beyond the sale of the first Edition—and *that* I *do* earnestly wish
for. There are few persons who can afford to buy a two guinea Book,
merely for admiration of the Book. The edition has no chance of
being sold except to the wealthy; and they buy books much more
for fashion's sake than anything else—and alas we are not yet in the
fashion. I guess you are not going to Binfield before your return
home, as you speak of being at Bocking in the first week of next
month. It is three or four months since we heard any thing about

[1] *Poems*, 1815.
[2] Francis Jeffrey (1773–1850), editor of the *Edinburgh Review*.
[3] Editor of the *Quarterly*.

my Uncle's family and at that time my Aunt was in bad spirits having just lost her sister. I wish you had been likely to see them. I should like very much to know from you whether Mary[1] has quite got the better of her disappointment. I wish, poor Girl! she had never seen Mr Sandys; but having been so unfortunate it is a great blessing that she has escaped a closer connection with him. All who know him [?say] that he is a weak young Man; his Mother is odious and his Father, I believe, little better. Add to this that probably they would have been in narrow circumstances for the best part of their lives. Your account of your son John[2] is delightful. I wish I could send you a similar one from this quarter; but we do not produce scholars. John is without exception, unfortunately the slowest Boy at his books that ever I was acquainted with; yet he has a good understanding, and as just a sense of right and wrong as the best philosopher. He is tall, strong, and well-looking, a good player and well liked among his schoolfellows for his sweetness of temper and his plain honesty; Dorothy is quick enough—but *she* wants steadiness—and that is all she wants. She likes reading for her own amusement; but is so fond of many other things that the love of reading is not yet a passion with her as it used to be with her Godfather (your husband) when he was her age. She learns latin and her quickness helps her forward very tolerably, notwithstanding the sad drawback of unsteadiness. William is a very clever child—No doubt you have heard of his dangerous illness, the Croup. I was in Wales at the time, and was hurried home on his account. He is mostly confined to the house, the weather having been very unfavourable this winter; but as he is quite well, we hope he will grow vigorous and blooming when he can be trusted freely to the open air. It is a sad pity that your children should be so far separated from their numerous cousins in this part of the world. The Lloyds are all very fine children. Your Brother is pretty well, and Mrs Lloyd's health much improved by her journey to Birmingham. We were very pleased with Mary Hawkin's letter—It is written with an appearence of much earnestness and sincerity. William has of course answered it. Oh! I had forgotten that he had sent the answer to Christopher to be forwarded by him—I should think that

[1] Mrs Cookson's daughter.
[2] Her eldest, b. 1805.

Mr Jameson was not unlikely to suit the Hoares as a Tutor—He is very religious and is a good Teacher, but he has not had a College Education.

If you or they should be inclined to write to him his address is

The Revd Thos. Jameson
Sherburne, near Ferry Bridge, Yorkshire.

The Bishop[1] is pretty well, he has not been worse lately.

[*Unsigned*]

50. *To* Mrs Thomas Clarkson

Sunday May 26. [1816]

My dear Friend,

Before this reaches you, you will have been informed by the newspapers of the death of our poor brother Richard, and for our sakes I am sure you have been affected by it though you did not know him personally. He left Sockbridge with his Wife in February, in a bad state of health, to transact business in London and at the same time to procure medical advice. We were not particularly apprehensive of danger as he had been so frequently ill for a great length of time though we heard that he did not cast off his malady;—but at the last Basil Montagu, seeing him grow worse and worse in confined lodgings, prevailed upon him to remove to his house—There he was very ill—and William set forward intending to go to London; but at Kendal he found a letter telling us that he was very much better; and for more than a week we had accounts of his convalescence. He was then with Christopher at Lambeth.[2] Last Saturday but once again he worsened. On the Wednesday an abscess burst on the Liver; and from that time, poor Fellow! he struggled—not I trust in great pain—until Sunday morning the 19th when he expired, nature being quite exhausted. His sickness and the anxiety attending upon it latterly affected us very much, the contemplation of the death of a *Brother* was solemn

---

[1] Bishop Watson of Llandaff.

[2] C. W. was Chaplain to the Archbishop of Canterbury, and now rector of Lambeth.

and distressing—and when all was over we felt it deeply, though we were very thankful when God had taken him from his sufferings—and heartily do we join in Christopher's prayer that God may give us grace to profit by the awful event. We have seen very little of Richard for many years therefore as a companion his loss will not be great; but when we did meet he was always amiable and affectionate; and there has been in all our connections with him a perfect harmony. It is a great comfort to us that he died in the house of his Brother and that his body rests where Christopher may probably also spend his latter days. He was to be buried in the Church at Lambeth on Friday. He made his will about three weeks before his death, and has appointed William and Christopher joint guardians to his Son and executors with his Wife. There is also another Executor, Mr Thomas Hutton of Penrith. We have reason to believe that the Will is a just one. I must add, which will give you pleasure, that my poor Brothers's wife has been a faithful and affectionate nurse to him. She is almost worn out, as Christopher says, with fatigue and watching. Poor thing! she means to return to Sockbridge as soon as possible. We are very much indebted to Montagu for his kind exertions.—Now my dear Friend I must turn to a subject which has been much upon our minds lately. Only I had not the heart to write to you while we were so anxious about Richard, and I am afraid you may have thought us careless or unkind. Sara promised me over and over again that she would write—and she much wished it—but you know she is idle—and I dare say persuaded herself every post day that we should hear from you,—as indeed I thought we should—respecting the Riots in Suffolk and the degree of apprehension you might entertain for the property of your Brothers and other Friends—that was the reason of our particular wish to hear from you. I trust that you, being out of the circuit of the Riots, are safe, and surely the Poor could not by any possible means take the fancy that Mr *Clarkson* was their enemy! but you cannot help having great anxiety and distress for others. Pray tell us how you feel—and what you fear or have feared—perhaps the newspapers exaggerate the mischief; but at best it must be very great. In this part of England we are happy—no public disasters seem to touch us. Labourers find the benefit of the cheapness of corn; and their wages are not much reduced; so that except from those who have property we have little or nothing of complaints—and they are only suffering under an evil which they can well bear, and which will certainly pass away. You sympathized in poor Southey's distress I am sure.[1] His loss is indeed irreparable; for it was impossible for any child more completely to satisfy the wishes of a Father. Herbert was in all pursuits likely to have grown up the Companion and friend of his Father—at nine years of age he had in study the eagerness of a fellow student, while he was as fond of play as an ordinary child—and his Father in his half-hours of relaxation made himself his playmate. Southey, you know, has uncommon self-command, and after the child was buried he addressed himself to his labours as before, and so has continued to do, but all agree that he is an altered man—his buoyant spirits I fear will never return and it will be very long before he regains his chearfulness. Mrs Southey supported herself wonderfully at first but she is in great dejection, and I fear that it will long continue; she is not of that turn of mind which makes her, under less afflictions than this, struggle through and bear up. Therefore how can we hope that she will speedily overcome this heavy sorrow? Poor Sara had the melancholy lot of being at Keswick during the whole of Herbert's sickness—she could not bear to leave them till all was over. Dorothy was with her and on the day of the child's death she came home with Edith[2] and Sara Coleridge, who stayed a week. Sara H brought with her a cough, the remains of her illness, and for some time she looked very ill; but she is now much better, and she has got her pony from Wales which will I hope set her completely strong again. Sara Coleridge is much improved in health and strength and is much grown. She is a delightful scholar, having so much pleasure in learning. I know no greater pleasure than to instruct a girl who is so eager in the pursuit of knowledge as she is—often do we wish that Dorothy was like her in this respect—*half* like her would do very well, for with all Dorothy's idleness there are many parts of her character which are much more interesting than corresponding ones in Sara, therefore, as good and evil are always mixed up together, we should be very contented with a moderate share of industry, her talents being quite enough. But I am perhaps mis-

---

[1] At the death of his son Herbert.
[2] Southey's daughter.

leading you. I have no fault to find with Sara in anything—but yet there is a something which made me make the observation—a want of power to interest you,—not from anything positively amiss, but she wants the wild graces of nature. Edith is a delightful girl—scholar good enough, and to me very engaging. I hope you got my Brother's Odes,[1] and the letter on Burns.[2] All are gone to Church but me, and I expect them home every moment. William and Mary are well; but Mary has had a bad appetite and looks very thin. I hope we shall hear from you immediately. May God bless you, my dearest Friend, Believe me

Ever faithfully yours,
D Wordsworth.

Herbert Southey died of an inflammation on the heart. I wish we could hear of Mrs Luff. All join with me in kind love and in begging that you will write.

51. *To* Mrs Thomas Clarkson

Rydal Mount. March 2nd [1817]

With a thankful heart, thankful for the blessings of a chearful home, and the society of my own dear Family have I dated this letter, yet not without some self condemnation that I have not exactly complied with your wishes, that I should write immediately after my arrival,[3] the more so as you were so very good to me when I was separated from my Friends. It was a fortnight yesterday since my arrival; and I have had so many employments, and above all such a succession of happy, I may say joyous feelings, that the time seems to be twice as long, and I have more than once set myself to recollect dates, in order to be persuaded in my own mind that I had not been much longer at Rydal Mount. I never had this feeling before after my absence from home, and I attribute it to the contrast in all respects between my manner of spending my time here and at Halifax, and the perfect opposition, if I may so speak, in all

---

[1] *Thanksgiving Ode ... with Other Short Pieces*, 1816.
[2] *A Letter to a Friend of Robert Burns*, 1816.
[3] From Halifax.

domestic manners and arrangements. There I was in a large house
with two old people,[1]—servants to perform the work as by
magic—no child's voice—all perfect stillness. True it is that they are
the most chearful and happy old people I was ever acquainted with;
yet how different the chearfulness of their fireside from the chearfulness of ours—and how different the seriousness! I was very happy
there, yet now that I am placed again in the perfect freedom of
home, I rejoice many times in every day that I am here saying, 'how
glad I am that I am among you once again'! Then notwithstanding
this is but the *second* fine day we have had since my return I have had
so much delight in the beauty of the country; I think the more from
having come from a country in some points resembling this,
abounding in vallies, streams, and gushing springs. When I was
there I thought the hills and vallies beautiful—and so they
are—and they reminded me of our mountain regions; but when I
came *home* again I was even struck with *surprize* at the excessive
loveliness of the objects before my eyes, the exquisite proportions,
combinations of forms, and richness and harmony of colours. I
stayed a whole fortnight at Kendal, having promised a visit to our
good friend, Mrs Cookson last summer, which I never paid, and
knowing how unwilling I should be to stir from home again after I
had once got here. I was met at the door at 8 o'clock in the morning
by Dorothy and Willy, who, thank God! are both now perfectly
well; but they then looked very delicate, having only just recovered
from very severe colds. Dorothy's was especially a serious indisposition, and I am very sorry to find that during the latter part of
this winter she has been more than usually susceptible of cold. She
is of a delicate constitution and her spirits lead her on to over-
exertion and fatigue, then comes relaxation and she catches cold.
Willy rides daily to school upon an ass, and this is of great use to him
both body and mind, and will in time, I hope, make a Boy of him
instead of a little Baby. After a five months absence I am astonished
with his babyishness; and really his Father fondles over him and
talks to him just as if he were but a year old; he has, however, so fine
a temper from nature that I think it is utterly impossible to undo it,
and by degrees he will be recovered from all leanings towards being

[1] The Rawsons.

treated as the little pet, 'the little darling'; for when he is amongst his school-fellows none are more active, independent, and manly than he, and he disdains all notice from Father, or Mother or any of us at such times. John is greatly improved. He carries his ingenuousness up with him, but the way of learning is to him steep and difficult; and he flags, or turns aside; yet I trust he will be a respectable scholar in time. He has a sound understanding and a good memory; and an intuitive sense of the just and honourable. Dorothy began music in Autumn and she is now fond of it. At first she was very desirous to learn, and we thought, if she would persevere, that a moderate share of skill might furnish amusement for her and sometimes pleasure to us in after times, but the benefit we looked to was chiefly collateral—unsteadiness is her master fault, and we thought that should she go on it could not be without steadiness and diligence. For some time (when the first novelty was gone) setting at the Pianoforte was irksome and she was driven to it, with the assurance that if she did not choose to take pains it should be wholly given up. Her backwardness is now conquered and she is fond of it; and the judges say she makes a remarkable progress. She learns to draw from one of Mr Green's[1] daughters and offers very well. As to her Latin she makes a poor progress, for she has no pride in it; but in time she will, I hope, make a tolerable Latin scholar, and at all events she has a much better understanding of what she reads in English from the little she does already know of Latin. Sara returned from Keswick the week before my return. She looks remarkably well and is very strong, she can walk to Grasmere and back without fatigue. Today we have all been at Church, where the duty is now most admirably performed by Mr Jackson's son; but, alas! we shall not have him long, and his father, the Rector, will take the office over himself. My sister's nephew, George Hutchinson,[2] is with him, a Boy of 14 years of age who has just had a fortune of 5000 per annum left him by his Mother's Uncle. Mr Wm Jackson (if his health permit, but he is very delicate) is to be George's private Tutor; and they are to go together to Oxford—Mr J—n as College Chaplain; and George, of course, will have nothing to do with the University at present. The education of this Boy is a

---

[1] William Green (1761–1823), of Ambleside.
[2] Son of M. W.'s eldest brother John. He took the name of Sutton.

serious concern. He is of an amiable disposition, sweet tempered, quick and lively; but very giddy and unthinking, and I fear might be easily misled. Mr de Quincey is married; and I fear I may add he is ruined. By degrees he withdrew himself from all society except that of the Sympsons of the *Nab* (that pretty house between Rydal and Grasmere). At the up-rouzing of the Bats and the Owls he regularly went thither—and the consequence was that Peggy Simpson, the eldest Daughter of the house presented him with a son ten weeks ago, and they were married on the day of my return to Rydal, and with their infant son are now spending their honeymoon in our cottage at Grasmere. This is in truth a melancholy story! He utter'd in raptures of the beauty, the good sense, the simplicity, the 'angelic sweetness' of Miss Sympson, who to all other judgments appeared to be a stupid, heavy girl, and was reckoned a Dunce at Grasmere School; and I predict that all these witcheries are ere this removed, and the fireside already dull. They have never been seen out of doors–except after the day was gone. As for him I am very sorry for him—he is utterly changed—in appearance, and takes largely of opium. My sister is very well; but miserably thin and eats very little. My Brother has had much vexation and anxiety respecting Richard's affairs and at this moment we are threatened with a Chancery Suit. If this cannot be put a stop to farewell to every farthing of the property I got from my Father (I have none else) and in the meantime we touch no Interest. Wm went this morning to attend the sale of furniture at Sockbridge. My dearest Friend, I have rambled on so long about ourselves that you will think I have forgotten the contents of your last most interesting letter, but not so I assure you. I was charmed with the account you give of your goings on at Playford Hall, and heartily congratulate you on the blessing of a bountiful harvest; and above all I was delighted to hear of your sister's happy prospects and heartily wish that it may please God to grant her all possible comfort as a mother. You will be glad to hear that Mary Hutchinson[1] has got a Daughter. She and the Children both well. Farming concerns wretched—year by year they grow poorer. What do you say to the suspension of the Hab: Corp: Act?[2] If it *be* necessary I can only think that the feeble

---

[1] Of Hindwell.

[2] The Habeas Corpus Act, suspended following agricultural riots.

execution of the Laws which we have already is the cause of that necessity, and it is greatly to be lamented. Nothing can so much tend to irritate the minds of the people, I hope you will be able to give us a good account of Tom, to whom I beg my kind love and to your dear Husband, your Father and Sister, and remember me to Mrs Kitchener. The Kirkby Lonsdale business[1] was with great trouble and fatigue settled without loss. I pray you write soon—Farewell, my dear Friend, yrs ever   D. W.

Oh, that you would come and see us next Summer!

Have you seen Coleridge's 'Bible the Statesman's best Manual'.[2] I think it is ten times more obscure than the darkest parts of the Friend.

52. *To* Thomas Monkhouse

Kendal, March 3ᵈ, 1818.

My dear Friend,

Knowing that you do not grudge a shilling that pays for tidings of old friends, and that if you can get a little sound good-government doctrine into the bargain, you will think the shilling well bestowed, I send you this paper;[3] which I think you will say is pretty well done. There is nothing comes out on the other side of the question worth reading, though every day brings out something fresh on both sides. The Broughamites evidently abate in their hopes, and the opposite party has *well grounded* hopes of success; but the misguided mob, including almost all of the lower classes who have no votes, cry aloud for Brougham, expecting that if he is but returned for Westmoreland, meal will be reduced to fifteen shillings a load. So they cry out! and no lady would venture to appear in a yellow[4] ribband in Kendal streets, though you cannot walk thirty yards without meeting a dirty lad or lass with a blue one! and the

---

[1] The bankruptcy of W. W.'s sub-distributor.

[2] *The Statesman's Manual*, 1816. S. T. C. had now become a permanent inmate of the Gillman household at Highgate, where he was to remain for the rest of his days.

[3] An election broadsheet containing part of W. W.'s second *Address to the Freeholders of Westmorland*. Henry Brougham (1778–1868), the radical, was standing against Lord Lonsdale's sons, Lord Lowther and Col. H. C. Lowther.

[4] Yellow was the Tory, and blue the Whig colour.

ladies of that party also have no fear of displaying their colour.

I am detained at Kendal by bad weather. I came in the coach on Thursday, and shall return upon Neddy to-morrow, if the day be fine. All are well at home. We often wish you had a vote to bring you down at the election. H. Brougham is expected about Easter, when it is much to be feared that there will be fresh disturbances.

I am called to dinner, so excuse this scrawl, and if you put this paper into any one's hands, pray erase all my scrawling. God bless you!

Ever your affectionate,
D. W.

I should have sent you the last Kendal paper, but it contained nothing but the London tavern dinner and some villainous writing in which there was no sense, on the other side.

53. *To* Mrs Thomas Clarkson

Sept. 18, 1818.

My dear Friend,

By a note from Mrs Coleridge we heard of you yesterday; and of your having been engaged in the trying office of nursing your good Father during a dangerous illness; I am thankful with and for you that he has recovered and you have my earnest wishes that it may please God to prolong his life for many years to come, in that happy state in which I know him,—though in times suffering in body, yet not grievously—and always blessed with chearful spirits which made him enjoy the Happiness spread around him, yet ever looking forward to another state of being. I never think of your dear Father without sentiments of love and reverence. I saw him first at Eusmere, but did not then perceive what he was. To know him perfectly he should be seen at home, with his Family and long established connections around him. Do not think, my dearest Friend, that I only write to you now because I have chanced to hear of your Father's illness—I certainly should have written this very day. So far, last Monday—It is now Friday, therefore alter the word 'written' for 'begun to write'. How I was prevented from going on I do not recollect; ever since, however, we have been engaged in some way. But indeed, my dear Friend, I am hurt when I review the many months which have passed since we had any communication with each other. It is like wilfully wasting means of comfort and happiness and of social intercourse of that best kind where true friendship and true love exist. At our time of life why be guilty of this folly? Old Friends must needs be diminishing year by year and new ones cannot now become like the old. We may value, esteem, admire them, but something is still wanting. To what does all this tend? You may well call it prosing, the truth, however, is that I want to make an *effectual* resolve never again to be so foolish, and to induce you to do the like. We talk of engagements, and of business—of domestic employments, and out of doors pleasures; but we all know very well that the fault is in ourselves.

You wrote to me last—this I know but *when* I cannot say, only it was some time before the West^d Election, and that was three months ago. I really think that our Party have carried themselves with moderation on their triumph, and it may be hoped that private enmities are subsiding; though indeed they were very bitter in some instances at Kendal and even at Grasmere—as to us Rydal people some Friends we have gained—for instance the Norths who I believe formerly never looked upon us with a friendly eye give us always a cordial greeting—and Mrs North during the whole of the Election sent her own Son to me every day with the earliest intelligence of the state of the Poll. All the rest of the family except Dorothy, were at Appleby.[1] As I say we gained some new Friends and I do not think we have lost any of our old ones—at least we have had no sparring and have met one another at all times with 'accustomed cordiality'. A few weeks ago Lord Lowther spent three days with us and my sister and I liked him much. He has very good sense and was pleasant and chearful in a quiet way. He is certainly very discerning in the characters of men and seems to have no *bitterness* in his judgments. This contest must have been of infinite use to him. If he did not know it before he must now perceive that much will be and is already required of him, and that rank and great professions must be upheld by personal character and a judicious attention to the

1 The election took place at Appleby Castle.

interests of the people with whom he is connected, and indeed he seems disposed to give his mind to the acquirement of knowledge, especially in connection with these two Counties. Col Lowther and his wife, Lady Ellinor, called on Tuesday. He is a fine brave Fellow and has seen much of active service abroad. He is painfully shy. The first time he spoke to Mary and me he seemed quite daunted—like a Rustic from one of our mountain vales, but on Tuesday we thought that he had gained courage during the late struggle for his shyness seemed to be much worn off. The Wilberforces have been at Rydal rather more than three weeks and are delighted with the country. Their houses (for they have two) are at the bottom of the hill by the road-side, just opposite to the road turning up to Lady Fleming's house and ours. But these two houses (though we have borrowed a press-bed which is placed in a parlour) are not sufficient for their needs. They have no less than 5 beds at different houses in the village. The family amounted to 19 when they first came, but three are gone—two schoolboys and a Secretary. The arrangements were first begun by Letters between Mr W. and my Brother—but the business was soon given up by William to me and innumerable were the Letters which passed between me and Mr Wilberforce, and no little contrivance was required to get together Beds for so many, the cottagers, though they had rooms, not having beds of their own. First of all I had to receive 7 servants (William and Mary were at Keswick at the time) and on their arrival I was a little out of heart. With 7 servants came 5 horses—and there was no provender for them—and the Inns at Ambleside could not take them in—and packages and servants upon a wet and dirty day seemed at once to fill the small rooms—and when I said 'the Family will I fear be sadly crammed!' I assure you I was not encouraged to dissipate my fears—'Aye, if you saw our house! the first floor would far more than hold both these two houses.' Add to this, the old Cook's observation upon my answering to one of her questions 'such and such things must be sent for to Ambleside', 'Our men don't like going errands, they are not used to it'—and her exclamation 'what an inconvenient place!' when she found they could not get 'a drop of Beer' nearer than Ambleside—besides objections of the housemaid and kitchen maid to sleep upon a Mattress, and you will not wonder I was rather afraid, that our good Friends might find themselves not a little uncomfortable on their arrival,—but I assure you it was a pleasing contrast when they *did* come, all joy, animation and thankfulness. The rooms were larger than they expected—and so *many* sitting rooms it was quite delightful, and as to the garden—the situation—everything was to their minds. I desired the servants to send for me when the Family came. I found all at dinner except Mr W. and his two youngest sons who were not come. Mrs W. looked very interesting, for she was full of delight and talked as fast as any of the young ones—but I must say that she has never since appeared to me to such advantage. Yet I like her very well—admire her goodness and patience and meekness—but that slowness and whininess of manner—tending to self-righteousness, I do not like. Not a particle of this was visible that first day when they were all rejoicing over their dinner of Mountain mutton and West-morland Beef—and each telling,—and all at once—his or her separate feelings. Then came Mr Wilberforce himself and all ran to meet him—*I* must go to—and then indeed I was much affected, seeing his feeble body, which seemed to me completely worn out. This was the more affecting as I perceived at the same time that his mind was as lively as ever. Such were my first impressions. I soon however discovered with great satisfaction that he has yet no small share of strength; and it now seems to me that he *may* live many years.

The two daughters are very sweet Girls—remarkably modest and unaffected—lively, animated and industrious, in short just what well-educated girls ought to be. The weather has not been steadily fine, but they do not mind a few showers, and we have had many most delightful days, which they have made full use of—all except Mr W. who seems to have far too much to do.

We see each other very often—but have never eaten a meal to-gether till yesterday, when my Br. dined with Mr W. and all came up to tea with us. The evening passed very pleasantly. Mr Fleming of Rayrigg[1] and his son were of the party. Thomas Monkhouse is with us, and we hope he will not be in a hurry to go away; for he is always happy at Rydal. He has brought a friend, Captain *Sertorius*, —how he came by that name I know not. He is a natural son of

---

[1] An old schoolfriend of W. W.'s, now curate of Bowness.

George Rose,[1] and through his interest, I suppose, was made post Captain at an early age. He is a pleasant, brave Fellow, and has seen much hard service. Trade goes on as it *should* do and T. M. seems now to have decided that it is better not to give it up, and I cannot but think he does wisely. He is in no danger of being so wedded to gain as to shut out good affections. It is above three weeks since Joanna left us to go to Hindwell; but we have not yet heard from her. Perhaps she is waiting to tell us of Mrs H's confinement, but this is not well; for we have been anxious to hear of Joanna as the weather was damp when she left us, and not favourable for a rheumatic person. Poor thing! her health is sadly broken. We do not much expect Sara this winter—at least Miss Dowling told us she intended to spend the winter in Wales, but she has said nothing of it to us. It is now, I believe, six weeks since we heard from her. She was then well and in good spirits. We have had the most delightful summer ever remembered—weeks of uninterrupted sunshine, genial showers, again weeks of sunshine. Our fruits have ripened and the fields have been for ever green. Strange this may sound to you; but so it was. In May and a part of June the drought was excessive, but the abundant dews I suppose prevented the parching of the pastures, and that you know is the time when the fern springs and that is always green is summer. We never had such an abundant supply of vegetables in our garden, while from all other parts of England we hear of the scarcity. I am sure that you will be pleased to hear that we are, so far, highly delighted with Miss Dowling's school. Dorothy is perfectly happy, and we have no doubt that she will greatly improve. No hour of her day is unemployed. She was at home last Sunday; and on account of her Cousin Monkhouse is to come again next Sunday. We do not go to see *her* finding that, when we have done so, she has been disturbed by the expectation of our going again, and has been on the watch for us from the top of the hill where Miss D.'s house stands. She grows much but will not, I think, reach her mother's height. She will soon be taller than I am. William has a sad illness in spring; but is now well and *for him* strong. John is a very fine-looking Boy. All strangers are taken with him from his ingenuous countenance, and the mix-

---

[1] George Rose (1744–1818), the politician.

ture of hardness and modesty in his deportment and manners. And now, my dearest Friend, it is time that I inquire after you all. How is Mr Clarkson? and where is Tom? I hope that by this time he has not only wholly regained his health and strength but cast off the traces from his Countenance of that dismal disease. Tell us that you both think about coming to see us and, further, that you talk of the time when, and the means how. This is a sad scrawl, I have been afraid of missing the post and now they come for my letter—God bless you, my dearest Friend,

Ever yours
D. W.

54. *To* William Johnson

October 21st, 1818.

... Sir George and Lady Beaumont spent a few days with us lately and I accompanied them to Keswick. Mr and Mrs Wilberforce and their family happened to be at K. at the same time, and we all dined together in the romantic Vale of Borrowdale, at the house of a female friend, an unmarried Lady, who, bewitched with the charms of the rocks, and streams, and mountains of that secluded spot, has there built herself a house, and though she is admirably fitted for society, and has as much enjoyment when surrounded by her friends as any one *can* have, her chearfulness has never flagged, though she has lived more than the year round alone in Borrowdale, at six miles distance from Keswick, with bad roads between. You will guess that she has resources within herself; such indeed she has. She is a painter and labours hard in depicting the beauties of her favorite Vale; she is also found of music and of reading, and has a reflecting mind; besides (though before she lived in Borrowdale she was no great walker) she is become an active climber of the hills, and I must tell you of a feat that she and I performed on Wednesday the 7th of this month. I remained in Borrowdale after Sir G. and Lady B. and the Wilberforces were gone, and Miss Barker proposed that the next day she and I should go to Seathwaite beyond the Black lead mines at the head of Borrowdale, and thence up a mountain called at the top *Ash Course*, which we suppose may be a corruption of *Esk*

Hawes, as it is a settling between the mountains over which the people are accustomed to pass between Eskdale and Borrowdale; and such settlings are generally called by the name of 'the Hawes'—as Grisdale Hawes, Buttermere Hawes, from the German word Hals (neck). At the top of Ash Course Miss Barker had promised that I should see a magnificent prospect; but we had some miles to travel to the foot of the mountain, and accordingly went thither in a cart—Miss Barker, her maid, and myself. We departed before nine o'clock, the sun shone; the sky was clear and blue; and light and shade fell in masses upon the mountains; the fields below *glittered* with the dew, where the beams of the sun could reach them; and every little stream tumbling down the hills seemed to add to the chearfulness of the scene.

We left our cart at Seathwaite and proceeded, with a man to carry our provisions, and a kind neighbour of Miss Barker's, a statesman shepherd of the vale, as our companion and guide. We found ourselves at the top of Ash Course without a weary limb, having had the fresh air of autumn to help us up by its invigorating power, and the sweet warmth of the unclouded sun to tempt us to sit and rest by the way. From the top of Ash Course we beheld a prospect which would indeed have amply repaid us for a *toilsome* journey, if such it had been; and a sense of thankfulness for the continuance of that vigour of body, which enabled me to climb the high mountain, as in the days of my youth, inspiring me with fresh chearfulness, added a delight, a charm to the contemplation of the magnificent scenes before me, which I cannot describe. Still less can I tell you the glories of what we saw. Three views, each distinct in its kind, we saw at once—the vale of Borrowdale, of Keswick, of Bassenthwaite—Skiddaw, Saddleback, Helvellyn, numerous other mountains, and, still beyond, the Solway Frith, and the mountains of Scotland.

Nearer to us, on the other side, and below us, were the Langdale Pikes, then our own Vale below them, Windermere, and far beyond Windermere, after a long distance, Ingleborough in Yorkshire. But how shall I speak of the peculiar deliciousness of the third prospect? At this time *that* was most favoured by sunshine and shade. The green Vale of Esk—deep and green, with its glittering serpent stream was below us; and on we looked to the mountains near the sea—Black Combe and others—and still beyond, to the sea itself in dazzling brightness. Turning round we saw the mountains of Wasdale in tumult; and Great Gavel,[1] though the middle of the mountain was to us as its base, looked very grand.

We had attained the object of our journey; but our ambition mounted higher. We saw the summit of Scaw Fell, as it seemed, very near to us; we were indeed, three parts up that mountain, and thither we determined to go. We found the distance greater than it had appeared to us, but our courage did not fail; however, when we came nearer we perceived that in order to attain that summit we must make a great dip, and that the ascent afterwards would be exceedingly steep and difficult, so that we might have been benighted if we had attempted it; therefore, unwillingly, we gave it up, and resolved, instead, to ascend another point of the same mountain, called *the Pikes*, and which, I have since found, the measurers of the mountains estimate as higher than the larger summit which bears the name of Scaw Fell, and where the Stone Man is built which we, at the time, considered as the point of highest honour. The sun had never once been overshadowed by a cloud during the whole of our progress from the centre of Borrowdale; at the summit of the Pike there was not a breath of air to stir even the papers which we spread out containing our food. There we ate our dinner in summer warmth; and the stillness seemed to be not of this world. We paused, and kept silence to listen, and not a sound of any kind was to be heard. We were far above the reach of the cataracts of Scaw Fell; and not an insect was there to hum in the air. The Vales before described lay in view, and side by side with Eskdale, we now saw the sister Vale of Donnerdale terminated by the Duddon Sands. But the majesty of the mountains below and close to us, is not to be conceived. We now beheld the whole mass of Great Gavel from its base, the Den of Wasdale at our feet, the gulph immeasurable, Grasmere[2] and the other mountains of Crummock, Ennerdale and *its* mountains, and the sea beyond.

While we were looking round after dinner our Guide said that we must not linger long, for we should have a storm. We looked in vain to espy the traces of it; for mountains vales, and the sea were

[1] Great Gable.
[2] i.e. the peak of Grasmoor.

all touched with the clear light of the sun. 'It is there', he said, pointing to the sea beyond Whitehaven, and, sure enough, we there perceived a light cloud, or mist, unnoticeable but by a shepherd, accustomed to watch all mountain bodings. We gazed around again and yet again, fearful to lose the remembrance of what lay before us in that lofty solitude; and then prepared to depart. Meanwhile the air changed to cold, and we saw the tiny vapour swelled into mighty masses of cloud which came boiling over the mountains. Great Gavel, Helvellyn, and Skiddaw were wrapped in storm; yet Langdale and the mountains in that quarter were all bright with sunshine. Soon the storm reached us; we sheltered under a crag, and almost as rapidly as it had come, it passed away, and left us free to observe the goings-on of storm and sunshine in other quarters—Langdale had now its share, and the Pikes were decorated by two splendid rainbows; Skiddaw also had its own rainbows, but we were glad to see them and the clouds disappear from that mountain, as we knew that Mr and Mrs Wilberforce and the family (if they kept the intention which they had formed when they parted from us the night before) must certainly be upon Skiddaw at that very time—and so it was. They were there, and had much more rain than we had; we, indeed, were hardly at all wetted; and before we found ourselves again upon that part of the mountain called Ash Course every cloud had vanished from every summit.

Do not think we here gave up our spirit of enterprise. No! I had heard much of the grandeur of the view of Wasdale from Stye Head, the point from which Wasdale is first seen in coming by the road from Borrowdale; but though I had been in Wasdale I had never entered the dale by that road, and had often lamented that I had not seen what was so much talked of by travellers. Down to that Pass (for we were yet far above it) we bent our course by the side of Ruddle Gill, a very deep red chasm in the mountains which begins at a spring—that spring forms a stream, which must, at times, be a mighty torrent, as is evident from the channel which it has wrought out—thence by Sprinkling Tarn to Stye Head; and there we sate and looked down into Wasdale. We were now upon Great Gavel which rose high above us. Opposite was Scaw Fell and we heard the roaring of the stream from one of the ravines of that mountain, which, though the bending of Wasdale Head lay between us and Scaw Fell, we could look into, as it were, and the depth of the ravine appeared tremendous; it was black and the crags were awful.

We now proceeded homewards by Stye head Tarn along the road into Borrowdale. Before we reached Stonethwaite a few stars had appeared, and we travelled home in our cart by moonlight.

I ought to have described the last part of our ascent to Scaw Fell Pike. There, not a blade of grass was to be seen—hardly a cushion of moss, and that was parched and brown; and only growing rarely between the huge blocks and stones which cover the summit and lie in heaps all round to a great distance, like skeletons or bones of the earth not wanted at the creation, and there left to be covered with never-dying lichens, which the clouds and dews nourish; and adorn with colours of the most vivid and exquisite beauty, and endless in variety. No gems or flowers can surpass in colouring the beauty of some of these masses of stone which no human eye beholds except the shepherd led thither by chance or traveller by curiosity; and how seldom must this happen! The other eminence is that which is visited by the adventurous traveller, and the shepherd has no temptation to go thither in quest of his sheep; for on the Pike there is no food to tempt them. We certainly were singularly fortunate in the day; for when we were seated on the summit our Guide, turning his eyes thoughtfully round, said to us, 'I do not know that in my whole life I was ever at any season of the year so high up on the mountains on so calm a day'. Afterwards, you know, we had the storm which exhibited to us the grandeur of earth and heaven commingled, yet without terror; for we knew that the storm would pass away; for so our prophetic guide assured us. I forget to tell you that I espied a ship upon the glittering sea while we were looking over Eskdale. 'Is it a ship?' replied the Guide, 'A ship, yes, it can be nothing else, don't you see the shape of it?' Miss Barker interposed, 'It is a ship, of that I am certain. I cannot be mistaken, I am so accustomed to the appearance of ships at sea.' The Guide dropped the argument; but a moment was scarce gone when he quietly said, 'Now look at your ship, it is now a horse'. So indeed it was—a horse with a gallant neck and head. We laughed heartily, and, I hope when again inclined to positiveness, I may remember the ship and the horse upon the glittering sea; and the calm confidence, yet submissiveness, of our wise Man of the Mountains, who certainly had more knowledge of clouds than we, whatever might be our knowledge of ships. To add to our uncommon performance on that day Miss Barker and I each wrote a letter from the top of the Pike to our far distant friend in S. Wales, Miss Hutchinson. I believe that you are not much acquainted with the Scenery of this Country, except in the Neighbourhood of Grasmere, your duties when you were a resident here, having confined you so much to that one Vale; I hope, however, that my long story will not be very dull; and even I am not without a further hope, that it may awaken in you a desire to spend a long holiday among the mountains, and explore their recesses.

55. *To* Mrs Thomas Clarkson

Coblentz 23rd July [1820]

My dear Friend,

I begin to write to you at Coblentz having just returned from the heights which overlook the City and the splendid vales of the Rhine and the Moselle. It is impossible to conceive any more delightful prospect of the kind than we have just beheld—but it is not for me to describe it—still less in the small compass of a letter such as can be written in the snatches which we take of rest—and no doubt your husband has been here—he will tell you how elegant—how beautiful looks the city of Coblentz with its palaces and spires and its purple slated roofs situated as it is at the junction of these majestic rivers on a plain formed into an angle by the rivers. Yesterday we travelled up the Rhine from Cologne, having spent a day there, and we came along the Meuse from Namur—the most enchantingly interesting and varied country that ever I travelled through. The Rhine is stately, rich, and for ever changing, but the Meuse is romantic beyond expression from the variety of the Rocks fortifications chateaus and cottages and the *trees* of the Meuse are superior to any we have seen elsewhere on the continent. They are not so fine as those in South Wales but very much like the trees of the North of England, though not the best of those. The woods on the Rhine are greatly inferior. But let me not disparage this majestic wealth-giving glorious river—its plains of corn, vines, fruit-trees—its stately convents—churches, villages. We were indeed through almost the whole of our ride yesterday in a perpetual state of excitement. Yet I think and more, if possible, delight in the memory of the Meuse, though I was unfortunately on that day so very unwell that I could hardly speak at all—and—from pure exhaustion, was obliged to sleep in the carriage even for miles of the most interesting parts of the road. The heat had become excessive two days after our arrival at Calais and I had been tempted at Ghent to walk so much that I was quite overcome. My Bowels were much affected, this brought on weakness.—At Brussels again I fatigued myself—There we stayed two nights—At Namur I did not go out as much as others but went slowly up to the Citadel, where I saw a beautiful view and the junction of the Sambre and the Meuse. This was too much for me and I was as I said overpowered and exhausted. Thence to Liège a miserable city of poverty and splendour enchantingly situated—forming a crescent on the hillside—with convents, spires, towers. Others walked before breakfast, but I took mine in bed, though I rose at 5 o'clock. It is my way now not to be able to sleep in the mornings—but my legs ached so from the state of my Bowels that I was forced upon the bed again. At Aix la Chapelle I took rest in the same way only went to view the Chair of Charlemagne etc. Rested in the carriage, and at Cologne did not stir out all day, while others were walking, only at night I viewed the magnificent Cathedral which has never been finished and the tower now stands as a majestic Ruin yet just as the workmen left it I believe every stone remains. The quire is perfectly beautiful and quite finished; but many of its painted windows are gone. The next day I rose quite well, but resolved to spare myself. The charming ride on the Banks of the Rhine seemed to give me strength as I went along—and I trust that (being resolved now to do always less than I *can* do) I shall know no more suffering. Today I have been the strongest of the Females yet I have resisted my inclination to take several tempting walks in the environs of this singularly happily situated city. I certainly am not so strong as I was twenty years ago. This I am now obliged to confess and I must manage myself accordingly. Five years ago I used to say I felt no difference. My Sister is an excellent traveller—all alive and full of enjoyment. So indeed am I—and, with a little better arrangement, I expect that I shall not be obliged to give up any important gratification in the delightful countries whither we are bound. William's eyes are much better—and except during two days when nothing would serve but he must write poetry, he has been perfectly well. The young people[1] are, as you may suppose, very happy—Mrs Monkhouse is a sweet good modest and amiable young woman, but she is not strong and is therefore unable to walk about like her sister and Mr Wordsworth, but not enjoying things in the same sort and degree that I do the privation is not so great for her as it has been for me. It is now Sunday the 23rd of July. How different from an English Sunday! but this is a quiet place and there is nothing unpleasing to me in the pleasuring of the sober people here. It is, however, painful to see labour going on on the sabbath day and the shops open. But at Brussels (which is of itself a gayer town) it was a time of Festival. One of the grandest of the Fêtes and lucky we were in seeing it—but at Brussels there was so much flash and bustle—and noise of carriages—so much finery—and everyone seemed so intent on pleasure—I was very glad at the end of the day that we had not another to spend there and longed for the stillness of an English Sabbath. In the morning was the procession—military and sacred music. In the square all day through rattling of carriages—the public walks for ever crowded—at night illuminations—and after all fireworks. We in the evening went in the string of carriages to the Hyde Park of Brussels and on the outskirts of the public place there was a fair and thousands of people—drinking—walking—what noisy laughing. But it is time to turn to England, where I hope you are all as well as we left you. It will be yet a fortnight before we reach Berne and till we are there we can have no letters, and this thought sometimes comes suddenly upon me and raises momentary fears. I cannot give you any other address than à la poste restante à Berne; for we do not know what our movements will be; but at Berne we shall desire that our letters may be sent after us—and pray my dear Friend, write immediately. When this letter reaches you our little darling William will I hope be under your care.[2] He is no doubt in most

---

[1] Thomas Monkhouse, his bride Jane and her sister.

[2] W. W. jnr. had recently entered Charterhouse. He left in 1822 on account of ill health.

of his leisure moments of rest from school studies and play, employed in planning his journey and thinking of the pleasures of it. That was a very hasty note which I wrote to you just before we left London, and I am afraid I did not half express the satisfaction which the Father and Mother felt when I first named to them your wish to have William at some of his holidays. I then said 'what if he can be received at the next (for it cannot be convenient for my brother Christ. to have him)' and they snatched at the idea greedily. William must put a word or two in your letter and give our kindest love to him and tell him that when we come home again we shall have a great deal to tell him of what we have seen. Journals we shall have in number sufficient to fill a Lady's bookshelf,—for all, except my Brother, write a Journal. Oh! Mine is nothing but notes, unintelligible to any one but myself; I look forward however to many a pleasant hour's employment at Rydal Mount in filling up the chasms. But it is grievous to pass through such a country as this only glancing at the objects in the broad high-way and leaving so many entirely unseen. I think of you all, of every Friend I have in England at night when I am in bed—often till I am obliged to endeavour to forget you and to keep down the strong wish which I and all of us have to hear from you all again. True it is that for months together no important changes trouble us—often so it is—but on the other hand how dreadful and how sudden are the changes that [?happen] in fancy and *have* happened three times in our [   ]. But I must not think of it. Trusting for good [?news] I entreat you to write. It is near ten o'clock (and tomorrow morning we are to depart at 6 o'clock). We go up the Rhine to Schaffhausen stopping a li[ttle on] the way.—I have written with perpetual [interrup]tions. William's and Mary's room is through this [and we] have eaten our meals in the common Room and dined at the Table d'hote, and as is the custom have all sate in our own bedrooms, and partaken of other customs of the country. In this room has been [   ] I have [?] each and all over and over [?] talk on all questions, or to ask me to interpret and it seems though I have scribbled so much I have told nothing when there is so much to tell of. This is a delightful inn so clean and comfortable in comparison with that at Cologne where we were assaulted by stenches at every turn. But on the other hand, the situation at Cologne was so amusing that I, who was a prisoner, was delighted with it. I sate at an open window all day mending my ragged cloaths and watching the immensely large Ferry boat which was emptied and re-filled every ¾ of an hour close to me. It has a square platform for passengers, and is covered with so many and so varied groups that it is like a piece cut out of a Market place. Fruit women with their Baskets, peasants with their rakes baskets etc. Gentlemen with carriages young ladies, children, soldiers, perhaps a cart laden with calves—a few sheep, a calf tied to a string. In short every thing comes and goes—and there are all the gay colours of the Rainbow. This Inn is the posthouse and is in a narrow street. The Landlord speaks good English and is a most sensible and intelligent man. The servants are clean and respectable. Every thing good in the house, and a quietness which I have seen in no other German Inn. I am going to give you a troublesome office. I must beg you to write a line to Mrs Hoare telling her that we are well and happy. You may say that I have been a little poorly, but am now quite well. I am anxious to hear of my brother Christopher, and Mrs H. kindly promised to write to me. Tell her that I have no other address to give than Berne, and that letters will be forwarded from that place to us. Say also that I have not forgotten my promise to write to my nephew John[1] but that must not be till we get into Switzerland, we have so little time for writing. Also I beg you will write to Miss Lamb and give my kindest love to her and her Brother, and say to them I will write from Switzerland. There we hope to meet Henry Robinson. After you have read and digested this letter (and less than one day, I think, will not serve for this, it is so badly written) pray forward to Sara Hutchinson. I wonder whether Mary Bell[2] goes to our Brother or not and very much do we long to hear every thing concerning Sara and Dorothy and John. And now my dearest Friend may God bless you and yours and preserve you till we meet again! My kind love to Mr Clarkson and Tom, and I pray you read this sad scrawl with indulgence. The fine-toned clock warns me it is time to pack for tomorrow. Ever your affectionate and faithful friend D. W.

[1] C. W.'s eldest son, about to enter Winchester.
[2] Servant at Rydal Mount.

56. *To* Edward Quillinan

Trinity Lodge, Thursday 20th May. [1824]

My dear Friend.

I have just written to Mr Monkhouse to tell him that Doro is now travelling northward with her Father, instead of southward with her Uncle. She was home-sick—the Father sick to have her at home, and so they settled it—and this morning at 7 o'clock I saw her seated on the top of the Stamford Coach by his side. Instead of going into Wales as before intended, at Midsummer, she is to accompany her Mother in the autumn, and my Brother will either go with them, or join them there to return with them. I hope Egerton Brydges[1] will find his way to the Lodge either this morning or at Chapel time in the evening. My Brother and Doro saw him since his return from London, but I happened not to be out with them. This house which seemed so chearful until to-day is now (deserted as we are) quite melancholy in its stillness; though the sun shines brightly, and the sight of it chears me a bit for the Travellers' sake. The Master[2] set off for London at ½ past 9.—I shall be at Cambridge again on my return from Playford with Mrs Luff, but probably only for one night.

I am sorry I was so careless as to bring away Miss H.'s letter, which I now enclose.

Poor Rotha![3] how anxious you must have been when she was so ill! I hope to hear from you while at Playford with good accounts of both your dear little Girls—and a pleasant history of your sports at Lee[4] with Mr M.,[5] visits to Ramsgate etc etc. Excuse this poor scrawl. I have many letters to write, and would much prefer musing in the Garden—or lying on a sofa with a Book from which my thoughts would wander far away—halting oftentimes at Lee—a place which will always be dear to my memory. God bless you and

---

[1] Quillinan's brother-in-law. His first wife, daughter of Sir Egerton Brydges, Bt. (1762–1832), the bibliophile, had died in 1822.
[2] i.e. C. W.
[3] Quillinan's younger daughter.
[4] Lee Priory, Kent.
[5] Thomas Monkhouse.

your bonny Lasses (I assure you Rotha was right bonny in my eyes long before they cast on her their last look). Do not fail to remember me to Mrs Lucas[1]—Yours ever truly

D Wordsworth.

Direct [to] Playford Hall n[r]. Ipswich.

57. *To* Henry Crabb Robinson

Playford Hall, near Ipswich.
Tuesday Morn[g]. 23rd May [1824]

My dear Friend,

In my way from Cambridge last Friday, as soon as I had secured my luggage etc I set off towards your Brother's house; stopped at Mrs Kitchener's to enquire after her, and just as I was setting out again your Brother and Sister were coming up the Square. Instead of proceeding to Southgate I turned in again with them, and Mrs R.[2] stayed till the Coach took me up.

—I was much pleased to see a chearful countenance when she met me, and though I marked the traces of age coming on—and of past suffering, on the whole she looked much better than I had expected. In fact she told me she had rallied wonderfully since her late distress.—I shall stop in Southgate on my return—Mrs Luff, who will be my companion to Rydal—going forward to the Inn—where she will take care of Luggage, etc. My time will be very short, as the Coach only remains half an hour at Bury—We shall travel with our Family cares—the whole of Mrs Luff's living Stock, three singing Birds of gay plumage brought from the Mauritius.

Thank you for your letter, which I received at Cambridge with the parcel and two Books for my Brother's use. He has taken them into the North, as, he told me, you were not in immediate want of them.

---

[1] Their governess.
[2] Robinson's sister-in-law, of Bury St Edmunds.

Your advice respecting my Continental Journal is, I am sure very good, provided it were worth while to make a Book of it,—provided I *could* do so—and provided it were my wish: but it is not—'Far better', I say, 'make another Tour and write the journal on a different plan!' In recopying it, I should—as you advise omit considerable portions of the description—These would chiefly be, what I may call duplicate descriptions—the same ground travelled over again either actually or by retrospect. Such occur several times. I should also omit or compress much of what is detailed respecting dress etc etc—and would insert all the poems.[1]

But, observe, my object is not to make a Book but to leave to my Niece a neatly penned Memorial of those few interesting months of our lives.

I have heard of your being at the Exhibition. I hope you liked Leslie's[2] picture of Sancho and the Duchess—We were charmed with it—What did you think of Mr Clarkson? and of the Master of Trinity?[3]

You will be surprized to hear that Dora is gone home with her Father. They left Cambridge on Thursday morning, and, I hope, reached Rydal on Saturday to breakfast. I expect a letter tomorrow.—My Brother was well and in good spirits at Cambridge, and we all enjoyed our visit there very much. The weather was delightful the first week.—Then came the Flood—a new scene for us—and very amusing—on the Sunday when the sun shone out again. The Cam, seen from the Castle Hill resembled one of the lake-like Reaches of the Rhine. The damage was, I fear very great to the Farmers; but though the University Grounds were completely overflowed up to Trinity Library, in the course of four days most of the damage was repaired. I think we shall remain here about a fortnight longer—We intend to stay two nights at Cambridge—two in Leicestershire—two in Yorkshire—and after that one day's journey, a night spent at Kendal, and a three hours' ride before breakfast will take us to Rydal Mount. Mrs Luff is a

---

[1] i.e. W. W.'s *Memorials* of the 1820 tour.
[2] C. R. Leslie, R.A. (1794–1859).
[3] Portraits by, respectively, A. E. Chalon, R.A., and G. F. Robson.

bad traveller—and short journeys and long rests suit her.—Adieu, my dear Friend,

Truly yours
D Wordsworth

I have had good reports from Mr Monkhouse of our friends at Ramsgate—I hope you and he contrive to meet when he is in Town—Dora is to go into Wales with her Mother in the Autumn. My Brother will either accompany them, or join them there.

58. *To* John Kenyon

Rydal Mount,
October 4th [1824]

My dear Sir,

About three weeks ago, on returning from a walk, a letter in which I instantly recognised your handwriting, was given to me. I knew it must have been left by a Friend[1] of yours, and was heartily grieved that I should have been absent, and the more so, as the servant told me he had neither visited the Terrace nor the Mount. Such was my first feeling and then I opened and read your letter. I am truly glad that both you and Mrs Kenyon are in good health, and seemingly in good spirits; and was reconciled to your having been compelled to visit the sea and the grey-green Fields of Bognor, instead of our brighter vallies, as you would have found neither my Brother, nor Sister, nor Niece at home; and I hope that you will have free choice next summer, and that choice will lead you hither. I am sure you will be glad to hear of us, and this reconciles me to sending a poor scrawl without a Frank; besides I ought to have written to you from London after the very kind letter which I there received; but you know how Country folks are bustled about in London, and will therefore excuse that failure in duty.

I need not say how glad we should have been to accept your friendly invitation, had it been in our power to visit you at Bath, and

[1] John Lewis Guillemard, F.R.S.

to take a ramble on the Quantock Hills, on which, through God's mercy, we can yet walk with as light a foot as in the days of our youth. But it is time to begin with what has been done. My Brother and Dora left me at Cambridge in May; they returned directly to Rydal Mount, and I followed them in June, after paying a short visit to Mrs Clarkson near Ipswich. Since that time we have had scarcely anything but fine summer weather, such as *you* ought to have when you first introduce Mrs Kenyon to these Lakes and mountains; and though as I say I am not sorry that you did not come in the autumn months I wish you could have been here in the summer. It will be six weeks to-morrow since Mrs Wordsworth and my Brother left us. Three of those weeks they spent in North Wales, thridding that romantic country through every quarter. My Brother, to whom it was familiar ground when a very young man, has been pleased beyond expectation and remembrance, and his Wife and Daughter (to *them* all was new) have been delighted. They have, however, had a sad draw-back from the agreeable thoughts and feelings which they carried along with them to *South* Wales. There, on the banks of the Wye, they met our friend, Mr Thomas Monkhouse, who by the advice of Physicians had come thither, to his Brother,[1] for the sake of quiet, dry and pure air, and chearful society, with strict injunctions to withdraw his mind from business. That injunction was totally unnecessary, for he is, alas! unfit for all business. My Brother and Sister were heart struck at the first sight of him. He looks like a person far gone in consumption, but as the London Physicians, attributing the disorder entirely to a derangement of the digestive organs, speak confidently of a cure, I am willing to hope, though the Surgeon at Kington holds out little or no hope of his recovery. You know what a good creature Thomas Monkhouse is, and how much he is valued by all his Relatives and Friends, and will, I am sure, rejoice with us if we have the happiness to see him restored to health. Removal to a warmer climate for the winter has been recommended, but I know not what will be done.

You will be glad to hear that my nephew William is, though not a thriving plant, what, but for his looks, we should call healthy at present—not fit for a public school, therefore he attends Hartley

---

[1] John Monkhouse of the Stowe.

Coleridge,[1] who has now fourteen Scholars—a flourishing concern for an Ambleside schoolmaster!—and he is steady and regular.

I have just had a letter from Mrs Coleridge, by which I learn that your Friends, Mr and Mrs Guillemard, are at Keswick. I shall desire her to say to them that I hope, if they return by this road, they will turn aside to look at Rydal Mount, though there is no chance of their finding my Brother and Sister at home. I think we shall hardly see them before the middle of November, as they think of paying a short visit to Sir George and Lady Beaumont at Coleorton, on leaving Wales, and most likely it will be the third week of this month before they leave Wales. You do not mention you Brother. I hope you hear good tidings of him. May I beg to be most kindly remembered to him when you write? With best wishes to yourself and Mrs Kenyon, believe me, dear Sir

Yours truly
D. Wordsworth

John[2] has been three weeks at Whitehaven with Mr Wm Jackson. I expect him home this week, to leave us soon for Oxford. My Brother's address is Thomas Hutchinson's Esqre, Hindwell, near Radnor. All pretty well at Keswick.

59. *To* Sir Walter Scott

Rydal Mount near Kendal May 30th 1825.

My dear Sir Walter Scott,

My vivid remembrance of your kind reception of me, along with my Brother, at Liswayde,[3] above twenty years ago, of our meeting under the Matron's Roof at Jedbergh, and of our pleasant travels together afterwards on the Banks of the Tweed mades me feel that I have still some claim upon your kindness, and, though it is many years since I had last the pleasure of seeing you I count on your not

---

[1] Hartley Coleridge had lost his Fellowship at Oriel College, Oxford, in 1820, and two years later returned permanently to the Lakes.

[2] W. W.'s son, now at New College, Oxford.

[3] i.e. Lasswade, in 1803.

having forgotten me, and shall therefore make no apology for this unexpected intrusion, especially as you are the only person now in existence who can solve a dispute—(be not alarmed, it is not of a very serious nature) between my Brother and myself.

It is, I think, sixteen years since you visited us at Coleorton[1] in Leicestershire;—we were then residing in a house belonging to Sir George Beaumont—you were going to Lichfield and do you not remember that my Brother and I accompanied you thither? Now we come to the point in dispute—Did we go with you to Miss Seward's[2] house? Did we see Miss Seward? If your memory enables you to give a decisive answer to these questions, perhaps you may also recollect some other little circumstances in connexion with the half-hour—for I think it was not more—that we spent together at Lichfield, and if so, you will take the trouble of noting *them* also in your answer, which may help to clear up the recollections of the one of us twain that are at present mistified.

We hear of you and yours from time to time, but how long is it since you travelled this road! We were then[3] living at Grasmere. My Brother and Sister beg me to say that it would give them great pleasure—so it would me too—and others of the Family, whom you have only seen as children, if you would yet again halt among the Lakes on your way southward—or come on purpose—with Lady Scott or any part of your household at liberty to accompany you.

Probably you have heard that my Brother has of late years suffered much from weakness and occasional inflammation of the eyes[4]—I am happy to tell you that for many months past his eyes have been much stronger in general, and he has had no attack of inflammation. He begs to be most kindly remembered to you, and adds again 'how glad I should be to see Sir Walter Scott here and any of his Family'.

Pray present our united regards to Lady Scott, and believe me, dear Sir Walter

Yours faithfully and with great respect
Dorothy Wordsworth

---

[1] It was in fact in Mar. 1807.
[2] Anna Seward (1747–1809) the 'Swan of Lichfield'.
[3] In Aug. 1805, when Scott ascended Helvellyn with W. W. and Humphry Davy.
[4] W. W. suffered from a form of trachoma.

60. *To* Robert Jones

My dear Mr Jones,

My Brother has commissioned me to write to you respecting a matter in which he supposes there may have been some mistake; but which I solve otherwise; however I am not sorry for the opportunity it gives me of inquiring after you, and of telling you something of our goings-on. But first to the point in question. Did you, or did you not remit to Masterman and Co the little sum (I believe about £8) which you owed my Brother? If you *have* done so there is an error in our Banker's accounts for no mention is made of it in my Brother's last half-yearly statement from them. I tell him (but he is not satisfied with my explanation) that surely enough the money has never been paid—that you are no more of a man of business than himself—and that you have intended coming this summer, and settling all in a much pleasanter and more convenient way than through the medium of Bankers—yourself by the fireside at Rydal Mount.—Well, however this may be, I hope it will secure us the pleasure of a letter from you—by *us* I mean my Niece and myself; for she and I are now sole housekeepers, and her Brother William is our only companion. John set off for Oxford this morning, with his Father and Aunt (Miss Hutchinson) who are to meet Mrs Wordsworth at Sir George Beaumont's in Leicestershire; where they will all stay a full month, except that my Brother talks of taking a week out of it for Cambridge, leaving my Sister and Miss H. at Coleorton; but I think it is more likely they will all go the round together, which, if it be done, will a little prolong their absence. The whole party are in good health, only my Brothers's eyes not quite so well as during the summer. Your Friend Dora was much out of health in the spring and summer, but is now as stout and strong as ever I saw her. We hope you will take next *spring* for your long-promised visit to us—arrange for the supply of your Church in good time, and come as early in May as possible. We really were not sorry that you did not arrive in the course of last *summer*; for you would have had no *quiet* enjoyment, and you are not made for *bustling* pleasures. We never in our lives had so many visitors. The newspapers (for I suppose newspapers are not excluded from the Valley of Meditation[1]) will have announced to you the names of some of them—Mr Canning,[2] Sir Walter Scott etc. etc.; but if we had kept a private register of the names of others of less note you would really have been astonished with their numbers. Dora regrets that she did not do so. Many thanks for your kind wish to see me in N. Wales. It is a country wholly unknown to me, [   ] you, if ever my wish of seeing it be gratified. [? It would be] no small addition to my pleasure to visit you, and your good Family at Plasy-Llan—a place of which I have heard so much in the days of my youth. My Brother has promised me, if all be well, and if no other scheme of travelling elsewhere prevent him, that he will take me the round of Snowdon next summer; but it is too soon to talk of this. We shall hope to see you in the spring, and then perhaps some arrangement may be made.

Dora begs her love to you, and kind remembrances to all her Friends in North Wales. Believe me, dear, Sir,

Yours faithfully
D. Wordsworth.

Will you trust yourself again to my guidance to the Top of one of our Mountains? Or did I give you too much of it the last time? For myself—and I am thankful for the blessing—I can walk as well as when but twenty years old, and can climb the hills better than in those days. The pure air of high places seems to restore all my youthful feelings.

61. *To* Mary Laing

29th March 1826
Brinsop Court
near Hereford

My dear Miss Laing,

I had been from home some weeks when your Second letter arrived—and here I still am, and probably may remain till the end

---

[1] Glyn Mavin, where Jones had a curacy.
[2] George Canning (1770–1827), statesman.

of June: for though it was my intention when I left Rydal to return
at the end of May, I feel now, while amongst my kind Friends, that
the time will be too short. This, however, will chiefly depend on my
Brother's convenience, it being his intention to meet me in North
Wales, and give me the pleasure of a Tour in the neighbourhood of
Snowdon,[1] and we are even ambitious enough to hope to reach its
summit. Mr Hutchinson's Family have removed from Radnorshire
into Herefordshire, (about 6 miles from Hereford). The Country is
fertil and pleasant—open yet not flat—and we have a view of some
of the Welsh Mountains. Miss Joanna H., as you know, lives with
her Brother and Sister, and she is here at present. Her health has on
the whole been much better since she was in Scotland, yet she is still
delicate—not equal to me in walking—but we drive out together in
a gig very often—and she is my chearful companion frequently on
a short walk. We talk of Edinburgh[2] with true pleasure, and of the
kindness received from every member of your Family; and both
wish we may be able to see you all there again—and we laugh over
our Staffa and Isle of Skye scheme—not, however, as a scheme
utterly hopeless and visionary—but years roll over out heads; and
perhaps neither of us has much hope that it will ever be accomplished. I had begun to think you very slow in writing—not however blaming *you* but myself; for I had given you too much reason
to suspect that you were forgotten. My dear Miss Laing, I am much
concerned to hear that your health is still so indifferent. Perhaps you
are to blame for confining yourself so closely to home. A little
change is often very salutary—not that I would recommend a journey to *London* as the best cure for a delicate constitution—and
perhaps you are right in refusing to go thither. In your former
Letter very long ago—(so long I am ashamed to tell it)—you talked
of your intention to go thither, and said you should be in Gloucester
place. Was that intention set aside? Or did you go? I was there in
the Month of April [18]24 but have now no temptation to repeat
my visit—our hospitable Friend[3] in G. place being dead. He was the
Brother of Mrs Hutchinson, an excellent Creature, whose loss is
deeply felt by every member of the Family. Mrs Hutchinson herself

---

[1] The plan was dropped, and D. W. never visited N. Wales.
[2] D. W. had toured Scotland again, with Joanna H., in 1822.
[3] Thomas Monkhouse.

is delightful, and has four as good and as fine Children as ever I saw. Mr H. is an excellent Man. They have a Farm that promises to answer perfectly if times be tolerable; but though the rent is low, if produce should go on sinking, the profits will never repay for the labour and anxiety. At present Markets and Fairs produce nothing. The neighbouring Banks have either failed, or even, if they have stood the heavy Runs against them, the country people are suspicious—so that Business is almost at a stand, and prices, consequently, are sinking. Notwithstanding, I see nothing here but chearfulness and comfort. Poor Sir Walter Scott! I was indeed truly sorry to hear of his name in the Gazette[1]—I did not *see* it myself—and was still in hopes there might be a mistake on the part of my informer. (It was at Manchester where I stayed a few days ago on my road hither that I heard of it)—But the Sale of his furniture, Books etc etc, too clearly confirms the truth. How *could* it happen that he should have so entered into *trade* as to be involved in this Way—he a Baronet! a literary Man! a Lawyer?—I wish very much for particulars both respecting what has led to this calamity and his present condition. How does he bear the Change? I hope well—but am fearful that Lady Scott may not be fortified to the needful point having heard that she was a person fond of distinction and expence—but this may not be true. No doubt Sir Walter, having retained his offices, will still have a sufficient income for a plain gentleman; but does he retain his *Estates*?

A few Months ago my Brother and Sir Walter exchanged Busts.[2] No doubt you have seen Sir Walter's? It is a fine work of art—a noble head—and an excellent Likeness. We prize it much at Rydal Mount, where it ornaments the Book-case in the dining-room. (By the Bye the dining-room has been enlarged since you were at Rydal and is now an excellent room). I wish my Brother's Bust may not have been subject to the stroke of the hammer; but I fear it may have shared the same fate as the rest of Sir W's moveables. Perhaps you have heard rumours of our leaving Rydal Mount:—*I* still hope that we may be suffered to remain there; and should we not, my Brother intends to build, being so unwilling to quit that beautiful

---

[1] As a bankrupt.
[2] Both by Sir Francis Chantrey, R.A. (1781–1842).

Village, where, a church having lately been built, there is every comfort that should make us desire to end our days there. He has purchased a piece of Land adjoining the Rydal Mount property, which commands the same prospect as our own Terrace. I mean the *further* Terrace, which I call our own because my Brother made it—and caused that bit of ground to be added to the pleasure grounds belonging to the house. For my part, I can as little endure the thought of building as of quitting Rydal Mount;[1] therefore let us turn from this unpleasant subject.

You will be glad to hear that all are well at Rydal. My Brother's eyes are much stronger than they were formerly, though still subject to inflamation in a slighter degree. My Niece is staying with Miss Southey and Miss Coleridge at Keswick. She is not hardy, and is grown very thin, and is subject to a cough; however there is at present no cause for anxiety, and I trust that in a few years her constitution will be established. William is quite well. John surprized us last week by his unexpected arrival from Oxford to spend the Easter holidays. He is in good spirits and looks very well. We have not his company now at Brinsop. He is staying with Mr Monkhouse,[2] Mrs Hutchinson's Brother, upon the Banks of the Wye where I have also been. It is a pleasant country, and a pleasant house to stay at. Mr Monkhouse is a delightful Man. I shall go to see him again in May with Miss Joanna. John Wordsworth will return to Oxford in about a fortnight; and we shall see him here on his way thither. He is to finish at Oxford this year and will take [his] degree at the *end* of [?].

I have thought of your good Father and Brothers in these disastrous times, and was truly glad to hear that the numerous Failures had not touched them. God grant that they may not hereafter suffer, for there seems not yet to be an end of the misery. My Brother has suffered nothing but a little inconvenience. He had prepared a new Edition of *all* his poems in five volumes, for the press; but the difficulties in which Hurst and Robinson have been placed have at present suspended the arrangement that he was making. My Sister will send you the Autographs before my return if she has an opportunity, which I think likely to occur, as some of

[1] In the end they were allowed to stay at Rydal Mount.
[2] John Monkhouse of the Stowe.

our neighbours have connexions in Edinburgh. It would not answer to send them by the Carrier.

Miss Barker is still at Boulogne, and the Borrowdale house just as you left it, except that the furniture is restored to its place. I was not at Borrowdale last summer. Mʳ H. Coleridge is still at Ambleside. He has one pupil from Ireland at £100 per annum. Now, my dear Miss Laing, let me beg you to write to me here very soon. Miss J. H. will not be less glad to hear from you than I shall—and pray tell us all particulars—public and private. Have you see Mʳ Wallace lately? I hope he will live as long as I do, for I can never expect any other Dentist to do me as good service as he has done—and as he is much younger than I am, I may calculate on his being the longer liver. Give our best respects to your Father and Mother and Brothers. How are your Mother's eyes? Believe me, dear Miss Laing, your affectionate Friend

D Wordsworth

62. *To* Henry Crabb Robinson

18th Febʳʸ [1827]

My dear Friend,

A Frank tempts me to slip in our united thanks for your zeal in the cause of our Friend, Mr Kenyon—I assure you, as the French say it has not been bestowed upon an Ingrate—as you will yourself perceive if ever you meet him at the Club.[1] He will then, I am sure be glad to hold discourse with you, and to tell you how much he has been pleased by your kindness and that of others of our Friends. It does indeed appear that he came in with a 'high hand'.

My Brother is much obliged to you and to your Friend Mr Rolfe[2] and for getting John's name put on the University Club's Boards and will be further obliged if you will place him on those of the Athenæum. It *may* be useful; and can do no harm.

---

[1] The Athenaeum.
[2] Robert Monsey Rolfe, 1st Lord Cranworth, lawyer.

He is now at Oxford studying Divinity, and we hope the result will be a steady determination to apply himself to the Duties of a Minister of our Church.

The printing of the poems[1] goes on rapidly. My Brother inserts your note (I believe with [out?] any alteration)—only perhaps something may be added to it; and, besides, one or two extracts will, I think, be inserted from our journals as notes to some other poems.

My Niece is much the same—not worse—but very delicate, and we are unceasingly anxious during this cold weather to keep her from injury. The present moon has brought that kind of fine weather which is delightful to the Strong for exercise; but very trying to invalids, though confined wholly to the house as she is. A heavy snow is now on the ground, and still falling;—We hope a thaw will follow—Nothing can exceed the purity of the scene now before my eyes—How different to you in London if the same snow is falling on streets and houses!

The death of Sir George Beaumont[2] is a great affliction to us, and was also a severe shock: for when he was at Rydal in the summer, and when I parted from him at Coleorton at the end of October, he was in as good health and spirits as he has ever been since we first knew him 23 years ago, and appeared as likely for life for eight years to come as any of our younger Friends, though his 73rd birthday was on the 6th of November.—Dear Lady Beaumont has been wonderfully supported hitherto; but I fear the worst *for her* is yet to come; and that strength and spirits may wholly fail; for she is of a weak bodily constitution, and after having lived with a Husband 50 years in perfect harmony, sharing in all his pursuits, the change must be dreadful—and *such* a husband!

Sir George Beaumont was buried on Wednesday—just a week after his Death—His illness was short—I believe not more than ten days. Charles and Mary Lamb will I know sympathize with us. They knew and highly valued our inestimable Friend. Give our love to them.

> In haste ever your affec^te
> D Wordsworth

[1] W. W.'s *Poetical Works*, 5 vols., 1827.
[2] On 7 Feb.

63. *To* Maria Jane Jewsbury

My dear Friend,

I had been thinking of writing to inquire after you when your welcome letter arrived. You wish to hear of our goings on, and though I have little leisure just at present I will not delay—nor will take up either your time or my own with telling truths that you can well divine—of forgiveness—or rather of offences having never come—of conjectures about you—of hopes and fears etc., etc.,—and last of all—of my own resolves to write—resolves made and broken. Happy am I that your state of health is so tolerable, and that you have no bad tidings for us of your Father or any other member of the Family: and am very glad that you have found so nice a plan for retirement and pleasure during the summer. Mrs Hemans[1] must be a sweet-minded woman, and I have no fears of disappointment on either side when you do actually see one another, and live together under one Roof. With my thanks to Mrs Hemans for her care in transmitting good Dr Channing's[2] message, pray tell her that I should have been happy indeed had our plans for the present summer led us into Wales. In that case, nothing should have prevented us from seeking out you and her. I distinctly remember Dr Channing, who was in bad health when at Rydal. My Brother was very much interested by him, and thinks highly of [his] Talents, and will, I am sure, be glad to hear that he is remembered with such pleasurable feelings by him on the other side of the Atlantic. I have not read any one of the new works you mention—nor indeed any thing that is new—and far too little of what is old; for I have been more than usually engaged by domestic duties during the winter and spring; and am now, at this very time, with Miss Hutchinson, engaged in the same way as when you first set foot at Rydal Mount, finding us on the grand-platform in the midst of old carpets and dusty Books: and, what is worse, we are new-papering—and making *new* carpets and about to have a new servant—

---

[1] Felicia Dorothea Hemans (1793–1835), popular versifier.
[2] William Ellery Channing (1780–1842), American Unitarian theologian.

But the week after next, we hope, will finish all—and we shall be quite ready for our dear long-absent Friends—not that we expect them *before* the third week in June—and hardly till the end of it. My Sister talks of leaving her Husband and Daughter in London on the first of June—but I should not be surprized if she were detained a few days longer—for they are overwhelmed with engagements. On the 11th they all went thither. Pray write to Dora. Their address is, 12, Bryanston Street, Portman Square.[1] There seems to be no chance whatever, of their passing through Manchester before the 17th nor do I even think they will take that road from Ashby, as you will not be at M. My Brother and Dora are to join Mrs W. at Whitwick (John's Curacy) adjoining Cole-orton Parish—and no doubt they will stay at least a week to see how John gets on in his new and important Station. Poor Fellow! he wanted me sadly to go with him; fearing that his Mother's anxiety to be at home after her long absence would hurry her away; but, now that he is a little settled, and his Mother is likely to stay not less than three weeks with him, he thinks it much better that I should enjoy the summer at home, and go to him, according to my promise, in the Autumn. Do you remember our homely Westmorland housemaid, Mary? She is an honest good creature, much attached to her Family, and is elevated to the rank of John's housekeeper. Anne, who was at Kent's Bank,[2] still lives with us at Rydal Mount. You will be glad to hear that John gave us much satisfaction in the pulpit and reading-desk of our little Chapel. His voice is very good—and his manner of reading agreeable. He now writes in excellent spirits, and aims to be satisfied with the nature of his employments—and even to like the *situation* of his parish—which, though populous, is somewhat lonely as to society; but he says there is plenty within three of four miles, and he much prefers being out of the way of—Tea visits—and Gossiping with the Ladies. His parsonage-house and garden are much to his mind, and as he is one of the best-tempered Men in the world I doubt not honest Mary and he will get on nicely through the summer.—She will be a right frugal house-keeper and he an easy

---

[1] Quillinan's residence.

[2] On Morecambe Bay, where Miss Jewsbury visited the Wordsworths in July 1825.

Master. Dora's health *must* be greatly improved, but she cannot walk—at least cannot do what her old Aunt calls *walking*—She is delighted with plays and operas—but I doubt not will return without the loss of one shade of her simplicity of character to Rydal Mount and her Doves, and the pony and Neptune.[1] Yet alas! her poor head has been submitted to a French Hairdresser!—This *does* vex me—I cannot condone the notion of seeing her decked (nay not decked—depressed) by big curls—and Bows and Giraffe Wires. Sir Walter Scott is in Town. They live near him, and many others—of whom the newspapers mention. It was a very great disappointment to Dora, when she went the day after her arrival in London to see Elizabeth Cookson[2]—and find her gone. Her father had arrived unexpectedly, and taken away dear Elizabeth—who is now at Liverpool—able to walk three or four miles as well as anybody. She is expected at Kendal tomorrow, and will probably the same night go on to Stourby, where Mrs Cookson and the whole Family are settled for the summer. Our dear William is still at [? home] but will probably leave us ere long—and if he passes through Manchester, and if you are there, he will see you. He has long resolved not to go into the Church. And what is he to do?—Here is his great difficulty—and his Father and Mother hope some prospect may open to him while in London. He is very tall and very strong—and of just the same loving disposition as when you knew him *little* Willy. Probably he may even go to France for a short time to hear the language. I am [?] is not the time to enter on such a subject. No doubt you have heard of his inclinations to the Army. These perforce have been given up. You do not mention Miss Kelsall—I want to hear of her marriage. My love to her. Pray write from Wales—Nor do you mention Miss Bosley—I grieved for her Father's misfortunes. God bless you my dear Friend—Ever yours

D Wordsworth

My kind regards to your Father—Excuse this hurried scrawl—

[1] Her dog.
[2] Daughter of the Kendal Cooksons.

64. *To* Christopher Wordsworth jnr.

Monday 21st October [1828]

My dear Christopher,

Mr Isaac Green[1] of Queens' College called for commands for Cambridge, and I *promised* to entrust him with a letter for you, which I intended should be a long one filled with all sorts of Rydal chit-chat, but visitors, coming in unexpectedly, have filched away all my time, and but that I would not disappoint the young man of the notion that he is doing me a service I would not write at all today. He is to stop the Coach at the Foot of the Hill to take up my dispatches.

My dear Nephews, I hope I may congratulate you all on a safe and happy return to Trinity Lodge, for no doubt Charles[2] would join you there (though but for a day or two) after so long an absence; but no doubt ere this reaches you he will have taken his place in Christ-Church. I was very much pleased with your Father's account of his excursion, and of the satisfaction and profit you had all shared. I will not say I envyed you, but should have had no objection to a Run through Paris with such good and Kind Friends, young and old.—I wish you would find time—you or John[3]—about three weeks hence to give me a long letter with a full account of your travels, to cheer my solitude at Whitwick, whither I am going, as soon as I can after the 6th of next month, to spend five months with John in his lonely Parsonage.—I will promise you in return all my adventures per Coach—through Manchester, or Liverpool, for my route is uncertain—and a full account of Whitwick arrangements, and of our Congregations in the ancient Church, our warfare with the Methodists, and our attempts—'feeble and ineffectual I fear'—to '*ameliorate the condition*' of the Poor.

I am anxious to hear of poor Charles, concerning whose health but indifferent reports reached us, through Mr Edward Hamilton,[4] who spent the summer at Bowness, and is soon to become a Member of your College. He is a pleasant young man, and I hope will be

[1] Later, master at Sedbergh.
[2] Charles Wordsworth (1806–92), C. W.'s second son, later Bishop of St Andrews.
[3] His brother, now at Trinity.
[4] Later, Fellow of Trinity.

among your acquaintances, if only because he is so fond of Bowness and the Lakes.

Dora has written to you I believe, and no doubt told you how much she was delighted with *her* tour.[1] I dare say she never once mentioned her health, therefore I must tell you that it is much improved. She can eat like other folks, and though still lamentably subject to cold-taking, is greatly improved in strength.

Your Uncle is just come in from a Drive. He says he hopes one or other of you will write him an account of your travels.

By the bye I must mention the Bearer of this, though I cannot expect you to take much nay *any* trouble; but if you should be in the way when he delivers this, pray be kind and civil to him. He is a very deserving and industrious young man, and I believe a good Scholar, the Son of our Butcher at Grasmere who has furnished you with many a good slice out of a leg of mutton. Excuse extreme haste and believe me dear Christopher, with Love to yr Father and Brothers,

ever your affectionate Aunt
D. W.

I was much gratified by your note and present of Poems,—The Mercer I like very much.

65. *To* Mrs John Marshall

[Whitwick] 26 Dec., [1828]

... The small living of Moresby, vacated by Mr Huddlestone of Whitehaven, has been offered to John by Lord Lonsdale, and he thankfully accepts it. The manner in which Lord L. has done this favour is not less gratifying than the favour itself.

Our rector, Mr Merewether,[2] is truly sorry to lose John, yet disinterested enough to be glad of his advancement.... He will remain here six months longer, and I of course shall remain with him. In fact, if he had continued here another winter, I should have done so also; as, in the first place, I am more useful than I could be anywhere else, and, in the second, am very comfortable. The walk

1 To the Rhineland the previous summer, with her father and S. T. C.
2 The Revd Francis Merewether, rector of Coleorton.

to the rectory and the hall at Coleorton is not too long for a winter's morning call. Therefore we have no want of society, and our fireside at home has never been dull, or the evenings tediously long. It gives me great satisfaction also to see that John does the duties of his profession with zeal and cheerfulness, and is much liked and respected by the parishioners. His congregations, notwithstanding the numerous dissenting meeting-houses, are much increased.

Perhaps you know that we are on the borders of Charnwood Forest. There is much fine rocky ground, but no trees; the road dry in general, so it may be called a good country for walkers. There is one hill from which we have a most extensive prospect, twenty–one miles distant from us. The air is dry though cold (for we are at a great height above the sea).... John was at Cambridge last week, to be ordained priest; my brother Christopher and my nephews are well, and in good spirits.... Five weeks have I been here, and not a single rainy day....

66. *To* Mary Lamb

Rydal Mount 9th Jan^{ry}, 1830

My dear Friend,

My nephew John will set off to-morrow evening to Oxford, to take his Master of Arts degree, and thence proceed to London, where his time will be so short that there is no chance of his being able to go to see you; but there is a *possibility* that your brother may happen to be in town at the same time, in which case it would grieve *him* and *us* at home not less, that he should not see him. Therefore, if it should happen that your Brother is in Town at any time from the 17th to the 26th of this month, pray desire him to inquire for the Rev^{d}. J. Wordsworth at Mr Cookson's,[1] No. 6 Lincoln's Inn. There he will be sure to learn where John may be found, of which at present he knows no more than that he will not *lodge* at Mr Cookson's though he will certainly call there, and leave his address immediately after he reaches Town.

[1] W. W.'s solicitor, son of the Kendal Cooksons.

I do not write *merely* for the sake of giving John a chance of seeing your Brother (and you also if you happen to be in London) but to inquire after you both, for now that our good friend Henry Robinson is absent *you* might as well be also living in Rome for any thing we hear concerning you; and believe me we are often uneasy in the thought that all communication seems cut off between us; and sincerely and earnestly do we all desire that your Brother will let us have a *post* Letter (no waiting for Franks or private conveyances) telling us minutely, how you live, what you both are doing, and whom you see—of old Friends or new—as visitors by your fireside. I do not ask *you*, Miss Lamb, to write, for I know you dislike the office; but dear Charles L., you whom I have known almost five and thirty years, I trust I do not in vain entreat *you* to let me have the eagerly desired letter at you earliest opportunity, which letter will, we hope, bring us tidings of H. C. Robinson. We have not heard any thing concerning him since his departure from England, though he promised absolutely to write on his arrival at Rome, and if his intentions were fulfilled, he must have been a resident there for many weeks. Do you see Talfourd?[1] Does he prosper in his profession? What Family has he? etc etc. But I will not particularize persons, but include all in one general inquiry (Miss Kelly[2] amongst the rest). Tell us of all whom you know, in whose well-doing you know us also to be interested; but above all, be very minute in what regards your own dear selves, for there are no persons in the world, exclusive of members of our own Family, of whom we think and talk so frequently, or with such delightful remembrances.—Your removal from London (though to my thought London is hardly London without you) shall not prevent my seeing you both in your own cottage,[3] if I live to go there again, but at present I have no distinct plans leading me thither. Now that Mr. Monkhouse is gone, we females have no absolute home there, and should we go it will probably be on our own way to the Continent, or to the southern Shores of England. *Wishes* I do now and then indulge of at least *re*visiting Switzerland, and again crossing the Alps, and even stretching on to Rome; but there is a great change in my feelings,

---

[1] Thomas Noon Talfourd (1795–1854) author and judge.
[2] The actress.
[3] At Enfield.

respecting plans for the future. If we make any, I entertain them as an amusement perhaps for a short while, but never set my heart upon any thing which is to be accomplished three months hence, and have no satisfaction whatever in *schemes*. When one has lived almost sixty years, one is satisfied with present enjoyment, and thankful for it, without daring to count on what is to be done six months hence. But, forgive me, I am prosing and do not say a word to satisfy your desire to know how we all are and what doing. To begin then with the heads of the house. My Brother and Sister are both in excellent health. In *him* there is no failure except the tendency to inflamation in his eyes, which disables him from reading much, or at all by candle-light; and the use of the pen is irksome to him; However, he has a most competent and willing amanuensis in his Daughter, who takes all labour from Mother's and Aunt's aged hands. His muscular powers are in no degree diminished; indeed I think that he walks *regularly* more than ever, finding fresh air the best bracer of his weak eyes. He is still the crack skater on Rydal Lake, and, as to climbing of mountains, the hardiest and the youngest are yet hardly a match for him. In composition I can perceive no failure, and his imagination seems as vigorous as in youth; yet he shrinks from his great work[1] and both during the last and present winter has been employed in writing small poems. Do not suppose, my dear Friends, that I write the above boastingly. Far from it. It is in thankfulness for present blessings, yet always with a sense of the probability that all will have a sudden check; and if not so, the certainty that in the course of man's life, but a few years of vigorous health and strength can be allotted to him. For this reason, my sister and I take every opportunity of pressing upon him the necessity of applying to his great work, and this he feels, resolves to do it, and again resolution fails. And now I almost fear habitually, that it will be ever so. I have told you she is well, and indeed I think her much stronger than a few years ago, and (now that I am for the whole of this winter set aside as a Walker) she takes my place, and will return from an eight miles' walk with my Brother unfatigued. Miss Hutchinson and her sister Joanna are both with us. Miss H. is perfectly well, and Joanna very happy, though she may

---

[1] *The Recluse.*

be always considered as an invalid. Her home is in the Isle of Man, and, with the first mild breezes of Spring, she intends returning thither, with her Sailor Brother Henry; they two 'toddling down the hill' together. She is an example for us all, With the better half of her property she purchased Columbian Bonds, at above 70, gets no interest, and will not sell. Consequently the cheapness of the little Isle tempted her thither on a visit, and she finds the air so suitable to her health, and every thing else so much to her mind that she *will*, in spite of our unwillingness to part with her make it her home. As to her lost property, she never regrets it. She has so reduced her wants that she declares herself to be now richer than she ever was in her life, and so she *is*; for she has always a little to spare at the end of the year—and in her little way can always assist the distressed. I believe you never saw Joanna, and it is a pity; for you would have loved her very much. She possesses all the good qualities of the Hutchinsons. My niece Dora, who remembers you alw[ay]s with the greatest affection, has lately been in much better health than within the last few years, she is very active and a most useful personage at home—her Father's helper at all times; and in domestic concerns she takes all the trouble from her mother and me. I trust that in course of a year or two she may become strong; but now she is no walker—cannot climb a mountain. It is not improbable that her Father may take her to Cambridge in the spring, and if so to London—and in that case they would see you: but no plans are laid, though now and then Dora amuses herself with talking about it. As for myself you will be glad to hear that I am perfectly well; but after this pleasant assurance I must tell you that my health had a sad shaking last April, when I was with John in Leicestershire. The disorder was inflammation of the Bowels. In June I left that country—and from want of care have had two or three attacks, but neither so severe, nor of the same kind; however, enough to convince me of the necessity of great care; and therefore *now* though perfectly well I am acting the invalid, never walk except in the garden and am driven out whenever weather permits by my Niece in the pony chaise. By this means I hope to resume my former habits next summer, during the present winter laying in a stock of strength. My dear Friend your eyes are weak, and you will find this a sad troublesome prosy letter, and vexed I am, for (using proper discretion) I might have told you all I *have* told in one half the number of lines—pray forgive me and entreat your kind Brother to send me a written assurance that you do so and with that to send us a minute account of all that concerns yourselves and as much about mutual Friends as he has leisure for and inclination. My Brother, Sister, Miss H., and Dora unite with me in sincerest good wishes for the coming year, and every succeeding one of your lives, and that they may be many.—God bless you both, and my dear Miss Lamb,

Believe me your affec^te Friend

D Wordsworth

Strange that I should have written this long letter without a word of our absent William to whom you were so kind when a London Schoolboy.[1] He has been at Bremen since last June. When he left Rydal Mount his health was but indifferent—but in Leicestershire he recruited and left *England* in good health but at first the change of climate, habits etc etc disagreed with him and he was very unwell, yet always wrote in good spirits and I am happy to tell you that his late letters have onl[y] spoken of 'excellent health'. But it [is now] nearly two months since his last and we are anxiously expecting letters. He is much attached to the excellent Family with whom he lives; and we have reason to believe that his time passes profitably.

Do you ever see Mr and Mrs Thomas Clarkson? Mr Clarkson's health is improved, but his wife is less equal to exertion than formerly.

John makes an excellent parish priest, other particulars, if you meet, he will tell you himself.

67. *To* Christopher Wordsworth

Rydal Mount—April 27th [1830]

My Dear Brother,

I make haste to thank you for your kind letter which would have given us unmingled pleasure had you not reported rather less favorably of your health than we wished—or indeed *expected*; for latterly

---

[1] In 1819, when Mr Johnson was preparing him for Charterhouse.

we have had pretty good accounts of you; however it is not worse than we *might* have reckoned upon; for, excepting your rheumatic pains, you seem to have no ailments that Rest and Relaxation will not speedily cure—but of these, before the end of June, you will sorely stand in need. Now my reason for not letting a day pass over without acknowledging your letter is this—that I would be beforehand in our proposal in order that Rydal Mount may have its fair chance when you make your decision as to whither you shall turn your solitary steps—(for it does not seem that any one of the *young* Men[1] will be with you)—You can here have constant possession and command of a quiet sitting-room above stairs, and as pleasant a bed room as heart could desire—for any part, or the whole of the next summer; and it is not possible for me to say what pleasure it would give to William and Mary myself and every other member of the Family if you would take possession of them for as many weeks of your holiday-time as you can afford. William says, after such a severe winter and such a deluge of spring-rains that we may expect a dry summer, and he hopes you would not have the same cause for complaints of our moist climate as when you were at Ivy Cottage[2]—and—even at the worst—this situation being so elevated, we have, comparatively, a bracing air; in the hot and damp season always very different from that of the Valley below us. You need not dread the idleness of the 'Idle Mount' for you may always shut yourself up from it in your own apartments; and, further: I can assure you that we have less and less every year of that sort of bustle; you would have no want of Books ancient or modern—Lady Fleming allows W^m free access to her old library, and would really be proud of your making use of it. There is also the Hawkshead School Collection of Divinity and other Books—and Southey's large library—not to speak of the miscellaneous assemblage on our own Shelves. All other motives for directing your steps hitherwards I leave to your own suggestion—only my dear Brother I pray you never lose sight of that strong one the pleasure you would give to William, Mary and me and your God-child Dora, who would be half wild with joy to ride about with you among her and your native Hills— Remember, too, how many summers are gone

[1] C. W.'s sons.
[2] In 1822.

by and how few yet remain for *us* who are fast travelling towards our final home. Though I have been so speedy in urging my plea do not suppose we look for an equally speedy reply—we only wish to have the start of other claimants; and shall require but very short notice if you at length determine to come to us.

William, of course, now gives up all thought of visiting you next month, or in June with Dora, which he would have been inclined to, had the time better suited. The young Men's important occupations quite put it out of the question; he hopes, however, that at the time you mention there may be no obstacles—and, if so, he would be very glad to turn his steps towards Cambridge, accompanied by his Wife and Daughter. I say *at least*—for though they are fearful in prospect of a long journey for *me*—I cannot at once say it would be absolutely impossible for me to accompany them. However: being all three past the planning age, we will for the present let the matter rest under this assurance; that William, Mary and Dora will gladly accept your kind invitation if time and circumstances allow of it—and if I cannot be of the party I shall remain very contented at home with one kind companion.

My first wish is that your dear Son John may be elected Fellow of Trinity[1]—without much further anxiety: labour I suppose he *must* have to the very last. My next that Chris. may also be elected, and thus spared the going through so much as has fallen to his Brother's lot. You do not mention Charles's prospects—John told me he was not very hopeful of reaching the First Class; but I do expect to see his name there; and shall be anxious for the Oxford paper (which pray desire him to send me whether he be first, second,—or *un*named). Whatever be his place I shall have no misgivings—no doubts about his well-doing.

We have been anxious about the King's health[2]—but the papers tell us he is recovering—which could hardly be expected if what they first told us were true. I do not recollect any thing having happened among us since I last wrote, therefore will leave the rest of my paper, hoping our dear Brother will fill it up—Give my kind love to John and Chris—with a thousand good wishes for a

---

[1] He was elected later this year, along with Christopher.
[2] George IV died on 25 June.

happy end of their Labours—and the like to Charles when he is written to—and believe me, my dear Brother,

> Your ever affectionate Sister
>> D. Wordsworth.

Dora is still at Moresby.

68. *To* William Pearson

> Rydal Mount,
> Wednesday. [?29 Dec. 1830]

My dear Sir,

I am glad to hear that you had not a troublesome journey home, and were no worse for it in health.

My Brother and Sister write from London and Hampstead, in good spirits. All three are well. No fresh news from Heidelberg[1] or Moresby. This weather is charming for the young and strong—Moonlight and at Christmas used to be delightful, thirty years ago. I now enjoy a short, sharp walk in the garden, and a peep out of doors, on the Evergreens and sunshine, from a warm fire-side. Many thanks for the straw, I shall pay the bearer.

> Believe me, my dear Sir,
>> Truly yours,
>>> D. Wordsworth.

69. *To* Elizabeth Hutchinson

> Tuesday—about the 14th Sept [?1834]

My dear Godchild

This is not one of my vigorous days, therefore you must take it kindly though I send you a short, unentertaining, and ill-penned letter. For the last mentioned failure my excuse is, that I lie upon my back in bed and with uplifted knees form a desk for my paper.

---

[1] i.e. from W. W. jnr.

Do not suppose, however, that I spend all my time in bed—It is only that I rise late and go to bed before sunset, because it tires, and in other respects disagrees with me to sit up more than from 4 to 6 hours in the day.

I hope you will find the green gown useful: but I wish I had also been able to send you some *book* to help you to adorn the mind, while the Body is gaily dressed in its 'gown of green'. My dear Elizabeth, I hope your good Father and Mother will consent to allow you to visit your Friends at Rydal very soon—*I* say the sooner the better—but am afraid we must not look for you till George's[1] return at Christmas—and indeed it would be unreasonable to expect you to leave home before the end of the holidays, when so large a troop of your companions will be assembled there; but we all (your Uncle and Aunt W. Aunt Sarah, Dora and myself) join in the wish and the request that your Parents will spare you to us when George returns. Probably Cousin Dora will not be at home during the first part of your visit, and you will in that case, be a lively companion and useful help to us, the old, and for myself I must add the *infirm*.

I trust you may gather much improvement among us with your own pains-taking; but cannot promise you any regular instruction, and indeed if Dora should be at home (which I trust she will *not* be) when you arrive, she has not health or strength sufficient for a Teacher. You may however, learn much, indirectly, while contributing both to my amusement and instruction by reading to me, which will be to me of great use and comfort. I can promise to do nothing more for you in the way of instruction than drawing out your comments and remarks and making my own: and further; it will be a pleasure to me to point out whatever may appear to me amiss in you manner of reading. It would fatigue me to instruct you in French—and indeed perhaps you *need* little instruction except in the pronunciation—and *that* I could not give: but a French-master has been fixed for some time at Ambleside, and we hope, and even expect, that he will *stay*, as he has a number of scholars, and there will be no difficulty in having him here to attend on you, if we cannot get you introduced into some friend's house where he may have other pupils.

[1] Her elder brother, now at Sedbergh.

I feel as if I had much to say both to you and Mary,[1] and to your dear Mother: but as I took too much exercise yesterday (tempted by the fine weather) I must spare myself and conclude with this one assurance that I have it much at heart to have some intercourse with you, my dear God-daughter before I quit this world—Do not suppose however, that I have any feelings which make me expect this speedy approach of death. Far from it—I suffer comparatively little, and have a full enjoyment of all the blessings with which I am surrounded: but life is uncertain even with the strongest—and still more so with the old and feeble, therefore I hope the time for your coming (if all be well at home) may be fixed for next January—I send you a God-mother's Blessing, with sincerest wishes that you may not waste the happy days of Youth. Make the most of them. They will never return, and if you do not profit by present advantages you will bitterly repent when it is too late, but however happy you may be in the enjoyment of youth, health and strength never, my good child, forget that our *home* is not here and prepare yourself for what will come, sooner or later to every one of us.—Give my love to all the Inmates of Brinsop-Court—not forgetting the unseen little Sarah[2]—I have had many anxious thoughts concerning your Uncle Monkhouse:[3] and it is with a thankful heart that I congratulate him on the hopes of a complete restoration of his eyesight. Pray give my affectionate regards to him with earnest wishes that all may end as it has begun.

Again God bless you! Believe me
ever your faithful and affectionate Friend,
Dorothy Wordsworth.

Remember dear Elizabeth, that my penmanship affords no example for you. How I wish I could ever again climb the Credenhill hill with all of you—young and old!—or visit that old Tree on the top of the Hill opposite to dear Brinsop! Tell Mary I hope she will not fail to send me a sketch of your little Church—and mark Aunt M.'s[4] grave.

---

[1] Her elder sister.
[2] Her younger sister.
[3] John Monkhouse.
[4] Miss Elizabeth Monkhouse (d. 1828).

70. *To* Dora Wordsworth

[Spring 1838]

My dearest Dora

They say I must write a letter—and what shall it be? News—news I must seek for news. My own thoughts are a wilderness—'not pierceable by power of any star'[1]—News then is my resting-place—News! news!

Poor Peggy Benson lies in Grasmere Church-yard beside her once beautiful Mother. Fanny Haigh is gone to a better world. My Friend Mrs Rawson has ended her ninety and two years pilgrimage— and *I* have fought and fretted and striven—and am here beside the fire. The Doves behind me at the small window—the laburnum with its naked seed-pods shivers before my window and the pine-trees rock from their base.—More I cannot write so farewell! and may God bless you and your kind good Friend Miss Fenwick,[2] to whom I send love and all the best of wishes.   Yours evermore

Dorothy Wordsworth

[1] Spenser, *Faerie Queen*, I. i. 7 (misquoted).
[2] The Wordsworths' closest friend in their later years, with whom Dora W. was staying.

Suggestions For Further Reading

*

Where possible, the latest available edition is cited.

Letters and Journals

The Letters of William and Dorothy Wordsworth, ed. Ernest de Selincourt, 2nd enlarged edition: *The Early Years*, ed. Chester L. Shaver (Oxford, 1967). *The Middle Years*, Part 1, ed. Mary Moorman (Oxford, 1969). *The Middle Years*, Part 2, ed. Mary Moorman and Alan G. Hill (Oxford, 1970). *The Later Years*, Parts 1, 2, 3, and 4, ed. Alan G. Hill (Oxford, 1978, 1979, 1982, 1988). Supplement to *The Middle Years*, ed. Alan G. Hill, forthcoming.

Journals of Dorothy Wordsworth, ed. E. de Selincourt (London, 1952), 2 vols.

Journals of Dorothy Wordsworth, ed. Mary Moorman (Oxford Paperback, 1971).

Letters of William Wordsworth. A Selection, ed. Alan G. Hill (Oxford, 1984).

Poems

The Poetical Works of William Wordsworth, ed. T. Hutchinson, rev. E. de Selincourt (Oxford Paperback, 1978).

Biography, Criticism, etc.

JOHN BEER, *Wordsworth and the Human Heart* (London, 1978).

THOMAS DE QUINCEY, *Recollections of the Lakes and the Lake Poets*, ed. David Wright (Penguin English Library, 1972).

ROBERT GITTINGS and JO MANTON, *Dorothy Wordsworth* (Oxford, 1985).

JOHN E. JORDAN, *De Quincey to Wordsworth, A Biography of a Relationship* (Berkeley, Calif., 1962).

H. M. MARGOLIOUTH, *Wordsworth and Coleridge, 1795–1834* (Oxford, 1953).

MARY MOORMAN, *William Wordsworth, A Biography*: I, *The Early Years*, II, *The Later Years* (Oxford Paperbacks, 1968).

NORMAN NICHOLSON, *The Lakers* (London, 1955).

VIRGINIA WOOLF, 'Four Figures', from *The Common Reader, Second Series* (London, 1932).

The Illustrated Wordsworth's Guide to the Lakes, ed. Peter Bicknell (Exeter, 1984).

Index

*

193

OXFORD

MORE OXFORD PAPERBACKS

POETRY FROM OXFORD PAPERBACKS

Oxford's outstanding range of English poetry offers, in a single volume of convenient size, the complete poetical works of some of the most important figures in English Literature.

WORDSWORTH

Poetical Works

This edition of Wordsworth's poetry contains every piece of verse known to have been published by the poet himself, or of which he authorized the posthumous publication. The text, which Thomas Hutchinson based largely upon the 1849–50 standard edition, the last issued during the poet's lifetime, was revised for the Oxford Standard Authors series by Ernest de Selincourt.

The volume preserves the poet's famous subjective arrangement of the Minor Poems under such headings as 'Poems Referring to the Period of Childhood', 'Poems Dedicated to National Independence and Liberty', and 'Sonnets Upon the Punishment of Death'. *The Prelude* is given in the text of 1850, published shortly after Wordsworth's death, and *The Excursion* as it appears in the 1849–50 edition. Two poems of 1793 are included, 'An Evening Walk' and 'Descriptive Sketches', and a group of other pieces not appearing in the standard edition. The text reproduces Wordsworth's characteristic use of capital letters and in most cases his punctuation, though spelling has been regularized. The poet's own Notes to the 1849–50 edition, as well as to some earlier editions, are reprinted, along with his Prefaces.

The edition also contains a chronological table of Wordsworth's life, explanatory notes on the text, and chronological data for the individual poems.

Also in Oxford Paperbacks:

The Prelude   William Wordsworth
Poetical Works   John Keats
The Golden Treasury   Francis Turner Palgrave